RIDING ON THE EDGE

A MOTORCYCLE OUTLAW'S TALE

JOHN HALL

m
motorbooks

First published in 2008 by MBI Publishing Company and Motorbooks, an imprint of MBI Publishing Company, 400 First Avenue North, Suite 300, Minneapolis, MN 55401 USA

Motorbooks titles are also available at discounts in bulk quantity for industrial or sales-promotional use. For details write to Special Sales Manager at MBI Publishing Company, 400 First Avenue North, Suite 300, Minneapolis, MN 55401 USA.

To find out more about our books, join us online at www.motorbooks.com.

ISBN-13: 978-0-7603-3276-4

Editors: Darwin Holmstrom and Mariam Pourshartari

Design Manager: Tom Heffron
Cover Designer: John Barnett
Layout Designer: Liz Tufte
Cover image: *Michael Lichter*

Printed in the United States of America

CONTENTS

Christianity—and this is its finest merit—subdued to a certain extent that Germanic lust for battle, but could not destroy it, and if some day that restraining talisman, the Cross, falls to pieces, then the savagery of the old warriors will explode again, and with it that mad berserker rage about which the Nordic poets have told so much. This talisman is decaying, and the day will come when it will crumble. Then the old stone gods will arise from the forgotten ruins and wipe the dust of centuries from their eyes, and Thor will at last leap up with his hammer and smash the Gothic Cathedrals.

— Heinrich Heine

INTRODUCTION

The first world to exist was Muspell. It is light and It is hot. It flames and It burns. Those who do not belong to It, and whose native land It is not, cannot endure It. The One who sits there at the Lands End to guard the gates is called Dark Surt. He has a flaming sword, and at the end of the world He will come, He will harry, and He will vanquish all the Gods and burn the whole world with fire.

—Snorri Sturluson, *The Norse Edda*
Thirteenth century Pagan Iceland

And there He sat.

Horned and cross-legged, and holding His flaming sword like a cross. The grim image of Dark Surt, embroidered under the name on the backs of the sleeveless blue denim vests that we wore over our well-worn black leather motorcycle jackets. Frank Friel, the head of the Philadelphia Police—FBI Organized Crime Task Force, called us the most "violence-prone motorcycle gang in America."

We called ourselves "the Pagans," the baddest of the ass-kicking, beer-drinking, hell-raising, gang-banging, grease-covered, roadkill-eating, 1960s motorcycle clubs, chromed cavaliers and swastika-studded scooter jockeys. Spawned on the marshy flatlands of Southern Maryland, we were a band of motorized highwaymen who ruled the roads from the pine barrens of Long Island and New Jersey to the glistening moonlit peaks of the Allegheny and Blue Ridge Mountains. Across the Dutch farmlands of Pennsylvania and down the Great Valley of Virginia, in the back alleys of the old steel, mining, railroad, and paper-mill towns of the Appalachian rustbelt, it was all Pagan country.

By the late '70s we had wormed our way from the wide-open roads and cornfields of the Dutch country clear down to the narrow streets and crowded stalls of the Italian Market in South Philly, where some of the brothers were getting caught up in the shadowlands of the Philadelphia underworld and popping up on the radar screens of Frank Friel and his FBI task force.

The shit finally hit the fan on a March morning in 1980, when someone put a gun to the head of Angelo Bruno, the man they called "the Gentle Don," because he believed that he could run a criminal empire by peace and persuasion rather than violence and coercion. When the gunman squeezed the trigger, Bruno's head burst into a river of blood, and so did the streets of Philadelphia. All peace and persuasion died with Bruno and the city was engulfed in the most violent crime war in American history.

When the bodies stopped falling and the river of blood dried to an occasional trickle, Nicodemo "Little Nicky" Scarfo emerged as the new head of Bruno's criminal cartel, which has been called, among other things, the Society of Men of Honor. Physically, Nicky Scarfo was little more than a dwarf, but he had the ambition of a giant. He dreamed of becoming the biggest crime czar in America, ruling an empire that stretched from the sunny casino-studded boardwalk of Atlantic City to the dingy smoke-filled backroom betting parlors in the bars and clubs of Scranton and Wilkes-Barre. Gambling, drugs, entertainment, extortion, labor unions, construction firms, trucking companies, vending machines; from tattoo parlors and pizza joints to pool halls and massage parlors, whatever the enterprise, legal or illegal, he wanted to run them all.

In building his empire Little Nicky did not have the patience of the Gentle Don. He believed that there were quicker and more efficient means of putting people in line than peace and persuasion. From his throne room in the back of a rundown warehouse on South Bancroft

Street, Little Nicky issued an edict demanding that every drug monger, bookmaker, tattoo artist, titty-bar owner, pizza twirler, and chop-shop grease monkey in Philadelphia pay tribute for the privilege of doing business on the streets of his empire.

To collect this tax he dispatched a band of thugs, who determined the rate by how scared their victims looked and how much they thought they could squeeze out of them. Those who didn't pay were beaten senseless with baseball bats, usually on the open street, as a warning to Little Nicky's other subjects who might prove recalcitrant. But when Nicky's tax collectors paid a call on the Pagans, the bearded bikers did not look scared at all. In fact they laughed right in the faces of Scarfo's clean-shaven Wops.

Little Nicky considered this an insult, and he ordered his enforcers to teach these rude cycle-bums a lesson they would not soon forget. But Scarfo's stooges wanted no part of the chain-wielding Pagans. They told Scarfo that these guys were even crazier than the *Mulignanes* and that there was no telling how they might retaliate. So nothing was done; the dispute settled into a stalemate, with Little Nicky seething in his warehouse and the Pagans doing pretty much whatever they wanted all over Philadelphia.

Relations between the Pagans and the mob festered like a swollen abscess, which finally burst on a spring night in 1984, when Little Nicky's hard-drinking underboss, Salvatore "Chuckie" Merlino, staggered out of a restaurant in South Philadelphia and saw a Pagan sitting on a motorcycle. Fortified with the kind of courage that comes out of a bottle, Scarfo's drunken underboss rammed his car into the bike and sent the Pagan sprawling into the street.

While he was lying in a hospital bed, the Pagan was visited by his bike-riding brethren. One of them found an accident report lying on the table next to the bed where the police had left it. When he picked it up, the name Salvatore Merlino jumped up in his face. And underneath Merlino's name there was a South Philadelphia address.

"Look at this," he said, as he began stabbing the paper with his finger right under the address. He then passed it around the room, and his bearded brethren all began grinning as they read it.

The next night a band of Pagans pulled up at that address and shot over two hundred rounds of ammunition through the walls, windows, and doors, while Merlino's terrified mother crouched on the floor, peeing herself under a shower of lead and glass.

As Detective Friel later put it: "The incident went unavenged. This brazen insult to the majesty of the Men of Honor was never punished. The Mafia bullies had been bullied by the bike riding bullies and backed down." In fact, Scarfo's people ultimately coughed up five grand for bike repairs and hospital bills.

Years later I met the Pagan who orchestrated the attack on Merlino's home.

It was a fluke encounter. I was working as a bartender. He walked in and ordered a drink. We recognized each other's tattoos, and we both asked ·the same question: "Who the hell are you?" He was a leader of the Pagans during the Philadelphia mob wars in the early '80s. I went by the name "Stoop" and ran the New York club back in the late '60s.

He told me about the war with the Dwarf Don and about the attack on Merlino's home. Actually it wasn't really Merlino's home, the guy told me. It was his mother's. The guy had put her address on his driver's license to confuse the cops, but he had only confused the Pagans instead.

"'Who's a dare? Who's a dare!' we heard her screaming right before we started firing." We both laughed.

Then I told him that I had been the leader of the New York Pagans from 1967–1969. He was as interested in my story as I was in his.

"I always really regretted that I wasn't a member back in those days," he said. "You guys back in the '60s were crazy. I missed all that. But those were the days when you guys did the shit that 'the Legend' was hatched from. In fact it was the shit you guys did back then that helped guys like me scare the shit out of those greaseballs later on."

We talked some more, about gang wars and about the '60s. Then the place closed. He left, and I began to clean up. I thought about what he said.

"Crazy?"

Actually I thought it was all pretty routine stuff back then. Sure, we got into some shootings and serious shit. But most of it was just good clean fun, like drinking beer all night and standing up on the seat of your motorcycle, drunk and without a helmet, at three o'clock in the morning, while you blew every red light on Hempstead Turnpike. Dawn coming up over a line of motorcycles on the front lawn of the clubhouse, and a bunch of brothers covered with stale beer, blood, barroom dust, and road grease, all curled up with their old ladies on damp and dirty mattresses on the floor of the clubhouse basement. Beating a bar full of citizens unconscious with chains and rendering the place to splinters in a matter of minutes—and for what? Because somebody said the wrong thing to a brother who couldn't even remember what was said the next morning. Walking into a courtroom with black leather jackets, knee-high boots, earrings, chrome chains, and swastikas, then sneering through your beard at a jury of straight citizens and defying them to convict you. And all of you getting handcuffed together and carted off to jail in the end, howling and laughing about it like all hell, but not having put a dime in your pocket. Then getting out and scraping together gas and beer money so you could do it all over again.

Crazy?

Maybe he had a point.

Today every department store in the country sells black Harley-Davidson t-shirts that proclaim: "The Legend Lives on." But it wasn't Harley-Davidson that made "the Legend;" it was the people who rode them during a time when Harley-Davidson was working hard to disassociate itself from the people who were building "the Legend," that later saved the company from bankruptcy. The Legend transformed country music singers from crooning cowboys into longhaired rednecks. The Legend transformed the fashion industry so that middle-aged professionals no longer went to country clubs on weekends dressed like Johnny Carson, but instead dressed up like '60s outlaw bikers, with bandannas, denim vests, and knee-high leather boots as they putted around the block on $40,000 machines. And the Legend enabled outlaw bikers to displace Nazis as the number one bad guys popping up in the neurotic nightmares of suburban middle-class Americans.

Crazy?

I thought about all of this as I washed the beer glasses, wiped the bar, pulled up the rubber mats, and began mopping the floor. Soon I forgot what I was doing and I was thinking about a lost time when things were different. A time before helmet and drunk-driving laws. A time when America was still half free. A time when the Jersey Meadowlands wasn't a sports complex, but a real meadowlands with grass and flowers that we roared past on the way to Pennsylvania. A time when Reading wasn't the world's largest factory outlet, but a real hard-ass Pennsylvania Dutch working town, with mills and breweries and railroad yards. A time when Blackie wasn't dead and decomposing under a black granite tombstone behind a factory in Laureldale Cemetery, but riding past that same cemetery with the sun in his face, the wind in his hair, and a black pointed beard like a Persian caliph. A time when Jane wasn't yet a grandmother, but when her own kids were just out of diapers and she herself was still an auburn-haired little Pennsylvania Dutch teen-angel with soft green eyes and the sweetest little Dutch futz that ever warmed the passenger seat-pad on a chopped hog.

I was thinking about all this, and suddenly everything was changed. Changed utterly. The place no longer smelled like stale beer and it wasn't dark and late on a winter's night. No. Now the sun was shining brightly in the late morning sky, and everything smelled like fresh spring grass as a pack of custom choppers roared through the Jersey Meadowlands in a blur of chrome, polished candy apple lacquer, black leather, blue denim, grease, sweat, exhaust fumes, long hair, beards, and swastikas. The sun was shining in our faces, Dark Surt was grinning on our backs, and the Pagans were on the run.

The year was 1967. The year the Legend was born.

CHAPTER 1

*People with courage and character always seem
sinister to the rest.*

— Hermann Hesse, *Demian*

MEMORIAL DAY WEEKEND 1967

The weatherman had predicted clear blue skies over the entire East
Coast. And he was right; it was already hot when we rolled out
early Saturday morning.

Like the Dark Legions of Muspell, we rolled out of the damp, wooden,
dirt-floor garages in Maspeth and Greenpoint, Long Island. Out of the
parking lots of all-night neon truck-stop diners on U.S. 1 in Rahway and
Linden, New Jersey. Out of the dying corrugated steel and mining towns,
beside the quiet rivers in the rolling mountains of Pennsylvania. Out of
the moonshine hollows of West Virginia and the second-floor crash pads
over waterfront bars in Baltimore. Out of the mist-shrouded oak and
hemlock forests of the Blue Ridge and Allegheny Mountains, down the
wide-open asphalt highways of the great Shenandoah Valley of Virginia,
and even down the quiet Saturday-morning streets of the nation's capital.

The Pagans were on the run.

The Pagans, with names like Big Dutch, Apple, Satan, and Little Jesus.
Indian Joe, Renegade, Crazy Joey, Pappy, German, and the Whiteknight.
Sweet William and Saint Thomas. Chuck, Blackie, Wild Flea, and Amish.
Animal, Stoop, Dizzy, Ozark, and Oakie. J.P. Soul, the Preacher and the
Rabbi, Tom Thumb, Friar Fuck, Baby Huey, Righteous Fuckin' Elroy, and
the Galloping Guinea.

The leather-clad Teutonic Knights were on the run, their pony-tailed Guineveres clinging to their backs. First in small bands of five or six, they rode down the quiet morning streets of sleepy little American towns and cities, where the roar of their unmuffled straight pipes rattled the window panes of small wooden-frame houses. Then, in larger packs, they roared down the highways, flying past wary motorists and puzzled cops, who sat dunking donuts in paper cups and spilling coffee on their laps. By evening, the packs had formed a caravan, an army of bearded barbarians on souped-up, chopped-down, raked-out hogs, gleaming chrome tailpipes, well-worn black leather jackets, and greasy denim vests with the image of Dark Surt grinning on their backs.

Their destination: Reading, Pennsylvania, where 12,000 straight motorcyclists were gathered for the Grand National 12-Mile races. A month earlier, when the same Reading Fairgrounds had been the site of the Billy Huber Memorial Races, the Pagans had been just one of many East Coast outlaw clubs, along with the Heathens of Reading.

The outlaw motorcycle club was a monster spawned unintentionally by the American Motorcycle Association (AMA), which claimed to represent 99 percent of the motorcycle owners in America. In 1965 the AMA published a pamphlet proclaiming that 99 percent of the motorcycle riders in America were hard-working, God-fearing, tax-paying, flag-waving, church-going, milk-sipping, cookie-eating, law-abiding citizens, and that the average American had nothing to fear from these people when they rode past on Sunday afternoons. It was the criminal element, the AMA claimed, the shit-kicking, beer-guzzling, gang-banging, ass-stomping, rock 'n' roll playing, hell-raising heathens and devil-worshiping hooligans who belonged to "outlaw clubs," which were not affiliated with the AMA. *Outlaw clubs*, the AMA again claimed, accounted for less than 1 percent of the people who rode motorcycles but accounted for 99 percent of all the crime, mayhem, and bad publicity that the public associated with motorcycles.

But the AMA had it all wrong. In the first place, I saw plenty of AMA motorcyclists raising hell, for which outlaw bikers later took the heat. Besides, there was a lot more to it than what the AMA claimed. It was part of what was beginning to be called the generation gap. Older motorcyclists belonged to the AMA clubs. They could remember when Marlon Brando made *The Wild One* and hamburgers cost a nickel. They wore black leather caps and '50s-style emblems, which they painted on the backs of their black leather jackets along with club names like Mercury Riders. They rode "garbage wagons," full-dress Harley-Davidsons equipped with windshields, saddle bags, *sesselfurzer* seats the size of living room chairs, and even radios and electric starters.

Outlaws were younger and leaner, longhaired rednecks and badass white boys with attitude. Many were Vietnam vets who still loved their country, but no longer trusted the government. Outlaws and criminals are not the same thing, as the AMA seemed to think. Criminals are crooks who manipulate the system to get rich. Outlaws simply don't give a shit. Al Capone was a criminal who died in bed a rich old man, his brain and wiener rotten with syphilis. John Dillinger was an outlaw. He died in a hail of bullets outside the Biograph Theater with his girlfriend on his arm. People came from all around Chicago with handkerchiefs to mop up his blood in the street like he was an American saint. That says it all about the difference between real outlaws and mere criminals. Outlaws like John Dillinger and Jesse James get cut down in the street but rise up from the dirt to live on as American legends, while the memories of wiseguys and mere criminals rot with their bodies in their expensive satin-lined coffins.

Outlaw bikers scorned helmets and Japanese motorcycles. We rode American, British, and German bikes with tiny bicycle seats and chopped-down fenders, stripped of all unnecessary accessories like windshields, saddlebags, mirrors, and front brakes. We souped-up the engines and raked-out the front ends. We wore our emblems and club names on sleeveless denim vests. That way we could wear the denim vest over our black leather jackets to proclaim our presence by "flying colors" (as we called it), or slip the denim vests under our leather jackets to avoid police detection. We reveled in our status as outlaws and began wearing swastikas just to piss off the world. And after the AMA published its pamphlet, we outlaws began wearing "1%" patches on the fronts of our jackets to disassociate ourselves from what we considered the "candy-ass" AMA riders.

Eventually the diamond-shaped one-percenter patches came to stand for everything the outlaw biker lived for and believed in. We guarded our patches with pride, and getting one ripped off was tantamount to castration. Not every club was allowed to wear them. On the West Coast only a handful of clubs wore them by mutual agreement. The Midwest, from the western foothills of the Alleghenies to the eastern foothills of the Rockies, was completely under the control of a Chicago-based outfit called simply the Outlaws who rode across the great prairies of the Heartland with a pair of crossed pistons and a grinning chrome skull named Charlie on their backs. But the East Coast was like a bunch of feudal baronies. Each town was dominated by a different club that went around ripping one-percenter patches off other clubs that they considered too candy-ass to wear them.

In 1966, the Maryland-based Pagans decided to change all that by building an East Coast outlaw empire. On December 23, 1966, the club rented an entire hotel in a dilapidated section of Newark, New Jersey, for a giant old-fashioned Yuletide celebration; they invited every respectable outlaw club on the East Coast. It was a good party, as outlaw parties go, and eventually the cops were called in. While the rest of the country prepared for the arrival of Saint Nick with visions of sugar plums dancing in their heads, the cops and the outlaws punched out each other in the halls and threw each other down the stairs for an hour. When it was all over, the cops had to commandeer a half-dozen busses from the local school district and drive the outlaws away handcuffed to the seats.

In an age when internet porn, violent rap lyrics, and pedophile priests have become everyday news items, it is hard to remember just how uptight, impressionable, and downright simpleminded most of the country was back in the mid-1960s. Imagine what it must have been like for average depression-born and World War II-bred Americans as they sat at the breakfast table in their new robes and slippers on Christmas morning, eating toast and sipping eggnog, while looking down at the barbaric images of long-haired redneck bikers and bandaged-up cops staring back at them from the pages of the Sunday paper. For an entire week, even the ultra-establishment *New York Times* treated it as a major cultural earthquake. On the pages of the *Washington Post*, one even detects a sense of municipal pride in Maryland's own infamous outlaw motorcycle club, as *Post* reporters actually hunted down and interviewed the Pagans for their account, which, not surprisingly, blamed the whole riot on the police.

The donnybrook apparently began about 1 a.m., when the hotel manager and special police officer James Robinson began to get antsy. The manager suggested that Robinson pull the plug on the band and tell the merrymakers to go home, which Robinson did.

"That's when they started emptying beer on me," Robinson later claimed, "and I called for help."

Help arrived in the form of two Newark police officers, who found Robinson "covered with beer" and surrounded by a crowd of shaggy revelers who were shouting "Heil Hitler!" at him. Someone draped a sheet over the shoulders of one of the cops as a joke, causing his partner to fly down the stairs and shout into his car radio: "Send everything!"

"Everything" turned out to be a phalanx of three dozen club-swinging cops charging up the stairs, and that's when the Yuletide festivities degenerated into a full-blown riot, which Newark Police Sergeant Roy Lane called "one of the most dangerous I have ever seen." The Pagans were driven off to the police station where, the newspapers reported, they were "stripped" of their iron crosses and "swastika charms," and "forced to take showers."

But perhaps the best performance was reserved for a buffoon named James Del Mauro, the Newark chief magistrate, who later in the week seemed more concerned with matters of hygiene than justice, as he dressed down the Pagans in a courtroom cordoned off by 35 plainclothes detectives.

"Never set foot in Newark again for any reason," he told the defendants. "This city doesn't want people like you." Then, in language reminiscent of how a red-faced Irish customs agent might have described Del Mauro's own people as they arrived at Ellis Island a half-century earlier, the judge continued, "You are the filthiest people I have ever seen. I look at you and wonder what has happened to the youth of today. I have been taught that there is nothing cheaper than soap and water to clean yourself with."

Perhaps he best described his sentiments after the initial arraignment, when a "shocked" Del Mauro told reporters, "I just don't understand these people."

The party may have ended in a bust, but for the Pagans it was a boom. The story was smeared all over the front page of the New York tabloids, and by the next afternoon, the Pagans were the biggest name in the East Coast motorcycle world. The site of the party, right across the river from Manhattan, had been deliberately chosen to antagonize the Pagans' biggest rivals, the Aliens. This club had resisted all offers to merge with the Pagans and considered the metropolitan New York area to be its exclusive fiefdom. For two years the Aliens had successfully ripped the one-percenter patches off every other club that tried to fly them in the metropolitan New York area.

At the party the Pagans announced that they had formed clubs in New York and New Jersey, as well as other cities like Bethlehem and Lancaster. By the next year, they claimed, the Pagans would be the only one-percenter club on the East Coast. Instead of fighting them, the Pagans invited the other clubs to join them in building an outlaw empire, from the frozen and snow-covered wastelands of northern Quebec to the swampy Everglades of Florida.

Starting a new club is one thing, but getting an established club to throw down its colors and patch over to your club is quite another. The Pagans were already negotiating with the big clubs in Baltimore, Wilmington, and Pittsburgh, but the Heathens of Reading were the big piece missing from the puzzle.

In those days Reading was still a hard-ass, blue-collar town. It was also a mob town. At one time it was the third-largest motorcycle manufacturing town in America. Its association with motorcycles continued, as every year it hosted races at the old Reading Fairgrounds. In the 1960s Pennsylvania had more motorcycles per capita than any state in the country, including

California. Reading was centrally located between the big East Coast cities: New York, Philadelphia, Baltimore, Washington, and Pittsburgh. And while the local Heathens may not have been the biggest club on the East Coast, they were one of the most respected, thanks to the leadership of a former paratrooper named Chuck Ginder.

The Heathens were a large club, and Chuck ran Reading like a feudal warlord. He had the cops scared, he had the mob scared, and he had the citizenry scared. Independent motorcyclists avoided riding in packs through his town, and they never wore denim jackets with cut-off sleeves, much less one-percenter patches, because they knew this was an invitation to getting hit in the head with a chain while sitting at a stoplight.

Chuck was a legend on the East Coast, and every club admired the way he had the town locked up. I even saw him stop ROTC cadets from Albright College and make them kneel down and unblouse their pants right on Penn Street. Sometimes I thought that as a former paratrooper he got madder at the bloused pants on college kids than at unauthorized one-percenter patches on motorcyclists. "At least they fuckin' ride motorcycles," he used to say. "Half these kids never even been on a plane, much less jumped out of one."

A month before the Memorial Day races, ambassadors from the Pagans had come to the Reading Fairgrounds for the Billy Huber Memorial races. They negotiated a deal with Chuck where his club would become Pagans but would be allowed to continue wearing small Heathen patches over their hearts. The week before Memorial Day, Satan rode up from Maryland with the new Pagan patches, which he handed over to Chuck in the editorial office of the *Berks County Record*. And the moment was recorded for posterity on the front page of the May 25th edition with banner headlines:

"Outlaw Motorcyclists En Route to Race"

"Reading Set for Grand National 12 Mile Contest"

"Local 'Heathens' Accepted as a 'Pagan' Chapter"

These headlines were followed by a half-page photo of three of the swastika-covered cavaliers, which ran the caption:

Heathens Join Pagans—It was quite an occasion last week in the Record office when several motorcycle buffs dropped in to join forces. For the "Heathens" cyclists of Reading, it meant being granted a Pagan chapter locally. Witnessing the transaction is "Big Jim" as "Pagan's" Satan, right, hands over the colors to "Chuck," president of the local group.

With the Heathens firmly in the pack, the Pagans were now ready for their first big show as the number one one-percenter club on the East Coast. We left New York early, rode down the dilapidated skyway they call the Brooklyn-Queens Expressway, over the Williamsburg Bridge, through Manhattan and the Holland Tunnel, then over the Newark Skyway, and into the marshy New Jersey Meadowlands, where we met the Jersey Pagans at an old bar stuck back in the high swampy marsh weeds.

When we pulled up, the Jersey brothers were coming through the door with their hands full of brown bottles of Rheingold beer. As they shoved them in our hands, we could feel that they were cold and covered with sweat. The swampy Meadowlands were already lush and green, but it would be another month before they started to stink. So we just sat on our bikes, sucking down the beer and fresh spring air. We exchanged the traditional outlaw greeting: a bear hug and a peck on the lips. Then after an outlaw breakfast of pickled eggs, dried beef jerky, and salted peanuts, we were off.

Like old-fashion cavalry brigades, outlaw motorcycle packs were followed by baggage trains, which were made up of pickup trucks, panel trucks, and cars with trailers. While it was mandatory that you show up for a run, it was not mandatory that you show up on a motorcycle. You just had to get there. Bikes got wrecked, or were impounded by the police. Brothers had just gotten out of jail, others were in casts.

The old '60s outlaws would do almost anything for a brother, but hauling one around on the backseat of his machine was not one of them. So the grounded brothers were condemned to ride in the baggage train with tools, stray women, citizen hangers-on, and the weekend supply of beer. If a grounded brother could not ride, he could at least get drunk.

Almost inevitably, Sweet William Parker rode in the baggage train, relentlessly sucking down one bottle of beer after another and titillating a party of ladies that he had picked up the night before. Sweet William found himself in the baggage train more often than not because he rode a motorcycle the way he drank beer and did everything else: to wretched excess. We used to tell him that he didn't need a throttle on his motorcycle—just an on-off switch. That's because the carburetor was either cranked wide open with the throttle nearly ripped off in his hand, or else he was standing on the brake pedal, all 230 pounds of him, trying to lock up the drum brakes and bring the screaming machine to a halt before he blew a red light and broad-sided a tractor trailer.

He blew head gaskets and burned valve seats, or just wrecked the thing and mangled it up like some dirt bike. Fortunately he had a Beeser, a British bike similar to a Triumph, manufactured by Birmingham Small Arms (BSA), and like Triumphs they were easy to repair and handled well. Had he tried some of his circus stunts on a hog, he would have wrecked a lot more often. It seemed his bike was in an almost constant state of repair—in someone else's garage. That's because we never let Willie work on his own bike. He had no mechanical ability whatsoever and he fixed bikes, like everything else, to wretched excess. He could apply enough torque to rip the head off a boar hog; ¼-inch aluminum bolts stood no chance against him. Eventually Geoff "PW" Quinn just told him, "Don't touch the fuckin' thing. Just bring it over here right away. It's easier to fix it before you go fuckin' everything up."

After a few breakdowns we arrived covered with grease and sweat at the rusty old steel bridge that spanned the Delaware River between Phillipsburg, New Jersey, and Easton, Pennsylvania. The Whiteknight was waiting for us with a contingent of Bethlehem Pagans drinking Horlacher beer from cans. The Whiteknight was a big Pennsylvania Dutch steelworker with tremendous tattooed biceps, a ruddy face, and brushed-back sandy red hair. He was a competitive weight lifter and an easygoing kinda guy, but strong enough to pick up a Sportster by himself and stick it in the back of a truck.

The Whiteknight gave us a hearty welcome and then led us to the clubhouse, which was sandwiched in a row of wood-frame company houses on a high hill overlooking the giant Bethlehem Steel mill. We got off our bikes and stretched. Car doors opened and brothers got out and cursed, while Willie staggered out and gave a wild yell. The Bethlehem brothers began throwing us cans of Horlacher from the porch. We opened them up and the beer spritzed all over the place. Then we stood in the street a while, drank beer, and talked. There were spring green mountains in the background, but down in the valley it was all grease and grime; the legendary Bethlehem Mill stretched out below like the smoldering carcass of a dragon with red brick scales. Steel and smoke, redneck bars, and country roads. The Pagans were in their element.

All three clubs—New York, Jersey, and Bethlehem—had strict orders not to go into Reading. The Mother Club did not want bands of drunken Pagans staggering around town getting into fights and getting arrested. They wanted every available member to show up at the fairgrounds, not to have half the club in jail for the races on Sunday morning.

The Whiteknight had been told to wait for a phone call, at which time we would be told how to go to Reading. In the meantime he told two prospective members to wait at the clubhouse for the call, and we collected the drunks who had staggered out to the cars and put them to sleep on couches. Then we rode in a pack to a Polack bar by the mill.

It was a classic Pennsylvania mill town bar—slightly greenish off-white paint, the color of old hard-boiled eggs. A couple of Phillies and a couple of Mets posters were scattered between other posters of American flags and sentiments like "Bomb Hanoi Now," and "America, Love It or Leave It." A yellowed, cracking photograph of General Douglas MacArthur decorated the front end of the back bar, and the back end was watched over by a photo of the former middleweight champion of the world, Tony Zale (whose real name was Tony Zaleski), the hardest piece of steel ever to roll out of Gary, Indiana—another hard-ass American town like Bethlehem and Reading.

There were old guys in beat-up caps with union buttons on them, sitting at the bar drinking shots of rye whiskey. In the back room a bunch of younger guys were shooting pool. When we walked in the older guys looked a little worried, especially the owner, a middle-aged guy who was tending bar. In fact, he looked like he'd just seen the angel of death walking through his door. The Whiteknight walked up to the bar with the Jersey and New York leaders and told him we were just there for a couple of beers and no trouble.

Actually, the Pagans rarely did have trouble in places like this. A lot of us were Teamster truck drivers, steel workers, and longshoremen, who had grown up around places like this. Trouble usually seemed to come from Italian mob wannabees in creased paints and patent leather shoes, college jocks—especially football players on steroids—and smartass middle-class mallrats who had not been smacked around enough when they were young. But in places like this, we were all forged out of ore from the same mine shaft, and soon everybody was pouring beer out of pitchers and shooting pool together. Then the phone rang and the owner handed it to the Whiteknight. "Let's go," he shouted as he handed it back to the owner.

The place emptied quicker than a courtroom after a not-guilty verdict. Outside, brothers were jumping on their kick starters and revving their engines. We rode back in a pack to the house on the hill, where there were more guys from Bethlehem and Allentown waiting for us. By the time we arrived, there were about 75 bikes all over the street in front of the house.

The Whiteknight came out of the house with Sleepy from New York and Updegraff from New Jersey. He held up his hands as a sign to shut off our engines. Dozens of engines shut off at once and our ears rang from the silence.

Then the Whiteknight spoke: "We are going to meet the rest of the club just north of Reading. We are going to ride in a pack. Stay in twos. Do not pass anyone. If a light turns red, do not stop. If a cop tries to pull you over, ignore him too. Stare straight ahead. Make him go to the front and pull over the entire pack."

Then he yelled, "Let's go."

First a few loud sputters, then a few roars, then the shit-kicking thunder of about 75 internal-combustion engines, a total of about 5,000 cubic inches of steel-lined cylinders, all roaring at once, each one revving at a different rate, each one bellowing through different lengths of tail pipe—some of which were swept up 4 feet in the air. It was like mechanical thunder roaring through every pipe of a Bach organ at once. Goose bumps would rise on your neck and your hair would try to stand straight up on your head. The only experience that ever came close was listening to the sound of thousands of Irish drums and war pipes coming up New York's Fifth Avenue on St. Patrick's Day.

We pulled out and rode double-file down old Route 222 through Kutztown, where people ran out on their porches to stare, as if we were an army of invading Huns. Just north of Reading, near a town called Moselem Springs, there was a large parking lot. Some of the old Heathens were already there. Others had gone to meet the Maryland and Virginia people and would be there in an hour. It was the gathering of the clan— the most Pagans ever assembled in one place at the same time. And this is where I first met the old Heathens, who for the past week had been the Reading Pagans.

There was Blackie, tall and lean, sitting on a raked hog with a chrome sissy bar. Half Sicilian and half Pennsylvania Dutch, he was dressed all in black, as was his bike. Even his hair and long pointed beard were black, as black and shiny as the hand-rubbed lacquer on his gas tank. On his forearm he had a topless bikini girl tattooed over the word "Honolulu," a souvenir from his army days.

Behind him sat his wife, Baby, a Mexican girl from Fresno. He had brought her back as a souvenir from his California days. She was as tall and lean as him—same height, same weight, same black hair. In fact if they had been mules, they would have been a matched pair.

Next to him was Righteous Fuckin' Elroy, a Mennonite farm boy from Leola, a Pennsylvania Dutch town in Lancaster County. Like Blackie, he was tall and lean, but with large hands and big bones, typical of the large component of Swiss and Alsatian blood in the Pennsylvania Dutch stock. He had dark brown hair, swept back in a mane like a wolfman, and deep-set, dark eyes.

Then there was Bob Rayel, or "Rayels" as he was called, Chuck's prime

minister and number two man in the Reading club. He wore a helmet—
not one designed for safety, but a steel Nazi helmet with red swastikas
emblazoned on the sides. It was the only kind of helmet an outlaw ever
wore back in those days.

But the most impressive thing about him was sitting behind him—his
wife. She had auburn brown hair, cut in bangs and falling in clean waves
over her shoulders. She was only 20 at the time, yet she had two kids
already out of diapers. Still, with her soft green eyes and pouting mouth,
she looked like a little Pennsylvania Dutch teen-angel herself. Sweet 16 and
Queen of the Hop. The two of them contrasted each other's appearance
as much as Blackie and his wife complemented each other. I remember I
made a point to check out the handle on her name patch as we waited in
the cool night air for the rest of the pack. It just said "Jane."

This was the beginning of the golden summer of '67. The Pagans then
looked nothing like today's popular media-generated stereotype of the
biker image: some middle-aged graybeard loon with a big belly who goes
around sounding like a cross between Burl Ives and your standard New
York City homeless-rights advocate, calling everyone "Bro."

The Pagans milling around the parking lot that night were much leaner
and younger. Members approaching 30 like Pappy, the Irishman from
Jersey with the big Teamster truck-driver beer-belly, were exceptions.
Their hair was long, but pushed back and greasy, and their beards were
trimmed. It was obvious that they spent more time listening to Johnny
Cash and Patsy Cline than to Bob Dylan and Joan Baez. But the beards
would grow shaggier and the hair more unkempt. In a few years when
the country scene moved from Nashville to Austin, the outlaw biker
would replace the cowboy as the fashion model for a new generation of
longhaired redneck country singers, and the motorcycle would replace
the horse as one of the redneck's three most prized possessions, along
with his dog and his gun.

Many of these guys also were veterans with their own brand of
patriotism. They wore swastikas, but they would stomp anyone in a minute
for burning an American flag. Most of them hated George Rockwell's
neo-Nazis as much as they hated war protesters. There were no ethnic or
outside group loyalties in the club. You were either a Pagan or you were not.

In a group of 200 Pagans, you might find two with some obvious African ancestry, or maybe two Puerto Ricans or two Jews. But at this time you could safely say that 99 percent of the collective ancestors of your one-percenters, clear back to the Stone Age, had lived north of the Alps and east of the Danube River. In other words, the outlaw bikers of the '60s were descended from the same Celts, Hunkies, and Germans who terrorized the shit out of the Greeks and Romans 2,000 years ago, with their long hair, tattoos, outlandish attire, and hard-drinking, violent behavior.

In the dim mist-shrouded past of history, these people had worshipped the swastika as a symbol of the raw, violent, creative, and masculine side of the divine force behind the universe. It was the symbol of a god who rode on the wings of the wind and hurled thunderbolts from the heavens. As such they could not have chosen a more appropriate symbol.

And then there were our women.

There were no women members, as such, and no women rode their own bikes in the pack. Remember, these were the days of mule-headed carburetors and defiant kick starters that could toss you over the handlebars in a heartbeat. And like the Pennsylvania Dutch religious sects, the behavior that the club expected from male and female members was radically different. Here again, these women had nothing in common with the popular media-generated image of the loud-mouthed biker bitch.

These were country girls who grew up in the valleys attending church on Sunday, but during the rest of the week they listened to songs like "He's a Rebel" and "The Leader of the Pack." After school, they drifted into town and either got pregnant or went to work in the mills, where the only air conditioning was an open window. As they bent over their machines and the sweat poured from their brows, they dreamed about cold lager beer, the smell of well-worn leather jackets, and riding through the cool night air with their arms wrapped tightly around a bearded barbarian with tattooed biceps. Just after dark, another pack rode up. At the head of it rode Chuck Ginder, leader of the Reading Pagans, and behind him sat Sweet Pea, his eight-month-pregnant wife. Next to him, his long greasy hair blowing in the night breeze, rode Fred "Big Dutch" Burhans, Grandmaster of the entire Pagan nation, the man who turned a loose confederation of rebel clubs from Maryland and Virginia into an outlaw empire. Behind them rode the Maryland and Virginia Pagans. The Southrons wore as much Confederate as Nazi paraphernalia, thus proudly embracing their Southern birthright at a time when pragmatic and ambitious Southern white boys were trying to run as far away from that heritage as they could.

After a brief huddle with the Mother Club, the individual club leaders called their brothers together and explained the rules. Our man Sleepy was a squat little guy with a Dean Martin hairdo and sunglasses, who walked with the wobbly gait of a slow-moving gas station attendant.

After he wobbled over, he pushed his Dean Martin sunglasses up over his forehead and explained the rules to us: "We are going to ride through Reading in a pack. There's 10,000 citizen bikers in town from all over the country. They're all going to be downtown. And we are going to ride from one end of town to the other. We are not going to stop. Chuck and Dutch are going to ride at the head of the pack."

Then he added that we would not be partying in Reading. The club didn't want any hassles with citizens the night before the big races. The Reading people had rented a cornfield out on the Lancaster County line and it was there that we were going to party. There would be guys flying patches from other clubs, and every one of them was in the process of becoming a Pagan. They were all to be treated just like brothers, and anyone starting a hassle would get his colors yanked right on the spot.

Then Chuck gave us the word and we started our bikes—over 500 of them—in a deafening roar like the coming of Ragnarok. Chuck and Dutch pulled out at the head of the pack and the rest followed. Before us lay one of the oldest cities in America.

Reading sits at the foot of Mount Penn, on the Schuylkill River, and along the old railroad line that connects Philadelphia with the old anthracite coal region. It was originally a Pennsylvania Dutch market town, and by the Civil War it was the capital of German-speaking America. But by 1900 it was becoming an industrial town with a large influx of immigrants from Eastern and Southern Europe. With the advent of Prohibition, it became the beer capital of America, as beer-baron Max Hassel continued to operate all five of Reading's breweries illegally, but at full capacity.

Hassel, a 19-year-old immigrant at the time the Eighteenth Amendment was passed, had the vision to see that the law would never work. He formed a real estate company and bought up all five of Reading's breweries, as well as night clubs and bars, which he operated as speakeasies. Under Hassel's reign, Reading became Sin City, with wide-open prostitution and gambling in the alleys off Penn Street. High rollers and revelers rolled in from New York, Philadelphia, Baltimore, and Washington. Night life in the clubs on Penn Street hummed, and at one time the city was home to the biggest floating craps game in the world.

By the mid-1960s a reform government had cleaned up most of that. There was still gambling and prostitution, but the high rollers were gone. Many residents now considered the night life dull and were looking for something to put some spice back into the town. Also because of the proximity to New York and Philadelphia, some of the country boys were starting to feel rebellious and sported a longhaired redneck image. Eventually they found their way into the Heathens, which became one of the largest and most respected outlaw clubs on the East Coast.

Now they were all Pagans. And for the next couple of years they would provide the locals with the excitement the town was looking for, until the locals decided that the Pagans were too hot and tried to clean them up like they had cleaned up the mob—but that was later. On this Saturday night of Memorial Day weekend 1967, the Pagans were about to burst into Reading as the undisputed outlaw kings of the East Coast.

The pack rode in from the north, out of the shadow of the Blaubarrick (Blue Mountain), past the silent graves of the Charles Evans Cemetery and the idle coal cars in the quiet railroad yards, all the way up to City Park, where Penn Street begins at the base of Mount Penn. Then, while the town was warming up to the sound of country swing bands with names like Dottie and the Dukes and Curly Smith and the Spadesmen, the Pagans descended down Penn Street. Two abreast, in a dark line of chain whips, earrings, gleaming chrome, straight exhaust pipes, and swastikas, with our women clinging to our backs, the bearded barbarians rode through town like a wave of thunder.

Today Laurie Hartmann is a little league coach who lives in central

Pennsylvania where her husband drives a mail truck, but she remembers that night well: "I was only 10 years old at the time," she says, "but we only lived a half block off Penn Street. I could hear them coming from the other end of town, and I remember sitting up in my bed watching them go by on Penn Street. All the kids in the neighborhood talked about it for years."

The adults talked about it for years too. The Pagans put some spice back into the town on that warm spring night in 1967, when a band of guys, many of whom had not known each other a year earlier, suddenly found themselves banded together in the number one one-percenter club on the East Coast.

The pack rode down to the end of Penn Street, where it crossed the Schuylkill River Bridge under the big yellow letters of the Sunshine Brewery sign. Then we rode out Route 222 for the Lancaster County Line, to the party that was on a farm they had rented. The fields had just been plowed, so everyone had to stay on the perimeter. We parked our bikes in the mud and cursed as the cars and trucks got stuck and had to be pushed out of ruts. Soon the spring mud was up to the tops of our boots. But finally everyone got parked and we settled down to party. There were hundreds of Pagans, as well as the other clubs that were about to become Pagans, clubs from Pittsburgh, Baltimore, and Wilmington.

Sleepy walked up to me with a can of Old Dutch beer in each hand, his slow-moving gas station attendant walk rendered even more ridiculous by the fact that he now had to suck his foot out of the mud with each step. Finally, huffing and puffing, he made it over to me and shoved one of the beer cans in my hand.

"Fuckin' shithole," he mumbled.

"I was thinkin' the same thing," I said. We sat down on the bumper of a truck.

"I mean," he said, "these guys come to New York, we take them out and show them the bars and clubs, and they can party and get laid."

"That's right," I said, "We don't take 'em to the garbage dumps in Greenpoint or the cemeteries in Maspeth."

"A whole fuckin' city with 12,000 scooter-jockeys in town," he mumbled, "just 10 miles up the road, and we gotta sit here in some fuckin' cornfield, where there ain't even a decent place to take a shit."

And so there we sat, two Brooklynites in Pennsylvania. A Dutchman from Ridgewood and Wop from Williamsburg, drinking beer we had never heard of and without even a decent place to take a shit, as Sleepy had put it. We had passed over the Aliens and instead joined an upstart rebel club, and here we now were sitting in a cornfield on the bumper of a truck, in Lancaster County, Pennsylvania, slowly allowing ourselves to be absorbed into the great rural Redneck Republic of America.

We sat quietly, resting for a while and absorbing the whole thing. Then Sleepy turned to me, slapped me on the arm, and said, "But you know what? I wouldn't have it any other way. I really like these guys. It's just this feeling I got in my bones that this is a great thing we got goin' here."

And he was right. I was thinking the same thing: it was a great thing. Thirty years later, the widow of one Reading Pagan described it this way: "I remember we had this club called the Heathens, and then we became Pagans back in '67. And then suddenly all you guys started showing up from New York, Jersey, Maryland, and Virginia, guys who had never seen each other before. But you were all acting like you had known each other all your lives. You were just like brothers. I never saw anything like it in my life, except maybe for the Mennonites."

I never heard it better put. The Pagans were a one-percenter outlaw motorcycle brotherhood, medieval and mystical, far more like the religious warrior brotherhood of Teutonic Knights than some sort of modern criminal cartel like the government and media were always trying to tell people it was.

The next day we arrived at the fairgrounds in a pack. It was hot and sunny. It was also the first year as a reporter for *Reading Eagle* columnist Joseph N. Farrell. He was one of the reporters assigned to cover the races. It was his first meeting with the Pagans, and he would later become an expert on them. Here is the way he remembers it:

> There's a picture that's been indelibly imprinted in my mem-
> ory for 30 years now, of a hippie girl, a flower child in beads
> sitting at the feet of a stern state police commander in full riot
> gear, offering peace and love to those around her.

None of whom was interested.

The state police commander and his squadron were blocking the gates to the old Reading Fairgrounds race track against a horde of mounted Pagans, the "outlaw" motorcycle gang in full force.

The Pagans wanted in, with their bikes, to the grandstand area, where hundreds or perhaps even thousands of respectable motorcycle enthusiasts were cheering on their professional motorcycle racers.

It was the clean shaven 99 percent under siege by the greasy, bearded one percent, or Attila at the gates of Rome, and the state police were having none of it.

The Pagans could go in, they were told, but not with their bikes—the cops feared, with good reason, the gang would literally ride roughshod over the clean-cut cyclists in the stands and create a riot.

Whether or not the Pagans had that in mind—and let's face it, they probably did—what they told the police was that they would never leave their bikes outside, out of sight, to be mauled over by vandals or curious cops looking for serious infractions.

It was in many ways a game no one could win. The Pagans never did get in, but the fear of future attempts put an end to motorcycle races at the Fairgrounds.

Reading Eagle
May 26, 1997

No one remembers who the flower girl was, but the state trooper standing over her was Harley Smith, an old-fashioned Pennsylvania Dutch cop, who was capable of drinking beer or swinging a truncheon as hard as any Pagan. It would not be his last run-in with the club, nor would it be Joe Farrell's.

When the Pagans disappeared out the other end of town, no one knew what to expect or where we would appear next. The locals had panicked and called out the riot police. Although the national guard would have been better, the riot police served our purpose. We could have left prospects—our term for wannabee members who were still on probation—to guard the bikes and then gone in without them. But had we done that, then everyone would have known what happened. This way no one knew what would have happened. They could only speculate.

At the time we didn't know all of this. All we knew is that we had rode all the way to Reading to hang out in a hot dusty gravel-covered parking lot for an hour, with dust flying all around us, pissing and moaning and cursing with no beer, only to break up into small packs and ride back to Bethlehem, where we sat on the wood-frame porch of the clubhouse all night drinking Horlacher and watching the lights in the mill.

But whether we guys from Long Island or the brothers from Bethlehem knew it or not, one thing was now certain. There were 12,000 motorcyclists inside the fairgrounds and the riot police had been called out to protect them. How could other clubs now claim to be real outlaws when the riot police had to be called out to protect them from the Pagans?

That weekend a legend had been hatched in Reading from an egg laid in Muspell.

CHAPTER 2

*The Spirit of the Lord is a raging fire in the breast of the
faithful that devours the impious.*
— Thomas Munzer, Patron Saint of Outlaws

The Pagans Outlaw Motorcycle Club was started by a bunch of
rebels from Prince George's County, Maryland, back in the days
when Prince George's County wasn't a bedroom community for federal
workers, but still a part of the Deep South. Lou Dolkin is generally
credited as the pied piper who hatched the idea. For their emblem they
wanted the image of an ancient god of Northern Europe. John-John
Griffith got the idea of Dark Surt, the demonic guardian of Muspell, from
a comic book. They drew him up with horns like a bull and feet like a
chicken, and then sat him in an arch of fire holding a flaming sword. And
the club was born.

Soon the Pagans had a half-dozen clubs terrorizing rednecks and bar
owners along the highways of Southern Maryland and Virginia. Hairy,
bearded, swastika-wearing, '60s-style outlaws, born to raise hell and have
a good time—it wasn't long until one of the rebels got in a hassle with
some punks from a local car club.

On a Sunday morning in June 1966, Samuel Duane Fredericks, a 21-
year-old Pagan from Montgomery County, took a ride to North Beach,
a small resort town on the Chesapeake Bay. There he was confronted by
members of a car club called the Avengers. The Pagan did not back down.
For his defiance he received a savage beating and stomping at the hands
of the car club, after which he staggered to his bike and tried to ride home.

It didn't work. As he was riding down New Hampshire Avenue in Prince George's County, he rear-ended a car that was stopped at a red light and later died of his injuries. According to the *Washington Post*, the Pagans blamed the Avengers and swore out "a blood feud."

The Southern cultural roots of the early Pagans cannot be overstated. The five counties on the peninsula between the Chesapeake Bay and the Potomac River are collectively referred to by locals as Southern Maryland. In the presidential election of 1864, only 16 people in all five counties voted for Abraham Lincoln, and one of them was lynched the following day. Throughout the Civil War the whole place had to be occupied by Union troops and kept under martial law. After shooting Abraham Lincoln, John Wilkes Booth deliberately chose this area for his escape route because he knew that he would be safer in Southern Maryland than the cops and federal agents who were sent to look for him under heavily armed military escort. It was only after Booth crossed the river into Virginia, where he mistakenly believed that he would be even safer, that the federal government was able to get someone to betray him. Memories of the Old South and the Civil War die hard in this region and persist until this day. Although the locals are really river and swamp rats, in many ways their clannish attitudes are similar to the mountain folk of Appalachia. Thus the Pagans and Avengers agreed to settle their differences in an old-fashioned hillbilly-style Reckenin'.

The chosen site was the parking lot of the Lee-Harrison Shopping Center in Arlington, Virginia. About sunset, heavily armed members of the Avengers began arriving in the parking lot, while the Pagans sat in the woods next to the parking lot, holding rifles and shotguns and waiting for the magic hour of 11 o'clock. The cops had been tipped off; they had the place staked out and were waiting for something to start, but they had overlooked a major flaw in their set-up.

"That's the oldest trick in the book," an Avenger's girlfriend told the *Washington Post* the following day. "When they [the police] change that old shift (11 p.m.), they're headed for coffee and the sack and you can do whatever you want for 15 minutes. Hell," she added, "the Pagans sat up in the bushes and watched the cops pull out."

Sure enough, as soon as the cops pulled out to change shifts, the area erupted into a hail of gunfire, with the Pagans firing into the parking lot and the Avengers firing back blindly into the weeds. Windshields shattered, shotgun pellets dented car fenders, people screamed, engines roared, and tires squealed as the parking lot began clearing out. Oddly enough, casualties were light, and police were back in force within minutes with both the early and late shift. By that time the Pagans had made their point and slipped off into the dense brush. However, according to the *Post*, the police did manage to round up about half the Avengers, along with two sawed-off shotguns, four standard shotguns, five cheap rifles, two revolvers, two automatic pistols, as well an assortment of tire chains, tire irons, billy clubs, and a "baseball bat bristling with dozens of nails and screws."

The following morning, red-faced police officers were busy trying to explain their snafu to the *Post* reporters. While admitting that they could have found a pretext for breaking up the gathering before it turned violent, one anonymous police officer claimed that "they just would have moved it to another place." He then added, "Besides, we're tired of chasing these hoods around. We wanted some arrests."

Nobody ever heard from the suburban car club again. But the Pagans were all over the *Washington Post* for a week, and the whole town was talking about them. "Suburban Washington is getting worse than Southeast Asia," the Beltway pundits were claiming.

The Pagans learned from this incident that one righteous brother willing to go down for the club was worth 10 hangers-on who were only looking for cheap thrills and loose women. Whenever a prospective member came along, the first question a Pagan asked was "Is he good people?" That meant if he got in jam, would he go to jail or would he talk and send a brother to jail in his place? They also learned that while a hundred people flying colors on a highway might impress motorists, you were better off with a small club of about 12 righteous people. You didn't want people who would show up for a party and then split when the shit hit the fan.

By the mid-1960s the Pagans had come under the leadership of Fred "Dutch" Burhans, an imperialist who had visions of ruling an outlaw empire spanning the whole East Coast, from the frozen parishes of French Canada to the rebel trailer parks on the sandy beaches of Florida. He established a half-dozen clubs in Southern Maryland and Virginia. Then he crossed the Mason-Dixon Line and went into the Amish farmlands of Lancaster County, Pennsylvania.

There he went after a well-established and respected club, the Sons of Satan. The leader was John "Satan" Marron, a man who listened to Dutch's imperial dreams and liked what he heard. The Pagans soon had their first club in Pennsylvania. If Dutch was the empire builder, the Caesar, then Satan became the ambassador, his Mark Antony. Satan could show up at a clubhouse on Friday night and talk nonstop until Sunday afternoon. And by the time he left, everyone's sides hurt from laughing and half your club would be ready to join his new outlaw empire.

Satan also brought something else to the Pagans. His roots went deep into the Dutch countryside. He had deep blue eyes and hair as black as shoe polish that he swept back in a thick mane like a lion. His jaw, his nose, his cheeks were square. Take away the swastikas and leather jacket, put him in a black hat and pastel blue shirt with suspenders, and he could be hawking shoofly pies from the back of an Amish buggy in rural Lancaster County.

The Amish are the strictest of the Pennsylvania Dutch religious groups that go by the Mennonite name. Any journalist or cop who spent time investigating the early Pagan clubs of Pennsylvania was shocked by their strong—but weirdly contrasting—similarity to the Amish and Mennonite communities: the sense of secrecy and brotherhood; the suspicion of outsiders and the whole outside world in general; the codes of dress that distinguish the brethren from outsiders; and the rigid distinctions in the behavior expected from male and female members of the community. Both communities believed in taking care of all the needs of its brethren, had a fanatical devotion to the community and its style of life, and had a similar manner in which they were expected to shun members who were thrown out of the community. Both shared an eighteenth-century, medieval, mystical, and thoroughly Teutonic outlook on the world. However the Mennonites were pacifists, and here the similarity stopped.

Historically, the Mennonite brethren were not always pacifists. They grew out of the largely peasant Anabaptist rebellion in Germany. In fact there was a time when they were not so different from the outlaw motorcyclists of the 1960s.

On Halloween night 1517, Martin Luther nailed a petition to the church door in Wittenberg that amounted to a declaration of war against the Italians who ran the Roman Catholic Church. Luther called on the Christian nobility of the German nation to drive the Pope's Italian agents out of Germany. This they gladly did—but they also confiscated the Church's property for themselves.

Inspired by Luther, Thomas Munzer organized the German peasants into the Kingdom of Zion, a religious brotherhood in whose members the Holy Spirit burned as a living flame that devoured the impious—the impious being all who got in the way of Thomas Munzer's new world order: priests, nuns, bishops, abbots, magistrates, nobles, Jews, Italians, bankers, merchants—that is, for all practical intents and purposes, anyone who was not a good, hard-working German farmer with beer on his breath and shit between his toes.

The Brotherhood of Zion sacked churches, monasteries, and cathedrals. They burned every painting and smashed every statue they got their hands on. They established a Mother Club at Muhlhausen in Thuringia, where they proclaimed polygamy and divided the women among themselves. Finally the imperial authorities raised an army to crush them, but the Brotherhood rallied under a banner with a hammer on it, the symbol of the ancient pagan god of thunder. On May 15, 1525, Munzer led his zealots to destruction on the battlefield of Frankenhausen, where they fought with a stubborn fanaticism right down to the last man. In the end Munzer was captured, tortured, and killed.

Later the Brotherhood was reorganized along the Rhine River by Menno Simmons, who introduced a new doctrine of pacifism. But the old spirit of rebellion still burned in the Mennonite's hearts, and they were arrested, tortured, and killed up and down the Rhine river valley for their obstinate refusal to recognize any spiritual or civic authority outside their own community.

Eventually William Penn invited the Brothers of Zion, along with every other religious fanatic in the Rhine valley, to his new colony of Pennsylvania. The Mennonites represented only a small portion of these German settlers, who were called Dutch because the English misunderstood the Germanic pronunciation of "German"—"Deutsche"—while the Lutherans and Reformed made up the majority. But all of them shared a common fanatical, rebellious, and mystical attitude that caused problems in colonial America.

Respectable theologians at Harvard, Yale, and Princeton lumped all the German religious groups together into what they contemptuously called "the Pennsylvania Religion." Highly inspired by the mystical teachings of Jacob Boehme and Hildegard of Bingen, the Pennsylvania Religion contained elements gleaned not just from Christianity, but also from Teutonic paganism, the Jewish Kabbalah, and what is today called homeopathy, pantheism, organic gardening, feminist theology, Wicca, Gaia theory, and, in general, New Age religion. As such it was the closest thing there ever was to an authentic all-American theology.

That outlaw mentality of the Pennsylvania Dutch is most graphically illustrated in the *Martyrsspiegel* (*The Martyrs Mirror*), the most popular book in colonial Pennsylvania after the Bible. It is an illustrated account of every German martyr who ever died for the Protestant faith. There are hundreds of them, but the story of Simon de Kramer captures the general point of the whole book.

Simon operated a produce stall in the market at Bergen op Zoom in the Netherlands. Shortly after the Netherlands were ripped out of the German Empire and placed under Spanish control, the new Spanish bishop made a pompous display of piety by parading through the market place holding a consecrated host above his head. Everyone kneeled in homage except Simon, who stood defiantly with his hands folded. For his stubbornness Simon was arrested and killed.

You don't have to be a literary scholar to see that the story of Simon de Kramer is a retelling of the story of Lucifer. Both Simon and Lucifer are outlaws who refuse to bend their knee to authority. For his insolence Lucifer was cast into Hell, and for the same offense Simon was tortured and killed. It's the same story, the same moral lesson. How you look at it only depends on which side of the law you happen to be on.

Early on, the Pennsylvania Germans got in a feud with the Quaker authorities in Philadelphia, and the Germans formed an alliance with another group of outlaws who were driven from their homes and settled in Pennsylvania and Maryland: the Scots and Irish. These groups then cemented their bond by forming gangs of militia and slaughtering Indians.

The protestants from Northern Europe who settled in America proved again and again that they could beat their plowshares back into swords when there was an ass that needed kicking. In 1776 a Lutheran minister, Peter Muhlenberg, ripped off his black robe while at the pulpit during the course of a Sunday sermon and stood before his congregation in the uniform of a brigadier general. "There is a time to preach, but now is the time to fight," he told his shocked parishioners. Muhlenberg then left the pulpit and led a Pennsylvania Dutch contingent to join George Washington's Continental Army. This Dutch contingent formed the largest component in Washington's army at Valley Forge, and fought and suffered as stubbornly under Muhlenberg in America as their ancestors had under Thomas Munzer in Europe. They were the first troops to cross the Hudson River and bring relief to the beleaguered New England colonies, and at Yorktown Muhlenberg's Dutchmen mounted the final American offensive of the Revolutionary War, crushing Lord Cornwallis' defenses and forcing the British surrender that led to American independence.

These were the kind of Germans who settled colonial Pennsylvania. Today they no longer practice polygamy or slay the impious with their hog-butchering knives, but otherwise very little has changed in the mentality of rural Pennsylvania Dutch towns. There is the same clannishness, the same suspicion, the same stubbornness. And there is the same contempt for authority, pomposity, and pontification that Thomas Munzer instilled in his followers 400 years ago. Only when you understand the kind of people who settled this part of the country can you truly understand the real outlaw mentality of Chuck Ginder, Satan, and the Pagans Motorcycle Club in Pennsylvania.

It was these same indomitable and defiant Dutch roots that gave Satan an invaluable asset in forming new clubs. When sizing up a prospective member, Satan was unimpressed by how big the guy was, how righteous he looked, or how loud he talked. Satan was looking for something more important, and he had an uncanny ability to spot it in a guy who was ready to bring to the club the fanatical commitment of a religious martyr. For better or for worse, this is what Chuck and Satan brought to the Pagans. They shaped the legend in Southeastern Pennsylvania, where it endures to this day.

This peculiar grafting of Pennsylvania Dutch fanaticism on the roots of rural Southern folkways had a lot to do with making the early Pagans different from any other outlaw club, and it also explains why fascination with the Pagans runs so deep in rural Maryland and Pennsylvania. I once spoke to the widow of a Pagan who told me that a few months earlier, she had been down at the local fire hall where some guy started hitting on her. He told her that he was one of the three guys who started the Reading Pagans back in the mid-1960s. What he didn't know was that her husband was one of the three guys. The other two were Chuck and Satan. She had never even heard of this guy.

"You have to understand," she told me, "you guys are all dead, in jail, or run out of town, but everyone you meet here tells you that they were a Pagan or at least good friends with one of them. I don't even bother explaining to them anymore who my husband was."

Notice that the graybeard old loon didn't try to impress this grandmother in the fire hall bar by telling her that he pitched for the Phillies, received a Medal of Honor in Vietnam, or made a million on Wall Street and then lost it in Las Vegas. No. He said he was a Pagan, because that's what he expected would impress her.

Thirty years ago, we terrorized the shit out of these hinds, and today they talk about us like we're William Tell or Robin Hood.

But like the t-shirts say, it's the Legend that lives on.

CHAPTER 3

I am the Spirit that denies.

— Mephistopheles, Goethe's *Faust*

Idrifted into the Pagans during the winter of 1966–1967.
In retrospect it seems a matter of fate. I was born in Brooklyn and grew
up in a section of Maspeth, Queens called Polack Alley. In the fall of 1966,
I was 19 years old, and I had been taking home $52.47 every week as a
produce clerk. Then my old man got me a union card in the Amalgamated Lithographers of America, Local 1, and I went to work as a press ten-
der. In the lithographing business at this time it was either feast or famine.
Right then it was feast, and I was soon working 12 hours a day, seven days a
week, and taking home over $200 a week. In order to have any sort of social
life, I often stayed up between shifts and showed up drunk 12 hours later,
which was no big deal back in those days. One Saturday night in October,
my buddy, Jimmy Tillman, and I decided, for whatever reason, to stop at
the Hicksville Farmers' Market while we were on our way to a bar. We were
walking down an aisle past a clothing stall, where I spotted a shiny black
motorcycle jacket.

That's cool, I thought, always having had a weakness, bordering on
addiction, for black leather jackets and western boots.

"How much?" I asked.

"Thirty bucks," the guy said. Given my newly found affluence as a
union man, I didn't even try to argue with the guy. I just pulled out my
bankroll, peeled off the money, and handed it to him. He looked shocked,

but didn't say a word, and I walked out sporting a new black leather motorcycle jacket. But a problem soon developed.

When we got to the bar a young lady about my age came up to me and said, "Oooooh, do you have a motorcycle?"

Shit, I thought. *This is embarrassing.* But then, remembering the kind of money I was making, I looked at her and said, "No, but I will in a couple of weeks."

So less than a month later, my buddy John Boos and I were down in Wantagh stuffing a beat-up, but serviceable, 1963 Triumph TR6 in the trunk of a car. And that was that.

Now this is what mathematicians call complexity theory, but the ancient Germans just thought of it as the way the three "women of the weird" wove the great rope of human destiny. Either way, had I not gone to the farmers' market that night, or had we not walked down that aisle, or had I been looking at the tits on a girl coming down the aisle the other way, or been bullshitting, or doing anything else to distract my attention, I may not have seen that jacket, bought it, been accosted by that young lady in the bar, and gotten a motorcycle. Then I would not have become a Pagan that winter, come to Pennsylvania, gone to jail, and gotten into Penn State, where I met my wife. In which case all six of my children would have never been born. *Schicksal* (fate) and *Verhangnis* (doom): two words in German which carry a weight of inevitability that cannot be translated into any other language. Sure enough, the course of my life was changed forever that night by a whimsical stop at the farmers' market, an impulsive clothing purchase, and an inquisitive young girl in a bar.

Now Harley-Davidson is forever associated with the outlaw image—and for good reason. When you saw a pack of outlaws, most of them were riding Hogs. Chopped Hogs had the mystique and looked great. But in those days, chopped Hogs were made by amateurs in garages with dirt floors, and they broke down a lot. The truth is if you rode a Harley chopper, you needed a truck or car. Besides, choppers with up-front cruise pegs and ape hanger handlebars could be hell on wet ground or snow.

The Triumph, or "Trumpet" as it was called, and the Beeser started in all weather, and the front ends were the best ever made. You could even ride them on snow and ice, just put your feet down and glide along slow. If the rear wheel went sideways, you caught your balance with your feet and straightened the bike out. Try this with a Hog, and you broke your leg. But best of all, the Triumph and BSA were also designed for British roads, which, back in the mid-twentieth century, for all intents and purposes, were the same as off-road. If a cop was chasing you down the back roads of Berks County, you could take off through a cornfield. You could never get away with that on a Hog.

I rode through the winter. And I froze. On weekends my Triumph was the only bike parked outside the Gaslight East on Hempstead Turnpike. In the summer the place was a motorcycle hangout with 50 bikes lined up in the street, but in the winter these guys traveled by car. They weren't outlaws.

Occasionally on those cold winter nights, another solitary rider pulled up on a BSA and backed up his bike to the curb next to mine. Over his black leather jacket he wore a sawed-off denim vest with a one-percenter patch on the front. His name was Richie Gavin, and the patches on the back of his vest identified him as a member of the Nassau Aliens.

He was impressed by the fact that, like him, I rode through the winter. It was the sort of thing that the old outlaws called "true class," something you either had or did not. And you simply could not make it up, like a lot of guys tried to do later. On the nights he showed up, we ended up sitting off in a corner talking by ourselves. We were different then the rest of the crowd. Real outlaws always manage to find each other. One night he picked up his shot glass, clicked it against mine, and said, "In the spring you gotta come around and ride with us." We drank to it.

This meant that I had found someone to sponsor me as a prospective member. If they were all like Richie, I figured I would be an Alien by Memorial Day.

Then one of the regulars at the Gaslight East, a guy from Levittown called Billy Koharet, told me to hold off on the Aliens. He told me that the guy who ran the Nassau Aliens, the Mortician, was a pain in the ass. He said that he had a better idea. He had his bike torn down for the winter. But he said that it would be back together in a couple of weeks. In the meantime he was having patches made up to start his own outlaw club.

"I figure we got about a dozen guys in here that would make outlaw material," he said. "The rest can go piss on themselves."

I didn't like the idea of passing up the number one one-percenter club in the number one city in the world for some Mickey Mouse start-up operation. With clubs in most of the New York boroughs and Long Island, the Aliens had established themselves a year earlier as the only one-percenter club in the metropolitan New York area. On a weekend the Aliens could ride to Rockaway or Coney Island with a pack of about 50.

The Brooklyn Aliens were the most colorful club, and that's where it all started with Johnny Pinstripe and Frankie Wheelchair. Pinstripe owned a shop in Bay Ridge, where he did the best custom paint jobs in New York. This was back in the days when it was all done with a brush by hand, so that's how he got his name. He even found a pair of Levi's with those real fine black and white stripes like railroad workers used to wear, so everybody would know who he was when they saw him riding down Cross Bay Boulevard.

Wheelchair is another story. He ripped his bike apart one winter in the back of Pinstripe's shop, where he found welding torches. Then he bought some steel and began making his own custom seat and sissy bar. All winter he talked about this project and what a "drop-dead good-looking" piece of equipment it was going to be. Finally, spring rolled around and the big night arrived when he had promised to show off his new custom seat and sissy bar all chromed and polished. He pulled up to a bar in Coney Island and everyone went out to have a gander at this drop-dead custom seat and sissy bar that by now had been played up like the Eiffel Tower on wheels.

But this was Brooklyn, the wiseacre capital of the world. When they got outside, people just shrugged their shoulders, and finally somebody just said, "It looks like a fuckin' wheelchair ta me." And that was that.

The Bronx was the biggest Alien club, and it was also the baddest. The guys had been together for 20 years. They played handball in the park together when they were kids. As teenagers they formed a street gang and stole hubcaps. The street gang became a car club, and the final incarnation was the Bronx Aliens Outlaw Motorcycle Gang. Now some bikers are offended by the word *gang*. They prefer *club* instead. To us, back in those days, a *club* was always a place where rich bastards went to play golf or bridge. But a *gang*, now that was a bunch of blue-collar guys hanging out drinking beer in a garage with a dirt floor.

The Queens and Nassau Aliens were relatively new, but they were solid. Partially because they thought they had something to prove to Brooklyn and the Bronx, but also because Nassau and eastern Queens really had better material because the communities lacked the tightness of the old ethnic neighborhoods, but the guys found that bond in the outlaw gang.

Manhattan was a joke. Like everything in Manhattan, it was all fad and showmanship, sort of like California. The Manhattan Aliens wore outlandish clothing and hung out in St. Mark's Place where they hoped they could get laid. In fact it was the little flower girls who first made up the word "biker" to distinguish these guys from the hippies and the heads.

I hung with Richie and Billy throughout the winter. Richie introduced me to some of the other Aliens, but I also kept my ears open. I heard that Nassau and Queens had some membership problems and were no longer the force that they used to be. There were even rumors that some of them were talking about starting a new club.

I asked Billy what was happening with his new club and told him that we might be able to pick up some of the Aliens and put something good together. It was then that he told me that he had something that was even better. He said there was a new club in New York, the Pagans.

"A bunch of hillbillies and rebels from Virginia," I asked him, "why would anybody want to ride with guys like that?"

But he insisted that wasn't the case anymore. They had new clubs in New York, Jersey, and Pennsylvania. By the summer they were going to be the biggest outlaw club on the East Coast, and they were looking for members. He had been down in Elmont partying with them and he liked the guys that he saw.

I still didn't like the idea of turning down a bunch of New Yorkers like the Aliens for an upstart hillbilly club from Dixie, but I agreed to go along with him. After all, they had put on a good show in that hotel brawl where they were tossing cops down the stairs.

We met them at a hole in the wall on Jericho Turnpike, where the party was going on in the back room. When we walked in the front door we were greeted by Sleepy. At the time he was still hoping to be called Little Caesar instead of Sleepy, since he was in his Edward G. Robinson mode.

He pushed his sunglasses up over his forehead and sneered at us. "This is bullshit," he said. "You're late. If you guys wanna ride with us, you gotta learn how to show up on time."

This is even worse than hillbillies, I thought. *Tomorrow I'll get Richie to sponsor me with the Aliens.*

We went in the back room, and I got my first look at the Pagans.

There sitting on a stool was Sweet William Parker. Sweet William was big, real big, with mischievous blue eyes, a mop of curly blonde hair, and a perpetual smirk tattooed across his face. He was the only marine, as opposed to what seemed like a whole company of paratroopers, that I ever met in the Pagans. I had gotten to know him from the bars along Hempstead Turnpike, where I had watched him bust up furniture and throw people through windows. The guy was a one-man wrecking crew. I was impressed.

He had a big, lumbering, awkward hillbilly gait, and he always seemed to be spilling beer or knocking over furniture. Someone would say something about it to Sweet William, and the loudmouth would end up getting carried out the door feet-first and covered with blood, that is if he didn't end up flying through a plate glass window head-first. Sweet William was one of those guys who would rather get in a fight than get laid.

He told me that his father and mother were both half Irish and half Indian. I guess that made him a barroom version of Jim Thorpe. And I told him that it was probably because of guys like him that the government passed laws against selling liquor to the Indians.

Sooner or later he seemed to show up everywhere. I later figured out that this was because he was constantly getting banned from every place he tried to hang out. He seemed to be steadily working his way down the entire length of Hempstead Turnpike. A couple of times I had helped him out in a fight, and he had gotten to like me.

When he saw me, he jumped off the barstool and picked me up and spun me around in a big bear hug. Then he planted a big kiss on my lips. This was the outlaw greeting back in the '60s, a big, sloppy French kiss on the lips, not some goofy thumb handshake or high-five. It was originally designed to blow citizens' minds, which it did. As for the outlaws, they were secure in their sexuality and didn't have hang-ups like normal people did.

Sweet William also brought his kid brother, Stretch, into the club. The kid was as tall as Sweet William, but he was a lot leaner, and also a lot nastier. Sweet William had done a good job teaching him how to fight. At 18, Stretch was a lot younger than most of the guys. In fact the Pagans had a rule that you had to be 21 to join, but like all rules they were made to be broken when there was a good reason. I wouldn't be 20 until July.

With Sweet William already in the Pagans and my buddy Billy about to join, I didn't have much choice. By Memorial Day I was on my way to Reading with the Pagans. It proved a smart choice. After Memorial Day the Pagans' star was rising over New York, and the Aliens' was about to plunge.

The week after the big Memorial Day show in Reading, we were having a meeting in the cellar of a clubhouse in Uniondale, when there was a knock on the door upstairs. Sweet William went to see who it was and returned with a big grin on his face.

"Wait'll you see this," he said.

Tommy Gannon tripped and fell down the stairs and rolled into the room. Les "the Rabbi" walked in behind him, laughing at Gannon sprawled on the floor. They were both Nassau Aliens, or had been. Their jackets were now bare where the club patches had been ripped off.

They said they both quit and wanted to become Pagan prospects. Other guys had quit too, they said, and in another week there would be no more Nassau Aliens. It was because the Mortician was a pain in the ass, they said. But that line was starting to get old. There was more to it than that. The big show in Reading had made its point. The Aliens had avoided the Reading races. They didn't want to confront the Pagans on their own turf 150 miles from New York. But the word had gotten back, and it was going around the motorcycle hangouts. The Pagans were now the only outlaw show in the East.

Tommy and the Rabbi became Pagan prospects, and what they said turned out to be true. A week later Richie Gavin was the only person in the world riding around with Nassau Aliens on his back. Even the Mortician was gone.

Richie soon became a joke. Everyone laughed at the Alien patches on his back and said, "That ain't no club no more." But Richie promised them that the Nassau Aliens would be back. He wore the colors everywhere, and soon the jokes stopped because they began to admire his stubborn determination. The joke soon became a legend: the "Lone Rider," they called him. Even the Pagans didn't fuck with him when he showed up by himself at our parties, because he was showing what the old outlaws meant by true class.

Every time I saw him, he asked me to throw down my Pagan colors and ride with him. He said he needed just one righteous brother to make a new start. As soon as he found that person, they were going to have weekly meetings and start paying dues. Then the two of them would find a third brother, and as soon as they could afford it, they were going to rent a clubhouse, because he said that not having a clubhouse was one of the things that brought the old club down. By next year, he said, the Nassau Aliens would be back.

I told him that I couldn't throw down my colors, but I also asked him to join us. I told him that the Pagans would have him in a minute. But he told me that he would fly Alien colors until he died.

And he did.

On the night of August 15, 1967, he stopped to see his wife at a hospital on Jericho Turnpike, where she worked as a nurse. When he pulled out onto Jericho Turnpike, a car clipped him and left him sprawled face-down in a pool of blood with the words "Nassau Aliens" on his back, staring up into the night sky. Now there were no more Nassau Aliens.

The funeral was in Williston Park. The parents were solid middle-class, middle-aged Irish with gray hair and red faces. In three generations, the family had worked themselves up from the bogs and the docks to a house in the burbs with lace curtains and cut crystal. His parents couldn't understand why their kid had chosen the life of an outlaw over the life of an engineer or accountant.

In New York we did not do outlaw funerals like they did in the rest of the country. We gave the guy back to his parents. This was New York, where family ties were stronger. Kids lived with their parents; even outlaws did. When you went to the guy's house, you respected his parents because they were family. And the family respected you because you were the kid's friend. All of us had grown up in Irish, German, Polack, or Italian homes. We could sit at the table, eat a lot, and praise the hell out of the food. A lot of the guys were veterans and could drink beer with the old man and talk about how the flower faggots, war protesters, and civil-rights niggers were going to ruin the country if they didn't start shooting them soon.

When we showed up at Richie's wake he was laid out in a blue suit. We said, "Sorry for your troubles," and Mrs. Gavin said, "Thank you boys for coming." She told us that she had placed Richie's colors in the coffin with him. Then she introduced us to the family. There were a couple of nuns there, and they seemed especially impressed to meet these friends of Richie's who, until then, they only read about in the newspapers. Sweet William wasn't raised a Catholic, and he was especially turned on by the reception he got from the nuns. He was playing up the role of the chromed cavalier and exuding as much charm as a gigolo. He even stayed to talk to the nuns while some of Richie's cousins took us across the street to a bar and bought us drinks. The priest was there and he seemed as impressed as the nuns to meet Richie's infamous brethren.

Pagans, Aliens, clergy, and citizens were all drinking together, and we all took our turns buying drinks and toasting Richie. In the end it was a grand wake. No one was about to let either a club or a religion stand in the way of 2,000 years of Irish tradition.

In other parts of the country, outlaws were not so tight with their families, and families were not so tolerant of the outlaw lifestyle. Many outlaws were estranged from their families, or they were orphans. When they died they had outlaw funerals, where they guy was laid out in his colors with a swastika flag over the coffin. Most of the other clubs had a guy they called "the Preacher," who officiated at these affairs. The Preacher would also propose toasts and say some appropriate words on New Year's Eve or Thanksgiving Day.

This caused a problem for the New Yorkers and some of the Jersey people, who had been raised Catholic. They may not have had any more use for the church, but the idea of a "preacher" was just *too Protestant* for them to digest. We got around this by having "the Rabbi," who had actually gone to shul and learned how to chant in Hebrew. He could always be relied upon to chant some Torah when the occasion called for it. Of course when the guys from Virginia came up and saw this, they howled and pissed themselves at the idea that, "the New York club ain't got no Preacher, they got a Rabbi instead."

After Richie's funeral the truce between the Aliens and Pagans began to disintegrate. Richie may have been the last of the Nassau Aliens, but there was still Brooklyn and the Bronx. Even some of the guys from Queens and Nassau were hanging around with them again and talking about reorganizing. The Aliens were hurting, but not gone. Only the Mortician seemed to be missing; it was like he just disappeared. By now the Aliens considered the Pagans not just a bunch of upstarts, but a real threat. And they were determined to hold on to the city and remain the undisputed lords of Cross Bay Boulevard and Ocean Parkway. The word was that they were willing to give Nassau and Suffolk County to the Pagans. The Bronx went to the Aliens without saying, and nobody gave a shit anymore about Manhattan. The Pagans from Maspeth and Greenpoint didn't like this arrangement of leaving Brooklyn and Queens to the Aliens, but the club had other problems it was working out. The Pagans were having growing pains.

The club operated under the *fuhrer* principle, having a strong leader who ruled with an iron fist and intimidated the shit out of everyone. At first some of the new clubs had tried to run their meetings under democratic principles, with elections and presidents and vice presidents and secretaries and sergeants at arms. They discussed business and decided things by votes. This didn't work. Trying to run a group of outlaws according to *Roberts' Rules of Order* was like trying to start a motorcycle by whispering sweet words into the carburetor. "Outlaw bikers and old motorcycles:" as Chuck Ginder used to say, "in order to get either of them moving, you have to stand up and kick the living shit out of 'em."

Sleepy was one of the leaders that had been elected. As it turned out, he wasn't a bad guy, but he didn't provide the kind of hard-ass leadership the Pagans needed. One night while he was asleep, they cut the patches off his vest. When he woke up they told him he was out of the club.

At the next meeting we were told that Sweet William was running the club. I had grown to like Sleepy a lot, and I argued that whatever his shortcomings were as a leader, they didn't make him a bad member and he should be given a shot a being a regular member. But Sweet William would have none of it. This was a palace coup and they didn't want the old leader around. They obviously had the blessing of the Mother Club. And, anyway, most of the guys just seemed confused.

The Pagan style of leadership was emerging in the new clubs. With guys like Sweet William in New York, Updegraff in Jersey, and the Whiteknight in Bethlehem, each club's leader was a guy who was physically big and mean enough to wrestle on TV and intimidate King Kong. The leader ran the club like Chuck ruled the City of Reading. Once a week he made a phone call to Washington and reported to the Mother Club. The leader had a number two man, like Rayels in Reading or Bucky in Jersey. He was selected for his diplomatic skills and served as an advisor to the leader, enabling the leader to bounce ideas off of him. That way most problems were already resolved and most decisions made before the leader walked into a meeting. The number two man also conveyed orders, implemented the leaders decisions, and more importantly, articulated the leader's decisions for the rest of the club and explained why things had been done the way they were.

The club also had two sergeants at arms, or enforcers. They were big and they supplied muscle. If the leader said we got to get everybody out of this place now, one sergeant at arms would run around throwing the guys out, while the other would wait in the parking lot counting heads as people came out, making sure nobody went back in. The leader also brought the sergeants at arms along to make an impression if he had to sit down and talk to someone. In addition to brute size, the sergeants at arms were chosen for their cool, an ability to think clearly in a crisis, and to keep their mouths shut.

In New York we had the guy we called Gypsy, the tattoo artist from Polack Alley. We also had Irish "Big Jim" Fagan. Both of these guys were over six-foot-two and 250 pounds.

In addition to sergeants at arms, each club needed a couple of crazies. Guys like Skip and Righteous Fuckin' Elroy in Reading, Domino in Maryland, Rocky in Pittsburgh, Dizzy and Crazy Joey over in Jersey, and Flipout—and later Bobo—in New York. These guys didn't show any common sense at all. Instead they brought that sense of religious fanaticism to the club. They were always on a mission. They were willing to do whatever they had to for the club, even if they risked getting themselves killed. These were the guys who really protected the leader, and the whole club for that matter. No matter what the problem, the leader always knew these one-percenters were behind him 100 percent.

Pagans were obviously not immortal. You could kill one or even run one down in the street, like the guy in South Philly tried to do. But everyone knew that if you killed, or even hurt, a Pagan, there was no telling how the others might retaliate. Everyone also knew that there would be no way to reason with them, or intimidate them, or even buy them off. The '60 s outlaws were not in it for money. Because they were like religious martyrs in their convictions, they struck fear into everyone. This was especially important when dealing with mobsters, wiseguys, and other normal criminals, who were motivated by simple greed and, therefore, could never understand what made us guys tick.

After assuming the leadership of the New York club, Sweet William quickly resumed his policy of getting run out of every police precinct and every town from St. Albans in Queens, to Lindenhurst in Suffolk County. The New York club soon developed a reputation for wrecking more bars than all the other clubs combined. A lot of this had to do with Sweet William's personality, but a lot of it also had to do with the fact that you could get away with it in New York.

As I said, Sweet William was the only marine I ever met in the Pagans, and this might have had something to do with his style of wrecking bars.

A paratrooper would be inclined to ask, "Can't we burn the place down, or at least wait outside and get the guys we want in the parking lot?" But for Sweet William this was out of the question. He only had one play in his game book: Come through the front door like you're hitting the beach at Iwo Jima, beat the crap out of the whole place, get your club the hell out, and let God sort the rest out.

Usually the Pagans did not start trouble, they simply retaliated. But because of the "all for one, one for all" policy, this retaliation was out of all proportion to the offense—some guy said something to a Pagan about spilling beer or being too loud, and the whole place was trashed in less than four minutes.

Four minutes, that was the key. You had four minutes to utterly destroy the place and beat everyone unconscious. Then the sergeants at arms began clearing everybody out, because four minutes is about how long it took for the cops to begin pulling up. As long as you got away, the cops never seemed to come looking for you.

Actually, I believe now that the cops back then kind of got a kick out of us. Most of the cops were Irish, Italian, or German back then, and since they didn't go to college, they thought all college kids were wiseasses. So when they heard some college kids started a fight and got their asses beat, they figured "good for the bastards." If the place was owned by some Italian mob wannabe, that was even better. The German and Irish cops hated Italian macho swagger because of the way they grew up, and Italian cops tended to hate wiseguys and mob wannabes even worse than the German and Irish cops. I now think that sometimes when the cops arrived, they only thought that we had done what they would loved to have done themselves, and therefore they conducted the whole investigation tongue-in-cheek and walked away with the usual report: the shit hit the fan, but no one was able to identify anyone.

The Pagans tended to get along real good with off-duty cops. Back in those days, cops were hard-asses too, not like the punks today. There were a bunch of New York City cops who lived in Suffolk County and owned motorcycles. They came around to hang out and made it clear that they worked in New York, so what went on in Suffolk County was none of their business. On the other hand, they respected the way we never talked about anything for which they could get in trouble by not reporting it to the Suffolk County Police.

As New York cops they worked rotating shifts, and there was a bar in Lake Ronkonkoma where the Pagans started hanging out with the off-duty cops on autumn afternoons. After a couple of hours of drinking, someone would get out a football and we all went out in the parking lot to play touch football. We were smart enough to split up sides so the Pagans would not end up playing the NYPD. So there we were, under the bright autumn foliage, the Pagans and the cops, running around in knee-high boots on asphalt, drunk, playing a friendly game of touch football like we were the Kennedys.

The cops wised us up, too. They taught us the four-minute rule. "Whatever you do, just make sure you get out of there in less than four minutes," they said. "That's how long it takes cops to respond to a call, and that's how professional bank robbers do it." So the Pagans were now wrecking bars with the same timing and precision that Willie Sutton used to rob banks.

It seemed to work, too. One time we wrecked a bar in East Meadow and I didn't get away in four minutes. There was a guy with us from the Chicago Outlaws, a French Canadian named Richie. His brother was called Cal because he spent some time in Southern California, where he built himself a kick-ass California-style chopper, the kind that looks great but ain't worth a shit on backcountry or mountain roads. The two of them just blew into town with Richie's wife and two kids that day. Richie didn't know where he was staying or even the real names of the people his wife and kids were with. I had a Triumph, he had a Harley-Davidson.

When we ran out of the bar that we had just wrecked, I leaped over the back of my seat cavalry-style. I flicked the switch, gave the starter one kick, and I was ready to go. Meanwhile, Richie was tickling his carburetor to prime it with gasoline. Then he jumped on the starter. Nothing. He jumped again, and the engine sputtered. He jumped again, and it sputtered again. Then he had to reach down and tickle the carburetor again. He jumped, and again it sputtered. Only this time it nearly threw him over the handle bars. I could only sit there with my Triumph revved up, waiting for the cops to show up and arrest us.

Which they did.

They impounded our bikes and threw us in the tank with the drunks and the piss-pants. They also confiscated my steel German *Wehrmacht* helmet with swastikas painted on the sides, which I had been using to knock people over the head. The next morning they hauled us all into court on a summer Saturday, in front of a judge who obviously just wanted to get out and play golf.

While I was waiting for my case to be called, an older Irish cop with gray hair came over and sat beside me. I saw sergeant's stripes on his uniform.

"You and your buddy seem like a couple a decent guys," he said. "Yous didn't give us a hard time last night when we arrested yous. And since nobody showed up to testify against yous, I'm going to tell the judge that yous've been very cooperative and maybe he'll forget the whole thing."

That sounded great. But later the guy came back and told me that his shift was over and he would be leaving soon. He also told me that he would tell the cop coming on duty to tell the judge that we had been very cooperative and maybe we should forget the whole thing.

The new cop was a young Italian guy, who didn't look too happy with me at all. When my case was called he told the judge, "Your honor this guy was running around a bar in East Meadow last night beating people over the head with a German helmet and knocking them unconscious."

Whoa, I thought, *that's not what the other cop told you to say.*

But it didn't matter; the judge looked bored by the whole thing. "Did you see this happening?" he asked the cop.

"No."

"Can you call any witness that saw it happen?" he asked the cop.

"But your honor," the cop said, "they're all probably still in the hospital."

"I can't run a courtroom like this," the judge growled. "Dismissed!"

I was dumbfounded. And boy did the cop ever look pissed.

"Do I get my helmet back now?" I asked him with a big grin on my face. "Follow me," he snarled.

I followed him through the labyrinth of the Nassau County Courthouse, grinning the whole time, but being careful not to say anything that could result in another bust. Finally we came to a small room, where I stood in the doorway. He walked over to a desk, picked up the helmet, spun around, and threw it at me. I caught it like a rugby football with both hands waist high. Then I held it up, tipped it to him in a mock salute, thanked him while I put it on my head, and walked out whistling "The Horst Wessel Lied."

This was the glorious summer of '67. There were no helmet laws. And there were no sexually transmitted diseases that a $5 trip to the doctor couldn't cure. Nobody cared about drunk driving as long as you didn't have an accident. And barroom brawling was as much a part of life as sex and rock 'n' roll.

We fought our way clear down Hempstead Turnpike from Jamaica Avenue in Queens Village, all the way out to Sunrise Highway in Lindenhurst. Sometimes we wrecked two or three places in one night. Bam, smash, boom. Four minutes and we'd be on our bikes, racing for the county line before the cops even found out who it was.

Under Sweet William, the New York club practically single-handedly built the reputation of the chain-wielding, bar-wrecking barbarians. The guys from other clubs used to come to New York just so they could wreck a bar on weekends. They got a big kick out of this, because in other parts of the country cops had a lot less to do and tended to take matters like this more seriously. Besides, bars elsewhere tended to be owned by normal people who the cops liked. In New York the Pagans had an innate knack for targeting bars that were owned by wiseass Italian mob wannabees, and the cops usually seemed glad to see these guys get their asses beat.

Contrary to what Hollywood likes to project, Italian wiseguys are not badasses. Sure, they kill people and they beat people with chains, but they like to do it when it presents no danger to themselves—in other words when they outnumber their victims 10 to 1. They do not have the

Pagans' "all for one, one for all" ethic. They hang out in the kind of places where wiseguys get respect without having to earn it. By staying in their own neighborhoods, their own clubs, and their own bars, they are not exposed to situations where someone says: "Yea you, I'm talking ta you, put up your hands and let's see you swing."

But there are not even that many real wiseguys. Most of the guys you saw strutting around with their cardboard-soled, patent leather shoes, expensive pants with the creases, and the Neapolitan pompadour hair-dos were not wiseguys, they were just wannabees. Occasionally their fantasies went to their heads and they needed to be taught a lesson, and sometimes that lesson took the whole establishment down with them.

There was a place on Hempstead Turnpike that was owned by a guy about 40 years old who made it a point to let everybody think he was connected. He talked the part, he wore the clothes, and since it was his bar, it was like his sandbox where he could play any way that he wanted. As part of the game, he always had about a half-dozen bouncers on duty, even if he only had a half-dozen customers. It was simply his way of indulging himself. With some men it's horses, with some it's boats, and with others it's women. With this guy it was bouncers. He kept them around like an Italian-Renaissance faggot bishop kept page boys. These guys strutted around like they were hot shit. They stuck out their pasta-stuffed chests, rolled up their sleeves, and wore religious medals around their necks that were big enough to take down Dracula from across the street. There were usually two at the door, one or two walking around the floor, and two sitting at the boss's table, nodding in agreement at everything he said and staring menacingly at anyone who approached his table.

We were always having problems with guys like them. The Pagans with their swastikas and these guys with the giant crucifixes around their necks, it was like the Vandals and the Romans all over again. They stared menacingly at us, and we spilled beer on the crotches of their creased pants and dared them to do something about it.

The time the shit hit the fan, it really did come about by accident. It was kind of a nice place and didn't really attract the kind of ass-kicking blue-collar clientele where the Pagans felt at home. But Sweet William was in love. He had met this girl who was afraid of the Pagans, so Sweet William agreed to go out with her to a nice place where there were no outlaws. He got out a decent pair of pants and a sport shirt. He even wore his old Marine shoes instead of boots. And he let the girl drive her car to this nice place.

Now Sweet William was the kind of guy who could pull this off. He didn't wear an earring or any jewelry because he was a marine, and his hair was cut short by Pagan standards, so he could pass for a citizen. Because he was half-Indian, he couldn't grow a beard, or hair anywhere on his body for that matter, other than his head. So in walked Sweet William with his date, like any other 23-year-old kid on Long Island.

Just because you could dress Sweet William up, it didn't mean that you could take him out. He had a way of moving around in a bar where you couldn't ignore him any more than you could ignore a rhinoceros. Everyone in the place knew where he was at all times and what he was doing. Meanwhile, the legion of pompadoured Neapolitans just faded into the crowd, like mere spectators in Sweet William's circus. This, of course, would never do. This is not how you play in the sandbox of an Italian mob wannabee. If Sweet William could ignore the legion of bouncers and disrespect the place like this, you would have the whole Hofstra football team in the next week doing the same thing.

Finally the owner turned to one of his bouncers and said, "Do something about this asshole." And they did. They hit him in the head with a club, kicked the shit out of him with their patent leather shoes, and threw him out in the street. The girl felt so sorry for him that she drove him home and screwed him all night.

The next day the Pagans were furious. Attacking a Pagan was like attacking a member of the Order of Teutonic Knights in the Middle Ages. The whole order would not rest until the insult was avenged. What made matters even worse in this case was that word quickly got around that the guy was a Pagan, and people were saying that the bouncers in this place were so bad that they threw the Pagans out.

Sweet William's brother wanted to go in with shotguns the next morning and take out the owner. But someone pointed out that it would be better to wait until Saturday night, when we could be sure of getting the whole crew that had attacked our man Willie. Then somebody said something about it while he was in Jersey, and Updegraff was on the phone pleading with us to wait a week because the Jersey people couldn't make it that weekend, but they were coming down the next weekend for a party.

We waited two weeks and the newspapers jumped on the events of that night like a horny brother on a hot mama.

According to the *Long Island Daily Press:*

> Between 50 and 60 leather jacketed black-booted members of a motorcycle group wrecked a Hempstead bar yesterday in apparent revenge for an incident in which several members were ordered out of the tavern a few weeks ago.
>
> When the two-minute melee was over, the group had demolished furniture and glassware, robbed the cash register of approximately $200, stabbed the owner and injured five others.

Meanwhile *Newsday* claimed that we attacked the bar in "commando fashion."

> The gang members, wearing dungaree jackets, motorcycle boots and helmets [he meant Nazi, not motorcycle, helmets], with swastikas around their necks, wielded baseball bats, tire chains, and lead pipes.
>
> The whole business took less than five minutes, [according to the bartender].
>
> It was so well planned it was ridiculous. They just came in and started swinging and stabbing.
>
> It was like a scene right out of a Hollywood gangster movie.
>
> It was like snapping your fingers, that's how fast it happened.

Both papers reported that the incident was in retaliation for an incident "a couple of weeks earlier when several members had been asked to leave in a gentlemanly fashion." Of course the investigative reporters never inter-viewed the Pagans for their side of the story.

All the newspaper articles about us were beginning to contain the same ingredients: black leather boots and jackets, Levi's, chrome chains and wrenches, long hair, beards, and earrings. And of course, the sinister and omnipresent swastika. No story on the Pagans ever seemed to be done right unless the word "swastika" appeared at least twice in every paragraph. It was like the reporters were writing a new kind of soft-core porn to titil-late their readers.

The Legend had found its troubadours.

CHAPTER 4

The World will end on the day of Ragnarok. It can not be otherwise because it is written in runes on the spear of the All-Father, Woden. On that day the great sky wolf will swallow the sun, a ship made from the nails of dead men will come to shore to rest, the frost-wolf Fenrir will advance with his upper jaw against the sky and his lower along the earth. His eyes and nostrils will blaze with fire.

All this will be foretold by the crowing of the three great roosters, one red, one black, and one brown. And their cries will awaken the dead in Hel.

Then the sky will burst and the sons of Muspell will ride forth. Dark Surt will be first, and with him fire blazing both before and behind. The wolf will swallow Woden and Tyr. Thor will slay the Midgard Serpent, but then stagger back and die from its poisoned breath. Heimdall will wrestle Loki to the death in the sky.

The world of the Gods, the world of men, even the dwarf-world and the world of the dead, all will become raging furnaces as Dark Surt hurls great fireballs over the earth and pillars of raging flames and swirling smoke rise everywhere. The gods will die. Men will die. Women and children will die. Giants will die. Monsters will die. Even the elves and dwarfs will die. The sun will be dark and there will be no stars in the sky. There will be only ashes everywhere, and the sound of black waters lapping at the ash rock as the Earth sinks into the dark sea.

— Twilight of the Gods, according to the ancient Pagan Eddas of Iceland

In the meantime nothing mattered except living with class and going out in style. We were the legendary '60s-style outlaws, and we tried to do both. On a Friday afternoon, if we had five bucks in our pocket, a well-tuned carburetor—no small matter in the days of the kick starter—and a softly purring engine, we were set for the weekend, and we expected to get laid, drunk, and in a fight. But not necessarily in that order.

Unfortunately, about this time, drugs, in particular speed pills, began to work their way down into the redneck class, and all hell was about to break loose, like on the Day of Ragnarok. Between drugs, the collapse of heavy industry, and racial violence, whole communities like Newark, New Jersey, Homestead and Norristown, Pennsylvania, and Greenpoint, Maspeth, and Ridgewood, New York, turned from being decent working-class neighborhoods into shitholes, often only in a matter of months. Bikers didn't make the shit, they just got caught up in it like everyone else.

Any woman, from plump to anorexic, only had to walk into a doctor's office and say that she wanted to lose weight, and out she would come with a prescription for hundreds of these little red, yellow, and blue amphetamine capsules, which enabled us to party non-stop from Friday night until Sunday morning. Some brothers jumped whole-hog into meth-heaven. They swallowed pills by the handful, and soon learned how to boil up the crystal powder on spoons and inject it right into their veins.

Often this went on for days, until they crowed like the three great roosters, howled like the frost-wolf, fought like grizzly bears, and, in general, behaved like wild swine. In the end someone got a phone call, often from jail. At this point the brother would be coming down, or crashing. His voice sounded like Boris Karloff's Frankenstein's monster, as he tried to grunt out that he needed bail money and that he was afraid he might have accidentally started a club war with the Aliens, or beaten the living shit out of some capo in the Gambino crime family, or some other such speed-caused shit.

Under Sweet William things calmed down a bit, but his now unbridled passion for trashing bars was causing problems of its own. The more sensible members, meaning guys who were reluctant to go to jail for something stupid, were now dropping out of the club. First to leave was

Ronnie the Chink, who was actually Italian but got his name because as a kid his friends found it easier to pronounce than Lacincia. Then it was Danny, and suddenly Sweet William was without a number two man.

It was obvious that the spot would be filled by either me or Davy Supermouth. Sweet Willie would have preferred Davy Supermouth, because that would have brought some common sense and stability to the leadership of the club. With me, he saw a loose cannon potentially more dangerous than himself. But the brothers would have none of it; they wanted me. Sweet William, like most good leaders, was capable of seeing which way the wind was blowing, and he also realized that, other than Davy Supermouth and me, there were no qualified candidates. So he graciously welcomed me into his confidence, and at 19 I was confronted with having to discipline, control, and lead a bunch of outlaws, some of whom had been riding motorcycles and getting their asses tossed in jail before I was old enough to jerk off.

Soon it was the Fourth of July, and time for another mandatory run. On Memorial Day the Berks County media had trumpeted the arrival of the Pagans for weeks, as if a rodeo was coming to town. That generated a lot of publicity, and it had served a good purpose. But it had also brought out the riot police in force, and the Pagans did not even get into the fairgrounds. This time we actually wanted to party the weekend away in peace, so we tried something different. The Mother Club merely gave the other clubs meeting points in Jersey and Pennsylvania and kept the final destination secret.

Thus the Pagans hit the highways to celebrate the nation's birthday in the usual motley caravan of vehicles, skulls, swastikas, and confederate flags. New York was a smaller, leaner, and a lot nastier club. Sweet William and I were told to have everyone on the road by nine o'clock Saturday morning. We rode out over the Verrazano Bridge and across Staten Island to Rahway, New Jersey, where we found Pappy, Updegraff, and Bucky from Belfast standing around, scratching their heads. They were as confused as we were. They had just gotten a call and were told to ride down Route 22 into Pennsylvania, and then wait for Pagans at the intersection where 22 meets the turnpike just outside of Allentown.

When we got there, we saw about three dozen Hogs and the usual assorted trucks and vans parked on the side of the highway by the cloverleaf. Now the New York and Jersey leaders were joined by the Whiteknight and the Bethlehem leaders. They too had been told to wait there for the rebels and the Heathens, who would be there in about an hour. Also, we were told that the big clubs in Baltimore and Pittsburgh had patched over and were now in. Although Philadelphia still belonged to the Warlocks, the Pagans were closing in with new clubs in Norristown, Wilmington, and Delco (Delaware County).

The Whiteknight scratched his head: "Well we know it's not Virginia or Maryland," he speculated, "Or else they wouldn't be coming here. My guess is Laconia. There's supposed to be a big rally up there this weekend."

Laconia, New Hampshire. We may have been outlaws, but we were still New Yorkers, and the guys from Jersey might as well have been. For us the world ended in Westchester. There was no such place as Upstate New York. Like New England, it was mythological. We had all grown up believing that civilization ended about 30 miles into Jersey in the west and Scarsdale in the north.

It was a great Fourth of July weekend weather-wise, with nothing but blue skies and blazing sunshine. It was a great day for the beach, and here we were in Pennsylvania, about to ride north across the frozen ice of Hudson Bay to some town at the North Pole. So we just laid down on the side of the road and dreamed about a good seven-hour ride deep into the primeval bowels of aboriginal North America.

About an hour later we were awakened by the telltale roar of a pack of several hundred 74-cubic inch engines. The clan had arrived. The usual outlaw greetings were exchanged. Then bottles of cold beer were pulled from the backs of pickup trucks: the usual Rheingold, Horlacher, and Reading "Old Dutch." But they were now joined by National Bohemian from Baltimore and Pittsburgh's famous Iron City. At the time Iron City was a matter of civic pride, even for outlaws. If there were 10,000 bars in Pittsburgh with 80,000 working tap handles, 79,990 or so were pumping Iron. You might be able to get a Wurzburger or Lowenbrau if you found an old German place on the North Side, and at the airport or a downtown hotel you might find a Bud or Miller High Life. That's "might find," because at the time 99.99 percent of all alcohol consumed by the working men and women of Steel City, the blue-collar capital of America, was Imperial whiskey and Iron City beer, affectionately referred to as "Imp 'n' an Eye-run."

We quenched our thirst and spritzed each other with beer to cool off. Then Chuck told Sweet William and I that we were going to Bloomsburg. At least everyone from New York and Jersey had heard of Laconia—but Bloomsburg? Where the fuck was that?

It turned out to be not so bad, only about another two hours away on the western end of the anthracite hardcoal region. There was some kind of weekend-long motorcycle drag race at some fairground that nobody ever heard of. But that was the point: start rumors that the clan was headed for the big show in Laconia, and have every state trooper in New York and Pennsylvania out looking for Pagan sightings in the wrong places. Then show up at some no-count affair in the mountains behind the coal region.

So we were off again, riding through the slate piles and rolling, stripped-off mountains of the Pennsylvania hardcoal region. Through former company towns with rundown wood-frame houses, where kids stared from the front porch with their fingers in their noses. And then through Centralia, a town sitting on a raging furnace burning out the bowels of a former deep mine that caught fire by accident. A town where the stench of Muspell seeps into cellars at night and where, as the Pennsylvania poet John Haag put it, "the trees in the yards die from the roots up and the birds are the last to know."

We crossed the East Branch of the Susquehanna and rolled through Bloomsburg. There is nothing sleepier than a college town on the Fourth of July when all the kids are someplace else. The few hicks on the street just stared open-mouthed like they were watching the Fourth of July Parade coming through. Things were different when we reached the fairgrounds. I could see it on the faces of the citizen bikers who had come for a quiet weekend. It was like they had just heard the crowing of the three great roosters announcing the world's end.

One thing was sure: no one expected us. The strategy had worked.

We settled down on a hill overlooking the racetrack and concession stands. I found Blackie and Rayels. As we broke out the Old Dutch and Rheingold, we could see that some people were packing up their trailers and leaving. These were the timid souls. Even citizen bikers like to effect a swagger, and the last thing they wanted to admit to themselves was that they had to split when the real outlaws arrived. Although everyone was kicking back and getting stoned and drinking beer, there was an element of tension that just seemed to hang in the still, stale summer air, like the feeling you get just before a late-afternoon thunderstorm in the mountains.

This was also Pennsylvania. Outlaw clubs tend to reflect strongly the region of the country that spawned them. And the Pagans were becoming as Pennsylvanian as shoofly pie or an Altoona-built K-4 steam locomotive. The old steel, railroad, and mining towns of Pennsylvania were hard-ass places. Until the 1970s even the Pennsylvania State Police and the Liquor Control Board were afraid to go into places like Scranton and Wilkes-Barre to shut down the bars on Sunday. A coalminer's daughter once told me that when she was a kid growing up in the 1950s in Coaldale, an old mine-company town in Pennsylvania's Shenandoah Valley, the kids used to go down to the ethnic clubs after church on Sunday and look around the parking lots for teeth that had been knocked out in brawls the night before.

Now if you believe what journalists say about outlaws, you hear all about awards that are given out for bizarre sexual acts performed in public to blow the citizens' minds. Red wings for public cunilingus on a menstruating white woman, for example, or black wings for a black woman. But I don't remember seeing much of this kind of crap hanging on Pagan colors. And that's probably because nobody would have been impressed by this kind of shit in Scranton, Altoona, or Pittsburgh. I don't know what works and what don't in other parts of the country, but back in the '60s you couldn't make it in Pennsylvania and West Virginia just by riding around with long hair and swastikas. When the shit hit the fan you had to be able to get down and dirty in the mud and the blood with the mill hunkies and the coal crackers, and swing your fists with the best and the baddest that Appalachia had to offer.

So here we were on the Fourth of July in the old hardcoal region, where brawling was as much of a barroom sport as pool shooting, less than 20 miles from Black Jack Kehoe's Hibernian House—the home of the legendary Molly Maguires—drinking Pennsylvania rye whiskey and Reading Old Dutch beer and just waiting for something to happen. And sure enough, it did.

The whole thing began as horseplay just about the time it started to get dark.

The Pagans were down at the track watching the drag races. Then a couple of Pagans rode their bikes out on the track while the rest cheered. Sweet William bummed a ride on the back of one and fell off on his ass, but stood up immediately and held a bottle of Reading Old Dutch beer high in the air to show that he didn't drop it. Everyone cheered as he poured the bottle down his throat.

But he had also ripped the seat completely out of his pants and torn up his ass into a bloody mess. This was something that he seemed to do regularly because the outlaw style of dress had not yet been firmly established. Today's bikers are as easy to recognize as Mennonites or Hasidic Jews, but in those days the style was still emerging. True, you had brothers like Domino, Rayels, and Blackie, who epitomized the lean, mean, and hairy, black leather and Levi's look that would eventually prevail. But you also had eccentrics like Sweet William and Gypsy, who wore khakis, and Stevie Hippie, who wore sandals made from recycled truck tires. Sweet William was also the only Pagan who didn't have his colors sewn on a blue denim cut-off. Instead he had his sewn on a brown leather cowboy vest. The big clean-shaven guy in the brown vest and beige pants stood out from the pack a mile away.

It was only after the leather vest fell apart and he got tired of buying a new pair of pants every Monday morning that Sweet William switched to a denim vest and denim pants. Frankly, he never looked quite right in denim.

Next someone got a rope, which he tied to a three-wheeler. Now Pagans began body dragging each other through the mud. Guys were getting up covered with mud, and then there were a few cuts and bruises and some blood. You could see the look in their eyes. They wanted more. Something harder, faster, more brutal. They began dragging each other more and more recklessly. They got up and slammed their heads together as hard as they could and then howled about it.

Perhaps someone mumbled something about these guys taking over the track. Perhaps it was merely the wrong look, or someone bumped someone, or just gave someone a dirty look. Or maybe it was even more serious, like some drunk pawing someone's wife. Fights soon started breaking out: fights between citizens, fights between citizens and Pagans. First there were isolated little incidents, then smaller brawls that ended quickly. But soon the area around the track erupted into a major riot. People were bloodied, people were beaten, and people were unconscious.

Tommy Gannon claimed that he had seen Domino stalking the area with a claw hammer in his hand and a deranged, blank look in his eyes. This was enough to make even a Pagan worry, because pound-for-pound Domino was probably badder than Sweet William. During the week Domino tied steel girders on the skeletons of the skyscrapers that were going up all over Washington during the Lyndon Johnson boom years. He never missed a day's work and had a reputation for being fearless. But from Friday afternoon 'till Monday morning he partied all-out. Twenty-nine times in a single year alone, he was arrested for disorderly conduct. It was only sheer lack of size and horsepower that kept him from becoming a more lethal demolition machine than Sweet William. If Sweet William was like a grizzly bear in a fight, Domino was a wolverine.

But Sweet William was the star of the show. He was decking everyone in sight, left and right, picking people up and throwing them over fences. And he stood out like a turd swimming in the champagne punch, this big half-Indian, half-Irish hillbilly, in tattered khakis with his bloody ass, busting people left and right. And people were actually coming up and challenging him, wanting to get a piece of him, like they were lining up to wrestle a circus strongman. But Sweet William was making short work of all of them. I never saw anyone like him. Like Jim Thorpe or Mozart, Sweet William was simply a prodigy.

After a while the area around the track began to clear out. And Sweet William was all tattered and sweaty and dirty, and huffing and puffing.

"I need a beer," he said.

So he and I and a couple of other guys walked up to the cafeteria to look for beer. When we got there, there were fights and scuffles and shouting matches going on all over the place. It was like an old-fashioned Irish wedding in Scranton.

It didn't look like we were going to get any beer. But while we were standing there talking, I noticed a hot dog go flying across the room and land on a picnic table, where a bunch of coal crackers were eating. One of the guys picked it up and just tossed it out into the room. But instead it hit Sweet William in the back of the head.

He spun around, saw it lying on the floor, and picked it up. "Who threw this?" he said.

"One of the guys at that table," I told him.

So over he went and started waving the weiner in the people's faces. "Did one of you throw this?" he asked.

One of the women at the table tried to make peace. "Somebody threw it on our table," she said. "And we paid good money for this food."

"Is that a fact?" Sweet William said.

Then I wondered, *what the fuck is he doing now*, as I saw him climbing up on the table, where he began doing a war dance, making sure to plant his big clumsy feet in the beans and pepper-slaw, with his bare bloody ass sticking out of his tattered pants right in the people's astonished faces. Before they could do anything, the table's legs broke and it collapsed with Willie on top of it and the legs of the citizens pinned underneath it.

Willie jumped to his feet like a startled cat and ran across the room to the food counter. The cook saw him coming, abandoned ship, and ran out the back door. Willie grabbed the guy's hat where it had fallen on the floor and put it on his head. Then he picked up the spatula and began flipping hamburgers on the grill, sticking them on buns, and handing them to the people in line.

"Here you go, it's all on the house tonight."

Everything was going fine until some wiseacre had to ask, "Who the fuck do you think you are?"

Willie used the spatula to flip a burger in the guy's face. Then he grabbed the soup pot from the counter and tossed it in the guy's face, scalding his own hands in the process. With that he jumped over the counter, tackled the guy, and began pummeling him on the floor.

It was contagious. Fights were breaking out all over the room. Soon it was another full-blown riot. Citizens and Pagans were even helping each other rip down walls and ceiling fans just for the fuck of it. But then someone shoved his head in the door and shouted, "The cops, the cops!" We all ran out the door.

We could see the headlights and flashing red lights coming down the dirt road. We ran across the road and up the hill to where we had parked the bikes. Brothers were screaming and cursing and pulling chains and wrenches out of car trunks and truck beds. I could hear the telltale sounds of slides on automatic pistols being pulled back and bullets being chambered. It all combined into a bone-chilling sense of horror. There we stood, like a bunch of cavemen, holding weapons in the dark and waiting to see what the police would do first. I can still remember the cold steel of a construction chain in the palm of my hand.

Car doors opened and the interior lights went on. We could see the gray uniformed state troopers, three in the front seat of each car and three in the back. There were a couple standing outside talking to blood-stained citizens and cursing, but most of them just stayed in the cars. Then some of us thought we heard them saying something like "nothing we can do about it tonight."

"They're leaving, they're leaving," someone whispered. And sure enough, they got back in their cars and left. The cops had backed down. The Pagans began dancing and whooping it up. The Imperial Guard had run off and abandoned Rome to the Vandals. The place was ours, even if for only one night, and it looked like the place was about to get sacked.

Then something strange happened: the whole place got real mellow. Pagans were wandering into citizen camps and citizens were wandering into Pagan camps, and everybody was sharing booze, weed, food, and beer. In some cases we even shared the women. Guys that only a couple of hours before were punching the shit out of each other were now sharing bottles of Old Overholt and hugging each other. It really was just like an old-fashioned coal region wedding, and eventually everyone just passed out drunk and exhausted.

The next morning I awoke early, tired, reeking, and hurting. No matter how drunk or tired you might be, it is nearly impossible to sleep with the bright rising sun in your face. I sat up and checked to confirm that nothing was broken. All around me I could see mayhem and destruction, wisps of smoke rising from the smoldering ashes of bonfires, burned-out car carcasses and demolished tables and buildings, beer bottles and beer cans everywhere, along with an occasional empty bottle of Jack Daniel's or Old Overholt. Like bodies on an ancient battlefield, sleeping leather- and denim-clad Pagans dotted the hillside.

At least they seemed to be Pagans from the faces I could identify. The club had a strict rule that you weren't allowed to crash (fall asleep) with your colors on. If you did, they set you on fire. So you had to roll them up and tuck them under your head or wear them under your leather jacket.

The bodies were beginning to move. All of them seemed to be as hung over and hurting as I was. We began rummaging around the back of truck beds and vans looking for more beer to quench our thirst and soothe our parched throats. Someone suggested that maybe we could find some coffee down in the ruins of the food pavilion.

"No fuckin' chance," Updegraff snickered. "They took care of that place good last night."

"We shoulda thoughta that before we wrecked it," Skip mumbled. He was genuinely bummed. You could see that in his face; morning coffee was to him what morning sun was to cold-blooded reptiles.

"Lookee, lookee," Flipout said. He was holding a bottle of Old Overholt with a few shots left. He took a drink and handed to me.

"Make sure it's not piss," Updegraff said as I started to drink.

"It's not," Flipout said. "I already tasted it."

I offered the bottle to Skip.

"I don't want to drink that piss," he said.

Then Apple, who was taking a real piss, turned around and pissed on him. "Here, drink this instead," he said.

Skip turned around and tried to smack Apple in the prick. And when Apple tried to jump away he pissed on the rest of us.

"You fuck," Updegraff screamed, as he shook a can of beer and snapped the pop-top and began shaking the can at Apple. Soon we were all spritzing each other with beer.

Then someone said, "Oh shit," and we all looked up.

It was descending on us from all over, like the crowing of the three great roosters. Cars were coming at us from every direction. State cops, local cops, cops from every municipality in the county, in cop cars and unmarked cop cars, and even civilians in big-ass Buicks and Oldsmobiles and Pontiacs, six people in each one. The cars stopped. The doors opened, and this time they all got out. State cops and local cops, sheriff's deputies and retired cops, the Veterans of Foreign Wars and the American Legion, the Kiwanis and the rotary clubs, the Knights of Columbus and the Masonic lodges, the Benevolent and Protective Order of Elks, and the Sons of Italy, the local Liederkranz and the Ancient Order of Hibernians. It was a regular militia, like the Revolutionary War. Armed citizens carrying hunting rifles, shotguns, clubs, and farm implements. But they weren't outlaws. They were citizens, and they were scared. They had wives and kids, dogs and cats, and lawns that needed to be mowed. They knew our reputation, and they were scared.

Dutch, Chuck, and Satan picked up on this immediately. Soon brothers were working their way through the crowd, whispering. I heard Flipout. "Be cool, be cool," he was saying. "Dutch says for everybody to be cool or I'm supposed to beat your ass."

"Shut up and just stand still," Davy Supermouth whispered in my ear.

We had been caught by surprise, but how could they know that? They probably assumed that we had as much common sense as they did and that we had sentries hiding in the woods with hunting rifles ready to pick them off. I could hear Satan talking a mile a minute to the state police commander. He could sound as down-home, warm, and welcome as a Dutch country kitchen on the first morning of buck season.

According to him, the place just exploded into a riot the night before. The Pagans hadn't started it, they had just defended themselves. He had been as scared as anyone and could understand completely why the cops didn't want to get involved and went home. He had wanted to leave, too. But the guys were too fucked up and drunk to leave last night. So now all he was trying to do was gather everyone up and get out.

"One hour," I heard him saying to the police captain. "Just give us one hour, and you'll never see any of these guys again. But I need one hour. You don't want us leaving anyone behind to cause trouble when we're gone."

The cop agreed. Satan had just handed him an opportunity to get rid of the Pagans as cheaply, safely, and quickly as possible. Monday morning he could tell the big shots in Harrisburg how he had run the Pagans out of town, and there would be no way for them to check. He had more than three dozen state police, armed professionals with shotguns, and he knew that we weren't going to start a gunfight in broad daylight. Then he ordered all the civilians and local cops to leave. He wasn't stupid. He knew that he had surprised us and we had no reason not to leave, but he did not want some hot-headed locals doing something stupid and provoking a riot.

Then Satan came over to me, his back to the cops and grinning from ear to ear. "We gotta get the fuck outta here before this guy changes his mind and starts arresting us," he said. "Where's Willie?" he asked.

"Anywhere," I said.

"Find 'im," he said. "You got 20 minutes to find all your people and have them standing right here by this truck. Any bikes that don't start, stick 'em in trunks or trailers. We're riding out of here in a pack in one hour, and I don't want anybody left behind for the locals to get their hands on when we're gone."

I found Willie in the backseat of a car with two girls he had picked up and brought along. He was sprawled out face down across their laps, his pants all ripped to shit and his bald Irish-Indian ass sticking up in the air, all bloody and ripped from when he had fallen off the bike and slid down the track. Even he looked ready to go home.

I dragged him out of the car as he was waking up, his eyes as blood-shot as his ass. But he got it together to round up all our people. Then he just stood by the side of the truck grinning, like he used to grin in the morning when we woke up in a jail cell. That impish grin of pride, like, "didn't we really fuck things up good and have a great time?" The grin that was the epitome of the proud leader of a band of '60s style outlaw bikers.

"Gimme that," he said as he grabbed the bottle of Old Overholt from my hand.

Finally we had everyone together. Willie climbed into the back seat of a car with the two girls, and I climbed on my bike and pulled out behind the car. I started to sober up as the wind blew through my hair. As we headed back toward Jersey through the stripped-out minefields, I could see Willie through the window, sitting between the two girls, each of them holding a brown beer bottle and alternately offering him sips, like two squaw nurses attending to a wounded warrior.

CHAPTER 5

And what rough beast, its hour come round at last,
Slouches toward Bethlehem to be born?
— William Butler Yeats, "The Second Coming"

Ater the Bloomsburg Races everything had changed—and changed utterly. A terrible beauty had been born. Born out of the claw hammer in Domino's clenched fist and the impish, incendiary glint in Sweet William's eyes. Born out of the blood that flowed from people's heads as they ran for safety in the woods, and out of the flaming pyre that had been the Bloomsburg fair's food concession.

Some of the saner guys were still dropping out of the club, and citizen bikers wanted nothing to do with us. We outlaws were becoming outcasts, but we were also rapidly becoming celebrities. The newspapers wrote us up like we were a pack of Vandals invading the postwar tranquility of the American suburbs. The Pagans were even featured in an NBC-TV documentary, *The Pursuit of Pleasure*. And we loved it. We were becoming increasingly intoxicated by our own notoriety, just as the women we tended to attract were. All of this naturally made us think that an occasional ass-kicking or stint in the can was well worth all the trouble. So we rode on through that glorious golden summer of 1967, listening to songs like "Harper Valley PTA" and "Ode to Billy Joe."

When all was said and done, Sweet William was not such a maniac as he might have seemed. If he wrecked two bars or concession stands in a week, this was actually less than 1 percent of his time. The rest of the time he could be downright likable and even *gemuetlich*.

When they got to know him, people honestly did like Sweet William, almost as much as they feared him, and many of them would do almost anything to be his friend. One of these supplicants was slightly gayish man with a goatee who owned a storefront rock club in a shopping center in Elmont, Long Island. The club was closed on Mondays, but as a gesture of friendship, the guy offered to turn the place over to Willie and the Pagans for a meeting place.

We set up a long folding table on the stage and hung a large red, white, and black swastika flag on the wall. Sweet William sat at the head of the table like the chairman of the board. Meanwhile, the owner stood behind the bar out of earshot and sold us beer when we needed it, which was often, because we were having fun and tended to drag things out as if we really had important business to discuss. Especially Tom Gannon: he liked to make long-winded speeches full of fancy words that some of us had trouble understanding. Eventually Willie cut him off and told him that he was nothing but a goddamn pain in the ass.

After the meetings we continued to drink beer. Hangers-on and girls came around, and soon Monday was the owner's busiest night. Between the hangers-on and girls, some of us managed to avoid work all summer. Willie seemed to be genuinely grateful to the owner, and he had put out the word that he didn't want anyone causing trouble.

But trouble loved Willie as much as Willie loved trouble.

Because the bar was in a shopping center and all the other businesses were closed at night, we had the whole parking lot to hang out. We sat out there on bikes sucking Rheingold beer from brown bottles. The only hassle came from the guys at the local VFW, who screamed "you Nazi bastards" from the windows of passing cars. Occasionally Flipout or Crazy Joey from Jersey threw beer bottles at them, but otherwise these Monday nights were laidback affairs with little worry about getting arrested or in a fight.

It was after a meeting on one of those hot, muggy Long Island summer nights when Stretch, Flipout, and I were sitting on a curb drinking beer and talking to the girls. The place was starting to attract a lot of young women who worked as secretaries in real estate and insurance offices by day, and who on weekends put on dresses and dated guys in suits from the office. These guys would drive them around in cars and spend money on them hoping to cop a feel on the way home, and would shit if they knew that Monday night the same women were down here screwing the shit out of greaseballs like us while paying our bar tabs and sometimes a motel bill, too.

It was weird. If we saw these same women on the street the rest of the week, we would not recognize them and they might be mortified if we did. But on Monday night they wore their hair differently, they wore more make-up, and they had special outfits—boots, tight jeans, trashy blouses, and leather jackets—that they saved for when they came down looking for cheap thrills. Maybe it just proves that most Americans are rednecks and outlaws at heart, but are afraid to admit it. In any event, it was just the sort of thing we needed to reinforce our atavistic medieval mentality.

So there we sat, just drinking beer and goofing, and Flipout was playing with a lock of some girl's hair. Suddenly his fingers stopped moving, and his mouth fell wide open, as he remained silent and motionless. We all heard it at the same time, faintly at first and several blocks away—a pack of motorcycles. We could also distinguish the uneven rhythm of a pair of headlights coming from two motorcycles riding abreast, even when they were just pinpoints several blocks away.

There was no mistaking the sound. It was a pack, and as we looked out of the parking lot, we could see them coming off the parkway and up Elmont Road. The front of the pack was already crossing Dutch Broadway and there were still more coming off the parkway.

"Oh shit," Flipout said as he dropped the girl's hair. "I don't like this."

Neither did I. It takes a lot of time and planning to put together a pack of a hundred or so motorcycles. We would have had to bring people from six states to do it. It always demanded some sort of occasion and purpose, and in this case, we somehow knew that we had something to do with their purpose. They were coming our way and it wasn't a social call, or we would have known about it already.

So we were all asking the same question, "Who the fuck is this?" But we all knew that whoever they were, they weren't Pagans and therefore it wasn't good. They were still coming off the parkway and crossing Dutch Broadway. Only now they were pulling into the parking lot. The parking lot was filling up with motorcycles, and I could still see them coming off the parkway.

Some of the bikes were ying-yangs: 450 Hondas and Suzukis. Those riders definitely weren't outlaws. But other guys were riding choppers, they had beards and the usual buttons, badges, and insignias. The three of us were looking around trying to get a hint of what was going on. We simply couldn't ask, "who the fuck are you people and what do you want?"

Then I saw it. A sawed-off denim vest on a pair of broad shoulders, and on the back of that denim vest was a white patch with red capital letters that said "Aliens." I knew then that it was not good. And then things got worse. There were more of the same patches, dozens more.

"Be cool. Be cool," Flipout was whispering. "There's nothing we can do now."

Flipout was right, there was nothing we could do but wait and see. Besides nobody was bothering us yet, but when they looked at us, it was clear they hadn't come for a party.

The car and truck train followed the pack. A green metalflake Corvette pulled into the parking lot. The door opened and out stepped the Mortician, erstwhile leader of the supposedly defunct Nassau Aliens. He was smiling like John Kennedy on Inauguration Day, and he was immediately greeted by two guys I recognized as leaders of the Bronx Aliens. Something was up. It was not good, but at least now we knew what we had to do: just wait and see what the Mortician did.

The Mortician wasn't big like Willie. He was average height and build. But he was a union roofer by trade and was hard as nails. He had a big nose, big bushy beard, and long, curly brown hair.

He strutted into the club looking as cocky as Joe Namath walking up to the line of scrimmage on Super Bowl Sunday. Everyone else followed. Inside, the place was now packed with bikers. I was surrounded by them, and not one of them was a Pagan. Then Tommy Gannon and Flipout wormed their way through the crowd and stood behind me.

The Mortician jumped on the stage, pranced around like Mick Jagger, then turned around to the crowd and yelled, "New York belongs to the Aliens, the Pagans ain't shit." He had issued his challenge. I figured we were now going to get our asses beat just by way of reinforcing that point. Then I heard Sweet William.

"Fuck the Aliens," he screamed. "The Pagans are where it's at."

A deadly silence descended over the whole room. There was Willie, lumbering across the floor with that big hillbilly gait. Not the jive-ass rooster strut of the Mortician, but the steady lumber of an ox not about to stop. In his khakis and brown vest he stuck out in a room full of denim and black leather. He was heading toward the stage and everyone was just moving out of his way.

When he got to the stage, he jumped up and stood staring in the Mortician's face. He stood a good 5 inches and about 50 pounds over the Mortician. It was obvious that this was not how things were going to resolve themselves.

Then someone started screaming: "Hold it, everyone just hold on a minute."

A member of the Bronx Aliens was walking toward the stage with his hands in the air. It could have been Harry, it could have been Mardo, I don't remember. But the guy was on the stage in a minute with two other important guys from the Bronx. One of them was Vinnie Girolamo, a guy about six-six and over 300 pounds who looked like a giant black muffball.

"They call him Gaga," Tommy Gannon whispered in my ear. "It's short for the Gorilla."

The two normal-sized Bronx guys were standing between Willie and the Mortician, and Gaga was towering over everyone, including Willie. Having let the Mortician strut and fret his moment on the stage, the Bronx was now taking control. And the situation was out of the hands of the Mortician.

This was a good thing for us, because we never had any real hassles with the Bronx people. Part of this was due to the fact that, like most Long Islanders, we had as little reason to go to the Bronx as the North Pole. But it was also due to the fact that the Bronx was getting sick of having to ride down to Long Island every time a Pagan blew a fart and some Alien fell off his bike.

Finally, there was the fact that as a long established club, the Bronx Aliens were real outlaws, they didn't have to invent ways of "showing class" to draw attention to themselves; it was in their blood. They were sincerely touched by someone who showed utter contempt for every normal instinct of self-preservation.

It was a berserker mentality. The ancient Germans hated the idea of dying in bed—the *strohtod* (straw death), they called it. Instead they looked for ways to die in combat. They formed an elite brotherhood called the berserkers. They wore bearskin shirts, drank beer, chewed on psychedelic herbs, pounded drums, and banged their heads together, until they worked themselves into a manic frenzy, and then they charged. They believed that they were now possessed by the spirit of the All-Father, Woden, and their subsequent recklessness scared the shit out of the Romans, who wanted to get home from the battle alive. On a fine sunny afternoon in September of 9 AD, they slaughtered 30,000 Roman legionaries, the toughest soldiers in Europe, and then nailed their heads to the trees on the Teutobeurg Forest mountain as a warning to anyone else with thoughts of defiling the sacred soil of their *Heimatland*.

Similar disrespect for personal safety impressed the old '60s outlaws the same way it did their ancestors. Other people thought that they were just plain crazy and stayed out of the way of these runaway trains. It was just this sort of reckless perverse piety—or "righteousness," as we called it—that had just bought Willie some time to talk. One of the two Bronx Aliens walked to the front of the stage, and shouted that everyone should relax and party, while they talked. Just have good time, and no fights. If anyone fucked up they would have to answer to the Bronx.

Then Willie walked to the front of the stage, put his arm around the Alien, and added that if any Pagan got in a fight he would personally come down off the stage and beat the shit out of the guy without even asking who started it. Behind the two of them there was still the hairy, menacing figure of Gaga.

The crisis was over. If anything was going to happen it would have already happened. The danger in these guys was in their spontaneity. That's when they acted with the abandon of the berserkers. If you could get them to start talking and engage their brains, you could usually get them to be reasonable. The result was a truce.

Pagans and Aliens would travel freely in New York and not hassle each other. In fact, if one of us saw a member of the other club in a hassle, we were supposed to jump in and help him out. And if any two members of the different clubs had to get into a fight, they would have to do it one-on-one with at least two witnesses from each club present—just like Alexander Hamilton and Aaron Burr had done. Finally, the rock club we were in was to be neutral territory, where everybody from any club, or no club at all, would be free to party on Monday night without hassle.

This last point was important. It was not easy to find a club, as opposed to just a bar, that would tolerate an outlaw club "flying colors." The only places that would were usually shitholes that were about to go under. Finding a place with a band that still attracted single girls was difficult. The Aliens had not failed to notice what we had going for ourselves, and they had seized the opportunity to grab a piece of it.

On the surface this was not a bad idea. At the time there were more than 7 million people in New York City alone, not counting Nassau and Suffolk Counties. This included cops, gangsters, psychopaths, blacks, and Puerto Ricans. In reality the New York Pagans and Aliens probably did not have 100 members between them in the same area at this time, but both clubs had enough enemies of their own already. There should have been room for both clubs, and they could have used all the help from each other that they could get. But many outlaws opposed, on faith alone, a peaceful solution to any problem, and they simply abhorred peace as strongly as any pacifist ever abhorred violence.

Some Pagans were already walking around muttering that, "this thing ain't over yet." Then there was this guy from the Bronx, with the muscles of a bull and the intelligence of Doberman Pinscher, who was walking around calling the Bronx leadership a bunch of disappointing "candy-ass chickenshit" fuckers. He was complaining that he didn't come all the way down from the Bronx for this shit, and that if they didn't have the balls to mop the floor with Sweet William's ass, he would just have do it all by himself. He was told repeatedly to "shut the fuck up," but it didn't work.

Finally Sweet William turned around to the Bronx leaders with whom he had just worked out the truce and threw his arms up in the air. He told them that he was going to have to fight this guy because he couldn't let him walk around talking like that any longer. The Bronx leaders agreed and said that the guy acted like a real asshole sometimes, so it might be a good thing if he got the shit knocked out of his head once in a while.

So less than a half-hour old, the treaty was tested—that is, the clause about Pagans and Aliens only fighting each other "one-up, with two witnesses from each club." Willie and the Bull went around to the back of the shopping center with two members from each club. Willie brought me and his brother Stretch. The Bull brought two guys from the Bronx who we didn't know.

I never quite understood the secret of Sweet William's style of fighting. He just picked people up and tossed them around until they were unconscious, and when that didn't work, he slammed their head on the floor or against the wall until the lights went out.

As for me, before I went into the club I was a sparing partner for heavyweight contender Bob Stallings, who actually beat the "Bayonne Bleeder," Chuck Wepner, at Sunnyside Garden. This meant I could pound the average bar patron into submission before he even knew what hit him. If that didn't work, I was also strong enough to work out on the mats with an NCAA heavyweight wrestler who went on to play offensive tackle for the Kansas City Chiefs for 10 years.

One way or another, I could demolish most people who were not professional athletes or martial arts experts, but I would have hated to fight Sweet William. The guy was like a machine with huge metal hooks and pinchers coming at you. As for hitting him, you might as well be punching away at a tractor as it was running you over, for all the good it seemed to do.

So the six of us went around the back of the shopping center, where there were dumpsters full of smelly, rotten food and the ground was covered with broken glass, rancid grease, and pebbles. Sweet William squared off with the guy from the Bronx, while the rest of us told each other that the whole thing was really stupid and unnecessary, and that the leadership of both clubs must be stupid if they thought this peace would ever last.

The fight started with Willie standing there in typical hillbilly fashion, knees slightly bent, arms slightly raised but just dangling in front of him like a Tyrannosaurus rex, and his head bent forward like a goat getting ready to butt. In spite of his fireplug build, the Bull from the Bronx turned out to be an accomplished boxer. As Willie came at him, the Bull shot a straight right hand into Willie's snotlocker. It landed like the Crack of Doom and should have been sufficient to stop a thoroughbred racehorse coming out of the starting gate at Belmont. But not Willie. He was all over the guy in typical Willie fashion. The two of them went down and rolled around in the rancid grease and broken glass. Before we knew it, Willie came up and was sitting on the guy's chest with the guy's arms pinned under Willie's knees and glass, grease, and pebbles all over the back of Willie's shirt. He had a hold of the guy's head by his hair.

"Now can we forget about this," Willie said.

"Fuck you," the guy said.

"Look I can smash your head on the parking lot, but there's no point in it."

"So fuck you and smash my head, you chickenshit piece o' shit."

"Would you cut it out, asshole," one of the guys from the Bronx finally screamed. "You wanted a fight, and he beat you. Now it's over."

"Let 'em go ahead and smash my fuckin head," the guy insisted.

So now Willie and the two guys from the Bronx were both screaming at the guy on the ground to stop being a jerk, but he just wouldn't listen. Eventually, the other guy from the Bronx, said to me "This is bullshit." Then he shouts at Willie, "Go ahead and smash his fuckin' head so we can throw him in a dumpster and go back and drink."

But Willie wouldn't smash the guy's head. He couldn't, because he was just as impressed by this guy's berserker stupidity as the Bronx people were an hour ago when Willie told them to fuck off.

Finally one of the guys from the Bronx kicked his own man in the leg while he was lying on the ground. "You fuckin' asshole," he yelled. "If you don't fuckin' stop we're gonna kick the piss outta you ourselves." Then he asked Willie to get off the guy and told the three of us Pagans to go back inside and leave them take care of the guy themselves. About 20 minutes later the two Bronx guys came back in with the Bull, who didn't talk to anyone the rest of the night but just walked around sulking.

Willie and I sat at the bar drinking beer. Then Willie turned to me and told me to sit next to him and not to take my eyes off him. He said that he thought the son-of-a-bitch had broken his nose and he felt like he was going to pass out. I told him to go home, but he said, "No I don't want those fuckers to think I might be hurt. I'm gonna sit here and drink all night. But watch me, just in case."

I did, and Willie didn't pass out.

The next week a few Aliens and some nomad bikers came back and hung out. For the most part members of both clubs and righteous nomads got along well, and most of the guys all around admitted that it was nice to have a place where you could go to hang out with *people*—which meant outlaws and kindred souls, as opposed to *citizens*—and not get hassled. Most of the guys who showed up in the pack the week before were not Aliens or members of outlaw clubs. They were just what would be called bikers today. And they were scared.

The Mortician had seized on this and spread the alarm throughout the biker community. It was whispered around motorcycle shops, claim bars, Nathan's hot dog stands, and the usual other biker hangouts. The Mortician whipped them up into a frenzy and told them the Pagans would run them off the road if they didn't join the Aliens in checking Pagan power in New York. With the security that comes from a pack, these guys banded together and rode with the Aliens for a reckoning.

But most of the nomads who rode up with the Aliens wanted peace, not trouble. They were relieved that the hassle was over, glad to have a standing invitation to hang out, and now just wanted to show that they were friends. A lot of these guys brought some good weed as a peace offering just to show that the hassle of the previous week was over.

But some of the Pagans would not let the issue rest. Davy Supermouth had grown up with the Mortician, and like the Mortician, he too was capable of duplicity and cunning. He was constantly trying to teach me how to tell the difference between situations when you fight and when you walk away and wait for tomorrow. Right now he was thinking about tomorrow, working on Sweet William, convincing him that everything was not OK, that the whole thing was symbolic and we could not let the Mortician go around thinking that he had put one over on us.

So Sweet William went to Jersey and sat down with Updegraff and Pappy from Jersey and J.P. Soul from the Mother Club to talk about the Mortician's big show.

When the situation called for charm and persuasiveness, you went to Satan. But when circumstances called for cunning and duplicity, you went to J.P. Soul, the man who Apple liked to describe as "the world's only uncircumcised Jew." Frank Rheinheimer from Newark, New Jersey. He looked and cut his hair like Sonny Bono. He wore a pair of wire-frame granny glasses with blue lenses, and he liked to stare out at you over the top. His favorite gig was walking into a black club, strutting up to the stage, and asking the band if he could sing a couple of songs with them. So here is this black band leader looking at this little Jewish guy from Newark staring at him over a pair of wire-frame granny glasses with blue lenses, and his hair cut like Sonny Bono, and on top of all that, a name patch on his shoulder declaring to all the world that his name is *J.P.* "fucking" *Soul* no less. And he is asking if he can sit in with an all black band in a black club. So what else can the bandleader do but laugh and say, "Give the white boy a chance."

But the punch line was that J.P. Soul was to black music what Charlie Pride was to white music; namely, he could sing it better than most blacks, and he always ended up bringing the house down. And Norman from a club called the Pharaohs came into work one day and said to Sweet William, "Where the fuck did you guys ever find that J. P. Soul? That man sure got *soooooome* soul." But in any event, J. P. now had more than black entertainment on his mind.

"Very good, I'm impressed with Mortician's work," J.P. said. "But can he do it every week? We can. And we'll soon see what kind of support he really has."

Two weeks later, while we were all there partying and trying out the different weed, several cars with Jersey license plates drove up. Every one of the occupants had a pistol in a shoulder holster or in his belt, and the trunks of the cars were loaded with shotguns and hunting rifles. The Pagans had remembered the lesson of the car club incident in Washington, namely that guns speak louder than numbers. But they had also brought along several hillbillies from the West Virginia and Virginia clubs. And that had been the real stroke of genius on the part of J.P. Soul.

All across the country, people from Main Street U.S.A. have this gut fear about Italian gangsters with their pinstripe suits, cardboard-soled shoes, and small caliber Berettas. People actually believe that if these guys have it in for you, you have no chance in the world against them, that they will hunt you down and find you any place in the world, and the police are impotent against them. People in New York know better. They know that if you can make it from Brooklyn to Poughkeepsie, or even Patterson, New Jersey, the stupid bastards will probably never find you.

But New Yorkers in turn fear their own boogeymen. They believe that if *Cousin Earl* and *Cousin Merle* come down from Cornhole County in the Appalachian highlands looking for you, the hicks can sit on a rooftop and shoot your eye out with a high-powered deer rifle from six blocks away, and then be safely back drinking moonshine on the front porch of a cabin in Shithole Hollow before the New York cops are even done drawing the white chalk lines around your body in the street.

And that was the point that J. P. Soul wanted to make. While the hillbillies walked around gawking at the black lights and psychedelic art like Gallic barbarians visiting the Roman forum, Pappy, Bucky, and Updegraff from Jersey were busy impressing the fact on the Aliens that they were a local club, and that everyone of the them was known to the Pagans. But there was no way the Aliens could ever know who all the Pagans were outside of New York. Meanwhile J. P. Soul congratulated the Mortician on a very impressive piece of work, but then he made sure to point out that there were, indeed, more Aliens than Pagans in New York, but that if the Aliens wanted to fuck with the Pagans, the next morning there would be Pagans in New York looking for them, Pagans with strange accents from places with strange names the Aliens had never even heard of.

Nothing happened that night, but from that point on everything was again utterly changed. For two weeks it had seemed that there might be room in the largest metropolitan area in the world for less than 100 Pagans and Aliens to live together as brother clubs. But now you could see it in Sweet William's eyes, in Upde's eyes, in J. P.'s eyes, in Davy Supermouth's eyes, in the Mortician's eyes: mistrust, suspicion, and the blank stare of a prize-fighter in the locker room just waiting for his turn to climb in the ring.

From here on in, it was to be tit for tat forever. It was only a matter of time, but one club would emerge on top in the end. A single Alien and a single Pagan could get along, but the two clubs could never share New York any more than two packs of baboons could share the same African savanna.

CHAPTER 6

*The ancient Germans believed that the gods had created the
world from the carcass of a dead giant named Ymir. And
only after they finished did they learn that the carcass was
crawling with maggots. The gods then gave these worms the
shape, and wits of men, and they became the dwarf races of
Swartalfheim* [Home of the Dark Elves]. *The miscreants
who inhabit the caves, mineshafts, and other cavities in the
Bowels of the Earth.*
— From the ancient pagan Eddas of Iceland

Andthat pretty much describes how outlaws saw the world around
them. There were "good people" who were made in the image of
the ancient gods of Asgard. And then there were the maggot people who
crawled out the arsehole of the dead giant. And naturally, in our world,
as in the Norse world, the maggots outnumbered the "good people" by a
ratio of about 10,000 to one.

But my mother had a different view of the world: a *Weltanschauung*
hatched where she had been born, in Ridgewood, a German city that
stretched from the Lutheran Cemetery in Queens to the Schaefer Brewery under the Williamsburg Bridge in Brooklyn. This city encompassed
seven breweries, most of the big meat-packing houses, and the best
machine shops in New York City. The whole thing had been built in 20
years between 1900 and 1920 as a home for German brewers, butchers,

and *handwerkers*. My mother remembered the days when mothers left their babies on the sidewalk in carriages while they shopped on Myrtle Avenue, where German shopkeepers prided themselves on stocking the best quality merchandise at the fairest prices, and where every Saturday morning the *hausfraus* (housewives) turned out to scrub the sidewalks in front of their homes on their hands and knees.

But those days were now gone. The neighborhood had long gone to shit in a handbasket full of drugs, piss bums, and wiseacres like me. Most of the old Germans now resided in the cemetery and the remaining *hausfraus* no longer scrubbed the sidewalks. Many, though, like my grandmother, waged a last-ditch defensive war, behind locked doors and clean curtains, on behalf of old-fashioned nineteenth century German Biedermeier values that had no place in modern day New York City, a place where only wiseguys and *scheissters* got ahead. For my mother these two worlds collided one July day in 1967.

New York had just passed the nation's first helmet law. Outlaws ignored it. We believed that America was still a free country and that there was no way that the Supreme Court would ever let such a stupid law stand. We were wrong of course, but in the meantime we just piled up tickets for this and other infractions. This was before they invented computers, and you could still thumbtack the tickets on the wall and laugh at them. Which is exactly what we outlaws did.

But the Town of Hempstead proved to be a problem. Here they issued bench warrants and turned them over to the Nassau County police for enforcement. I had an outstanding ticket, so about once a month a cop came to the house and asked for me. My mother was mortified.

But I had talked to a New York City cop who lived in Lindenhurst. A big German guy who rode a full-dress hog and liked to hang around with us—in the bars that is, not the clubhouse. Flipout had brought him around. He just introduced himself and said, "Look, I'm a cop, but I like to ride, and I'm just here for fun, but please don't say anything I'm not supposed to hear." So he was allowed to hang out once in a while.

I told him about it, and he said, "Just tell her to say you're not home."

"But can't they do anything?" I asked

"No, they can't. All they can do is ask for you, and if whoever answers the door, *even if it's you*, says 'he ain't here,' then all they can do is fuckin' leave. I'm telling you, I know, I'm a cop."

And that was it, they could kiss my ass as far as I was concerned. I tried to explain this to my mother, but it was no use. They had her number. They used to pull up in front of the house and leave the red light turning on top of the squad car, while the two of them stood on the stoop in uniform talking to her, real polite but also real slow and dragging the whole thing out. My mother was horrified, trying to get rid of them while looking up and down the block, hoping the neighbors wouldn't look out the window and see the flashing red light in front of the house.

They had her sick over it, and I was concerned that they were playing her for a sucker. I told her that she had to learn how to stand up to the bastards and not be embarrassed over something as stupid as a traffic ticket and twirling red lights. But it was no use; in the end I gave in. It was only a $10 fine to start with. And she insisted that "it can't hurt to go in and make a clean breast of it." Real German, I thought: *Be up front and straightforward about everything and other people will respect you and do the same thing. What was the worst they could do? Double the fine?*

The night before I left I told Billy Koharet about it. He looked at me like I was nuts. "You can't do that," he said. "They're crazy down there in Hempstead. There's no tellin' what they'll do ta you."

He offered to come over and try to talk some sense into my mother, but I told him it was no use. Then he said that I shouldn't go by myself, but he couldn't go with me because they had a warrant out for him, too. He said he would wait home all morning and I should call him if anything went wrong, and if nothing went wrong, come over as soon as I got done so that we could buy beer with what was left of the fine money.

When I left the next morning I could see that my mother was quite proud of herself. I rode my bike to Hempstead, chained it to a parking meter, and walked in the town hall.

"I'm here to pay a parking ticket," I announced to the clerk, who looked suspiciously like one of those maggot folk from *Swartalfheim*.

She asked me my name and looked up the ticket. Then she told me that I would have to see the judge because the ticket was more than 30 days old. I spent half the morning sitting in the courtroom. By the time the judge got to me, the clerk had found another ticket and the judge fined me $35 for the two, an outrageous amount in those days.

I told the judge that I only had $32. He told me that was no good—either I cough up 35 bills or go to jail. I told him that I could phone my buddy and he would be down with the other $3 in 20 minutes.

"Tell him to bring it to the county jail," he said. "We don't have any holding facilities here."

So they clapped me in handcuffs and carted me off to the Nassau County Jail. But first they let me use the phone, but only because the law said they had to. I could hear Billy screaming on the other end. "I told you something like this was going to happen," he said. "Tell them I'll be right there." But the cop said, no good, we can't wait, and then he carted me off to the hoosgow.

The Nassau County Jail is larger and more impressive than some state penitentiaries, and it is far more impressive than any hospital, school, or public park in the county that was built with taxpayer money. Here they mugged me, they fingerprinted me, they made me take a shower, and they made me spread my cheeks so some guard could look up my ass for drugs and shotguns. When he was satisfied that there were none, they gave me my jailhouse blues and took me to the barbershop.

I waited my turn outside. When it came, the guard escorted me into the room where they cut hair. I thought this was odd since the guard had not escorted the other inmates into the room. I knew what was up. Back in '67 prisoners needed *normal* short haircuts, but it was common to shave the heads of longhairs—hippies and bikers.

The barber pulled out the clippers.

"You gotta do that?" I asked.

"Sorry," he said. "But I got my orders."

I looked at the guard. "There's a guy probably out front right now with my fine money," I told him.

He just shook his head no, and the barber started shearing.

So sheared, shaved, and dressed in prison blues, the guard led me to a cellblock. It was loaded with niggers and Puerto Ricans.

This is nice, I thought to myself as I walked into my cell and plopped on the bed. These were still the days when single cells were the law. I just laid on my bed and ran my hand over my head and felt pissed. Meanwhile the niggers and Puerto Ricans walked by staring in and trying to look tough with their bottom lips sticking out.

Maybe they were just curious. After all, only lunatics and marines had buzzed heads in those days. But in any event, one of them finally stopped and stood halfway in my doorway. Now it was getting serious. I don't know what he wanted, maybe just a smoke, maybe just to see how much I would take.

But under the code of prison etiquette, he had no business crossing the threshold of my cell. With my shaved head he had no way of knowing that I was a biker, or prizefighter. He just saw a young white boy and probably thought they had shaved my head because I was some sort of longhaired hippie, war-protesting, drug-dealing college faggot. So he was going to shake down the college punk.

I was up and on him in a second.

We rolled out into the cellblock on to the floor. I turned his head around and began drilling my fist into his face, sledgehammer style. I could hear things squishing and saw blood spurting out. I was pissed at the world; it felt great and, at this point, it was better than getting laid.

Three white guys pulled me off him, while the niggers stood around shouting, "Be cool, be cool. What the fuck's a matter with him?"

The fight was over. The guy wandered off to the other end of the block with a bloody head. I went back in my cell and laid on my bunk. No one looked in at me after that. Then I heard a guard's voice asking, "What the fuck happened to him?"

I thought, *Shit, now I'm really screwed.*

Then I heard another guard's voice screaming, "Who the fuck told you to put him in there?" A few seconds later I heard the same voice: "I don't care what they told you, get him the fuck out of there, now."

The first guard called me. I soon figured out what was up. I was only 20 years old. I was supposed to be in a juvenile cellblock, but someone had been trying to screw me over, and they went too far by putting me in the hardest-ass cellblock they could find. Now they had trouble and had to cover their own asses. Since I wasn't supposed to be in that adult cellblock in the first place, there was no way they could report the fight. My luck seemed to be turning around.

They led me to a new cellblock—a juvenile block this time—and I was just settling in when a guard again came to tell me that I was getting out. Billy had showed up with their three miserable bucks, about five minutes after I got there, but they had taken forever to process the information and get me out. Then we had to go back to Hempstead for my bike. By the time we got back to my mother's house it was about five o'clock.

My mother had expected me back about noon. Intuitively, she knew something was wrong. Then I walked in with Billy and my skinhead haircut, and I told her the whole story. She was shocked, but Billy assured her that everything I told her was true and that they were crazy down in Hempstead, and I never should have gone there in the first place.

I could see it in her eyes. In her old-fashioned Teutonic world you did not abuse people who came forward of their own volition and sought to resolve a problem. Now that old world was crumbling like Asgard on the Day of Ragnarok. The bastards had sought to teach me a lesson, but all that they had done was to ensure that my mother would never again trust a policeman or public official.

By that time every Pagan's hair, except for Sweet William's, hung over their collars, but I rode through the summer of '67 as one of the first skinheads. With my shorn head, I stuck out among the Pagans the way a Pagan would have stuck out in a room full of Mennonites.

But it didn't make any difference. I was getting laid all over the place. There is something about the outlaw mystique and swagger that turns women on. It's like a movie magazine once said about Rudolf Valentino: He doesn't look like your husband, he doesn't act like your brother, and he doesn't in the least resemble the man your mother thinks you should marry. Now add to all that the simple mechanics of a ride on an old-fashioned motorcycle: a woman climbs on the back of a bike with her arms and legs wrapped around a hairy gorilla who is goosing the throttle on a 74-ci engine, rocking and rolling, laying it down on the curves, and jacking it up between the curves. His face is the windshield and his knees are the bumpers, and if he wrecks, both their heads are smashed pumpkins. But she's actually enjoying it, while the whole thing is wiggling right under her twat like a 500-pound, 60-horsepower Milwaukee vibrator. She's gotta be attracted to the guy before she gets on, and even if she's not, she will be after a couple of hours. Granted, it may not be for everyone, but it turned on more than enough women to go around.

Of course if you believe the media hype, you would think that all we did was ride around looking for young girls to rape. But who the hell needs to steal the milk when every farmer's daughter is giving the stuff away for free? In those days, when we outlaws wanted sex, we didn't have to look for someone to rape any more than we had to look for someone to fight. Of course there was a game that some girls liked to play. These girls came around and wanted to walk away feeling like they had a wild time getting roughed up a bit by some barbarian with swastika tattoos.

One of these was a Jewish girl from Syosset named Carole. She and a friend showed up one day at the beach in Oyster Bay. It was a Sunday and we were partying with a bunch of citizen bikers. After the sun went down we made a fire. I took a walk down the beach with the girl and we got into it. When we got back to the fire she began telling her girlfriend in an excited, but not alarmed, tone that she had just been raped.

The citizen bikers nearly shit themselves. They cranked up their bikes and split, yelling that they had to get out of there before the cops showed up. And then the outlaws split, just because they were conditioned to do so whenever they heard the word "cop." I left with them.

But the next night we were down in a parking lot on Old Country Road across from the Jolly Roger amusement park. I was talking to one of the citizen bikers who had been at the beach the night before. He was still shaken by the incident and still talking about it. Then I noticed an expensive late-model car pull up about 30 feet away from us.

"Who the fuck is that?" he said.

I recognized the two girls from the night before.

"It can't be," he said. "They wouldn't . . ."

But they had.

I walked over and stuck my head down by the window on the driver's side where Carole was sitting with a silly, half-embarrassed smirk on her face. I asked her how she found us and she said that she remembered one of the guys saying that we hung out here. Then she told me her story.

"When I got to school this morning, I told my boyfriend that I got raped by a Pagan last night. And do you know what the bastard had the nerve to tell me?"

"No, I don't."

"'What the hell do you want me to do about it?' I was so pissed, I just took off his ring and threw it in his face, and then I got my girlfriend and we came looking for you."

After that she came around every night, parked her father's car and rode around with us. Sometimes she stayed out all night. I don't know what she told the old man, but it couldn't have been the truth. She was also smart. She saw how the other women behaved and copied their style, not just behavior but dress, too. Soon she fit right in and nobody even knew that she was just a little Jewish princess. She actually wasn't a bad kid; in fact, she was pretty cool. The only thing that ever really shocked her was learning that Les the Rabbi really was Jewish.

We were having a hog roast or something like that. And somebody asked the Rabbi to say the blessing. He held his hands up in the air, closed his eyes, and began chanting something like he was speaking in tongues. With that the tip of Carole's chin fell down between her tits.

"Oh my God, that's Hebrew," she said to me, her mouth hanging wide open. "He really is Jewish."

"Why do you think we call him our Rabbi?"

She had trouble with that. In her world Jewish girls sowing some wild oats while hanging out with guys like us was one thing, but grown Jewish men wasting their time on such a *goyisher* occupation as this. That was another story all together.

As for her age, nobody every questioned the women we brought into bars with us. After all, the legal age was still 18, and in New York nobody gave a shit in those days anyway. So she became my old lady, and we rode around the whole summer. Up and down the turnpike, into the city, and clear out to Montauk Point where we camped in the dunes, ate shellfish, and drank beer at roadside clam bars. When September came around she went back to high school and I never saw her again.

One night during the course of the summer, Sweet William announced that we would be going to a Pharaoh party on Friday night. The Pharaohs were an all-black club. Not that it mattered. Here again, outlaw bikers weren't real racists anymore than they were real rapists. It's not like we didn't fight with blacks, we did that all the time, but for that matter we fought with everyone. And sure, we used to call them niggers, but so did every other red-neck on Long Island, and besides, we called each other greasy Guineas, dirty Wops, Nazi-bastards, Jew-fucks, dumb Polacks, and redheaded Irish pricks.

The Pharaohs were not one-percenters. In fact there was no such thing as a black one-percenter club at the time; it was pretty much a white red-neck thing. The Pharaohs belonged to the AMA and they had their name stenciled on the back of old-fashioned Marlon Brando type biker jackets, the very kind later worn by every gay artist, rock singer, and little punker girl with purple hair and a ring in her nose. But back in the 1960s these style jackets with all the epaulets, buckles, and dangling rabbit's feet were considered, like full dress bikes, to be strictly '50s shit. The outlaws wore those modified leather racing jackets without collars, without belts, and without epaulets. They looked more like a Lloyd Bridges scuba suit than a Marlon Brando biker jacket.

But everything about the Pharaohs was strictly '50s shit: the old biker jackets, the stenciled lettering, the big shield with all the Egyptian hiero-glyphics, and mostly the bikes. Just about everyone was on a garbage wagon. Not a stock garbage wagon but an embellished one: chartreuse, purple, gold, silver, and "titty-pink" paint jobs, with giant sissy bars, rac-coon tails, and extra lights strung all over the place—across the windshield, across the sissy bar, up and down the sides—more lights than a Christmas tree. In the dark you could tell a Pharaoh on a bike from blocks away. On one ungodly hot New York City summer night, the Gypsy, Sleepy, and I were coming back to Maspeth from Greenpoint in a car. We got stuck in traffic in the dark on the Kosciusko Bridge. While we were sitting there, with the marshy rotten stench of Newtown Creek worming its way up our noses through the stale night air, we suddenly heard the thunder coming through the lanes of snarled traffic behind us. Soon they were whizzing past us like an electric rodeo. The Buzzard, Bo Weevil, and Big Daddy— who was so big that they used to say his jacket was cut from a hippopotamus hide—the whole fucking pack, with their women perched behind them. Long lean women like South Carolina scarecrows, in peddle-pusher pants with scarves around their straightened Diana Ross Motown-style '60s hair-dos.

"Damn, they are fucking impressive," Sleepy said as we watched them disappear across the bridge in front of us.

The Pharaohs had a style all their own and it was a class act. We were as impressed with their electrified Frankenstein bikes as they were with our choppers. A couple of Pharaohs even started building their own choppers. One of these, the guy they called Norman who worked with Sweet William, began coming around our haunts on Hempstead Turnpike to check out our choppers and ask questions about problems he was having building his.

And then Sweet William told us we would be partying with the Pharaohs at their clubhouse in New Castle. He told us that Norman had taken him there the week before. He had met the Buzzard, who had invited the entire club to a party. Then he read us the riot act. There would be no fights, no incidents. We were not supposed to hit on their women and they would not hit on ours. If there was any dispute we were to bring it to him, and he and the Buzzard would resolve it. But under no circumstances were we supposed to swing.

Of course, Flipout had to ask what happens if someone does swing. Sweet William explained very patiently that if someone did swing, the club would back him because that was the Pagans rule: when one Pagan swings, they all swing—that is the Pagans prerogative. But then he made clear that he would be very embarrassed and afterwards he would personally beat the living shit out of the troublemaker because, as our leader, that was his prerogative.

So the night went fine. It was in the basement of a colonial-style house in Carl Place with a finished basement and a bar. The Pharaohs were older than us, about 30 on the average, while we were in our early 20s. In fact I think the Gypsy at 24 was the oldest Pagan in New York at the time. So in addition to race, we were also on opposite sides of the generation gap. And for the most part the Pharaohs were not native New Yorkers. They were displaced Southrons, and kind of reminded us of some of the Pagans in Virginia chapters.

In spite of all these differences, everyone got along. Sweet William and Buzzard parted with a handshake. Any Pagan was welcomed anytime at the Pharaoh clubhouse and at any bar or club in Carl Place, New Castle, or Hempstead where the Pharaohs hung out. Then came the more complicated part: Any Pharaoh was welcome anytime at the club in Elmont. Not only would Sweet William guarantee his safety among the Pagans, but if there were any hassle with the Aliens, or any white club for that matter, the Pagans would back the Pharaoh.

We rode through the summer and there was never any friction between the outlaw Pagans and the AMA Pharaohs. In fact Norman and a few others approached Sweet William and Davy Supermouth about breaking away and forming their own Pagan club.

Eventually the idea was shit-canned for two reasons: one, Sweet William felt that there would be no trouble in New York or Jersey, but the base of the Pagan power was still south of the Mason-Dixon line, and he felt that he could not guarantee that the black Pagans would be 100 percent accepted by the Southrons. Two, and more importantly, should the Pagans recruit members from the Pharaohs, Sweet William felt that it would be a betrayal of the Buzzard's trust, and it would certainly strain relations between the two clubs. The Pharaohs remained the only club in the entire metropolitan New York area with which the Pagans never had even the slightest hassle.

Overall, the outlaw attitude toward race was typical of many lower-class whites. They were well aware of the differences and dangers inherent in race relations. But as with most people who live on the dark side of the law, they were more concerned with *who you are* than *what you are*. In other words, when you got in a fight, you wanted to be with someone who wouldn't run. When you got pulled into a police station, you wanted a partner who would keep his mouth shut. When you got carted off to jail, you wanted a friend who came around to see what he could do to get you out and not try to screw your old lady. This is how outlaws tend to judge people. Racial prejudice, as most people know it, tends to be a luxury of the law-abiding middle class. Folks who are busting their hump everyday to make the nut and stay one step ahead of the law at the same time can't afford to reject "good people" on the basis of color.

In any event the summer of '67 rolled on. Sweet William continued leading us on bar-wrecking rampages that got us run out of one municipality after another. We had worked ourselves all the way into Richmond Hill to the west and Massapequa to the east. Every place in between, we had to hide our colors and travel incognito.

Davy Supermouth's wife finally had enough and moved out of their bungalow-style house in East Meadow. Then the club moved in. Davy slept in the bedroom, and Tom Gannon slept on the couch in the living room. Meanwhile, the rest of us began collecting mattresses and throwing them on the cellar floor. Eventually we managed to fit three double mattresses on the floor, where they quickly became cold and damp. But we were young, it was summertime, and we were usually either drunk, stoned, or both by the time we fell asleep. As often as not, we might have also had a slight concussion from being hit in the head, so we didn't notice any discomfort until we woke up in the morning. This cellar is where any number of Pagans from any number of clubs would sleep on any given night, along with their women, either steady old ladies or one-night pick-ups. We were like a pack of animals in a den, but we respected each other's privacy, and the girls were young too and thought it was cool. Today there are probably hundreds of normal middle-class Long Island kids who would shit if they found out that back when grandma was their age, she used to hump Pagans on the cellar floor in East Meadow.

Then one day Davy Supermouth brought home the two French Canadian brothers, Cal and Richie, the guy with Chicago Outlaw colors that got arrested with me in East Meadows. Davy put Richie, his wife, and two kids in the bedroom, kicked Tom off the couch, and slept there himself, while Tom and Cal shared the floor. This caused problems because Tom was uncouth and slovenly even by outlaw standards. He was another one of those great '60s outlaws who did his best to shape the Legend by their outlandish appearance and behavior. On the basis of his well-cultivated dirty and unkempt outlaw appearance alone, he was once arrested in Keansburg, New Jersey—he really wasn't doing anything at the time— and written up as "an Outrage to Public Decency." Tom's noise, snoring, and smell soon got on Cal's nerves, as it had gotten on Davy's nerves a long time before that, but Davy wasn't allowed to complain because Tom was a Pagan.

But soon Cal and Davy had a real case of the ass about Tom, and they began bitching that he was even a shit-ass chopper jockey, because nobody had ever seen him ride nothing but a little shit-ass 45-cc three-wheeler, the kind like the ice cream man used to have when we were kids. And they claimed that if he ever got on a real scooter, he'd probably get himself killed.

Then Davy took it upon himself to call the Mortician. They had gone through life since kindergarten alternating between being asshole buddies and kicking the shit out of each other. Right now the relationship was sort of in limbo, but whenever we needed to contact the Aliens, it usually went through Davy and the Mortician.

The Mortician said that now that Davy had mentioned it, he too could never remember seeing Tom ride anything but the little ice cream wagon. Of course I figured out that Mortician was probably playing Davy for a sucker, and Davy, who was usually just as sharp as the Mortician, was falling right into the trap because he was so pissed off at Tom that it was clouding his judgment.

And that was it. Outlaws have a thing about paranoia—not just fear but an ability to obsess on something, even if it's only a truckload of sewer workers who have been working down the block for a week. Now it was Tom. Davy and Cal mentioned the matter to Sweet William, and the whole club soon broke up into pro-Tom and anti-Tom factions. I was the leader of the pro-Tom, and Sweet William was leaning toward the anti-Tom people.

Then Cal brought that monster of a California chopper into play. It was originally a 74-ci Harley-Davidson that was now punched-out, souped-up, and machined to precision. The pistons had enough compression to squeeze coal into diamonds, and the carburetor could suck air like a

Hoover vacuum cleaner. These bikes were common in California, where most riding was done on wide-open roads. But they were virtually useless on Queens Boulevard, where they tended to overheat and blow up in snarled traffic. They also had trouble negotiating the winding roads of the North Shore of Long Island or the Pennsylvania coal regions. I had the monster out a couple of times and got it up to well over 100 on the Long Island Expressway, and a couple of guys claimed to have gotten it up to 140. Cal said he once got it to 150 and it still wanted to do more. It was like a bucking bronco. I once took it out and it started to rain on the way back. Every time I came out of a red light, the rear wheel was all over the road, and I was lucky to get it back without spilling it. Now Sweet Willie and Cal had gotten it into their heads that this California chopper was too much for Tommy to handle.

So one day on a hot Sunday afternoon in August, we were all drinking beer on the front lawn of the clubhouse in East Meadow. Cal pulled the monster out of the garage and parked it on the street in front of the house. Then he popped the question.

"Do you want to take a ride, Tom?" he asked.

Cal was grinning like the Devil. And Sweet Willie and Davy Supermouth looked like Beelzebub and Mephistopheles. Tom was on the spot, and he was already half drunk. But he was game.

"Shit yea," he said. Then he walked up to the monster and straddled it. His big Irish peasant hobbit foot came crashing down on the kick starter and fired it up with one kick. He let it purr for a few seconds—shit, it was 97 degrees in the shade. Then he cracked the throttle, popped the clutch, and brought the thing up on one wheel like the headless horseman. When it came down he took off like a rocket, with his long, dark, greasy red Irish hair blowing in the breeze like an Indian headdress. Then as he got to the corner we saw him stand up on the brake and bring the thing to a screeching skid. Just then, some lady came cruising right out of a side street where Flipout and Crazy Joey Vargas had gotten drunk the week before and ripped down the stop sign so they could play Frisbee with it.

The woman slammed into Tom. Cal's beautiful, black lacquer chopper went skidding down the street head-over-heels. Tom went flying up in the air and came crashing down on the lady's windshield. Then he bounced into the street where he laid on his back like a dead walrus.

The woman jumped out of the car and ran over to Tom, who was sprawled out in the street. Before she knew it, she was surrounded by two dozen bearded, swastika-covered Pagans. She became hysterical, wailing like a banshee and crying.

"I didn't see him," she screamed. "I didn't see him."

Willie had to grab her by the shoulders and shake her to calm her down. "It wasn't your fault," he told her. "Nobody here is blaming you."

In addition to being convincing, Willie was also the closest thing to a clean-cut All-American boy that the Pagans had. You could see it in the woman's eyes. When she realized that no one was going to hurt her, she was looking at Willie like he was Jesus Christ come back from the dead.

We took Tom to Nassau Community—the welfare hospital—where he had to sit in the emergency room for hours with all the niggers and Puerto Ricans. The rest of us soon got bored. They left me and Stretch with Tom and told us to call when he was ready to leave. We then left Tom with the niggers and Puerto Ricans and found a bar across the street.

They had a sign hanging up that read: Zombies $1.00. This was back in the old days before date-rape drugs, when they really made the damn things to knock girls on their ass. A single shot was still only 25 cents and every third shot was free, so for a buck, the thing must have been like strychnine. I had never had one, so I ordered one, and then another, and then a third.

"What's the most of these you ever saw a fucker drink," I asked the bartender.

"Three," he said.

"If I drink five, will you buy the last two?"

The deal was struck. He made them and he goosed them up real good. I drank them, but I don't remember paying for them. Of course, I don't remember going back to the hospital to get Tom or how we got back to East Meadow, either. The next day Stretch told me that when we got back to the clubhouse, I opened the back door of the car, got out, and fell down. I crawled up the front walk on my hands and knees. When I got to the front door, someone opened it like I was the dog wanting to come in. Then I crawled through the house on my hands and knees, and they heard crashing and banging as I fell down the cellar stairs just like Tom had done the night he came to join the club.

The next morning I woke up with a horrible hangover. When I managed to stagger out into the backyard, the big Irishman was sitting under a chair at the picnic table drinking beer. He had a cast from his right hip to his right ankle. He was also grinning like all Hell.

So for the rest of the summer, things went fine except for the next week, when we met some guy in a bar who wanted to impress us. He said he was the maintenance man at an apartment building, and if we wanted to go swimming he could get us in the pool. So we got on our bikes and in the middle of the night we showed up drunk at the pool. Tom kept climbing the ladder and jumping off the high board with his cast. The next morning it was hanging off him in dirty tattered strands, like the mummy in the old Boris Karloff movies. But the damn thing soon started to rot like a real mummy, and it smelled worse than Newtown Creek at low tide on a lazy August afternoon. Cal and Davy used to wake up gagging and retching all night long from the smell. Finally, they took him to the doctor and paid for a new cast.

CHAPTER 7

I promise the Chastity of my Body,
And Poverty, and Obedience to God,
Holy Mary of the Teutonic Nation, and to You,
The Master of The Teutonic Order, and Your
Successors, according to the Rules
And Practices of The Order,
Obedience unto Death
> — Oath sworn upon admission into the
> medieval order of Teutonic Knights

As the summer drew to a close, the Pagan empire was now spread out from the Eastern Shore of Long Island to the Pennsylvania– Ohio border and down into Virginia and West Virginia, with chapters in all the big cities. Pittsburgh proved to be an outlaw mecca. The new Pagan club quickly took control of the biker scene in western Pennsylvania. It absorbed the righteous clubs and disbanded the lame. Pittsburgh was still the Steel City at this time, although the industry was on its last legs and reeling like a punch-drunk prizefighter. But you could still walk into a Pittsburgh bar at eight o'clock in the morning and the night shift would be lined up, drinking Imperial whiskey and Iron City lager.

Pittsburgh was also the All-American blue collar town, combining the best—or worst, depending on how you wanted to look at it—of the East, the Midwest, and Appalachia. The Pagans soon became working class folk heroes. The papers couldn't get enough of them, and the cops couldn't get rid of them. They became a civic institution like Iron City beer, the Steelers, and Carl's Corner Taverns. Soon the Pagans had five large clubs in Allegheny and Westmoreland counties.

If you went to Bethlehem, Reading, or Lancaster, the brothers would get on the horn and an hour later there would be about a half-dozen guys sitting there drinking beer with you. But when you got to Pittsburgh, an hour later you couldn't move because the house was full of dozens of people, and outside they were still pulling up on the street. It was the outlaw capital of the world. There seemed to be more outlaws in Pittsburgh than Amish in Lancaster.

This set a new standard for Pagan clubs. Everyone now wanted to be like Pittsburgh. But Apple came around from the Mother Club and told us to cool it. He sat down and told us that we only had a dozen people, but that Big Dutch was very pleased with our club and we should not rush to recruit new members. A dozen righteous brothers are worth more than a hundred candy-ass party people who split when the shit hits the fan, he reminded us.

And Apple was right. When a Pagan was shot in the face by a member of the Rat Pack on Seneca Avenue in Ridgewood, New York, we didn't even have time to plan revenge. The following morning three members of the Rat Pack showed up at Stevie Hippie's front door with their patches in their hands. "Here," they said, "take these. We had no part in it and we want nothing to do with it. We're out."

That proved contagious. By the middle of the afternoon, Marcy, the leader of the Rat Pack, scuttled the club and everyone jumped overboard. Former members, if you could even find them, were professing to be outdone. Thus the gunman was left to deal with the Pagans on his own.

Meanwhile, over in Jersey there were the beginnings of what the hardcore members called the "Peace Movement." It had nothing to do with politics or Vietnam. It was all about Pappy, a man who was beginning to show a marked preference for negotiation over confrontation. Pappy had a family and a real Teamster job driving a flatbed rig, and his boss expected him to show up for work on Monday if he had a load of steel for him to haul. Pappy had discovered that you didn't have to go around pounding the living shit out of other clubs and ripping the patches off their backs.

When a new club showed up wearing one-percenter patches, Updegraff wanted to find out where they hung out and then go in and beat the shit out the members. Pappy had a different approach. He walked into the new club's hangout with his Pagan colors and his big Teamster beer belly and introduced himself to the leaders. Then he sat them down and explained that you could not go around giving yourself one-percenter patches like you were starting your own church. You had to be part of the great Outlaw Empire. He assured them that they were probably some very righteous dudes who deserved to wear them, but he had no way of knowing that. They simply had to remove the patches and hang out until the Pagans got to know them and brought them into the Outlaw Empire. The Pagans, he claimed, had no objections to other clubs flying one-percenter patches, but some form of control had to be exercised before the whole thing became a joke and every high school kid in the world ended up wearing one.

Invariably they agreed, because Pappy wasn't asking them to give something up. It was more like he was inviting them to become part of something big and nationwide, an All-American Outlaw Redneck Republic. He had assured them that they were probably a righteous bunch of dudes, and they were flattered. But in reality Pappy, Bucky, Saint Thomas, and a bunch of guys who Pappy considered more level-headed and sensible than the rest began an intense scrutiny of the new club. They quickly identified the three or four most righteous dudes in the club. Then in the middle of the week, each of these dudes would get a phone call from Pappy explaining that he needed a big favor, and could they meet him that night in some out of the way place to discuss it.

When the guys got there, they would be shocked to see each other. Then Pappy would sit the three or four of them down and explain that they were righteous dudes, but the rest of their club was a bunch of hopeless chicken-shit, candy-ass motherfuckers who would never get a one-percenter patch. He then told them that if they gave him their club patches, he was ready to sponsor them for Pagan membership.

It always worked.

As a result, Pappy's club grew until there were no other clubs left in central Jersey, and every righteous biker from Patterson to Asbury Park was flying Pagan colors. Soon Jersey had one of the biggest clubs, big enough in fact that the Jersey Pagans soon rivaled the Aliens on their own turf, and things settled down in the New York area. And for all this, Pappy was contemptuously dubbed "the Peacemaker" by the more violence-prone members of his club.

Meanwhile, the gap between us and the nearest Alien club was wider than ever, since by now Sweet William had gotten us completely run out of Nassau County. Now we were hanging out in Lindenhurst and Deer Park in the Pine Barrens of Suffolk County with about 2 million people and the Nassau County Police between us and the nearest Alien club.

Actually, it would be wrong to blame everything on Sweet William. His brother Stretch and I were probably worse than he was at starting trouble. At least we were far more arrogant. And Flipout could always be counted on to do something completely stupid to ruin a new hang-out. One time we were trying out a new place in Farmingdale. We had pulled up unannounced on bikes. The place was doing a robust business, and naturally the management shit themselves when they saw us. After a couple of beers I walked in the men's room to piss. I could see Stretch's leg sticking out of the stall door. He had some guy's head in the bowl face-down, and he was flushing and cursing like hell at the son of a bitch.

When I walked out I passed Sweet William, who was talking to some citizen dude. Here again, outlaw bikers saw themselves as medieval knights, and citizens were treated like peasants. Had the guy been a member of another club, or had he been at least dressed like a righteous-looking biker, I might have acknowledged him. But since he was a stone-cold citizen I just acted like he wasn't there.

"Your brother just flushed some guy's head down the bowl," I blurted out to Willie.

He just looked at me with his impish eyes and half a smirk. Then he shook his head like I was pathetic. "You just fucked everything," he said later, as he told me that the citizen dude was the manager. "I just got done convincing the guy that we were just here for a couple of beers and didn't want any trouble. And he was telling me that he had no trouble with us hanging out here. Then just as he says that, you have to come by and tell me that my brother just shoved one of his customer's heads in the bowl."

Needless to say that place didn't last long, and we continued our journey eastward. We had reached the end of Hempstead Turnpike and it was just a short jump over the Suffolk County Line, where we found a safe haven in Lindenhurst with an entire police force that had not yet had to deal with us. Davy Supermouth had been forced to move out of East Meadow and rented a house over the county line in Deer Park. At first he tried not to tell us about it, but we soon found out and turned that into a clubhouse, too. One night he got a hold of Sweet William and convinced him that we couldn't go on forever wrecking a new place every couple of weeks. Willie agreed. We were put on good behavior and told that if we wanted to fuck up we should do it in Nassau County or New York City. The club was going to winter over in Suffolk County without the police even being aware of it.

So by the time the Labor Day run approached, we were trying to be cool, and the Mother Club was trying to avoid unnecessary publicity. The number of Pagan clubs had more than doubled since the Fourth of July. Now we wanted a quiet place where we could all get drunk, get high, and get to know each other without a hassle. We finally found the place, on an island that could only be reached by boat in the middle of the Susquehanna River, just south of Columbia in Lancaster County, Pennsylvania.

Things did not begin well at all for us. A week earlier we had camped out on the Peconic Bay near Montauk Point on the south fork of eastern Long Island. Just before she went back to school and out of my life, Carole was coming on the run, but she was late. So I missed the pack and we had to ride out through the Long Island Pine Barrens by ourselves.

It was a pleasant summer afternoon. We stopped at a clam bar for beer and steamers. By the time I got there I had half a buzz on, but so did everyone else. We raced our bikes through the dunes and brush, wiped out, and fell down and slid through the sand. It was a lot of fun. Then we built a fire and got good and drunk and screwed in the dunes 'till the sun came up.

Unfortunately, I wasn't running an air filter on my carburetor. I only had a single barrel, so I was sucking straight air in order to make the thing run faster. Sand had gotten sucked right into the combustion chamber. The rings froze, and the engine died. I ripped the head off, and the walls were scored. I fought with a machinist to get it bored overnight. Then I got oversized pistons at Ghost Motorcycle in Port Washington, and by Friday afternoon I was trying to stick the thing back together by myself, when I realized I needed help.

It was six o'clock at night and everyone I called wasn't home. The only one I could get a hold of was my sister's boyfriend, Geoff Quinn. Quinn's old man was Irish, and his mother was an English war bride. There were about 12 kids in the family, and they lived in an old house in downtown Hicksville (that really is the name of an old German farm town on Long Island).

My sister brought Geoff home one afternoon when she was 15. He was not exactly what German parents expected for their only daughter, but it's what they deserved for leaving Ridgewood and moving to Hicksville. He was not the most ambitious kid in town, but his Irish wit, loquaciousness, and good-natured humor soon endeared him to everyone, and he had become a regular fixture around the house.

Geoff tended to drift from job to job, quitting after he had earned enough money or when it began to interfere with his social life. In the summer he worked as a gardener, in the fall he pumped gas, and then when the weather broke near the end of February he invariably showed up at George's Lawnmower Shop.

This was Long Island in the '60s, where after Labor Day the lawnmowers were tossed in the garage and forgotten about. Then as soon as the weather broke, everyone was down at George's with a lawnmower that wouldn't start. On a spring afternoon, George would have a dozen kids tuning up lawnmowers in the back of his shop, sometimes even out on the sidewalk.

Now there is a mistaken notion that good motorcycle mechanics begin working on cars and then graduate to motorcycles. But every good motorcycle mechanic on Long Island seemed to start in a lawnmower shop, where he worked in the spring until he could tear a small engine apart and put it back together drunk and blindfolded. Geoff had recently picked up a Beeser that he was putting together in his father's garage. But what's more important, he knew how to get my cylinder block back on without fucking up the rings. This is why I needed him now, and soon had him in the garage looking at parts scattered all over the floor.

"You ought to have a ring compressor," he said. "And I don't have one. But if you hold the cylinder I can get the pistons in." Unlike a Harley-Davidson with twin jugs, both combustion chambers on British bikes came in one piece. So you had to get both sets of rings in at the same time.

There we sat in the garage, me holding the cylinder and him sitting on the floor squeezing the rings until it went back together.

"You shouldn't be taking this to Pennsylvania," he said. "You're supposed to break a new engine in slowly for the first 500 miles."

"Fuck it," I said. "I don't have any choice."

As it turned out, I really didn't. When we got the thing back together, the engine was breaking up like all hell. "There's a short," he said. "You fucked something up in the electrical system, and I don't know anything about that yet."

"Who would?"

"Billy Benzino."

That was his boss down at the lawnmower shop, a Beezer-riding outlaw and one of the greatest mechanical wizards on Long Island. But he was out of town for the weekend. So now we were dealing with one of the Crown Jewels of British engineering: a Lucas electrical system. Anyone who has ridden a British bike will understand what I am talking about when I say that the reason the English drink warm beer is not because they like it, but because Lucas makes the refrigeration equipment.

So try as we might, we couldn't get the thing running. At about midnight, he said it was no use and he offered to give me a ride to Lindenhurst, where the clan was gathering. When we got to Lindenhurst, Tom Gannon was sitting by himself at the bar with the dirty, shitty, shaggy mummy cast on his leg, and a sleazy denim vest that looked like he had cleaned an oven with it. I walked up and slapped him on the back, and I could feel the grease and road dirt from his denim vest on the palm of my hand.

"My bike's all fucked up," I said. "I blew the engine up."

"So did everyone else," he said. "They all got sand in their engines last week and now nobody's bike will run." As it turned out Gannon was there by himself and everyone else was either picking someone up or waiting to be picked up. All I could do was wait.

Geoff sat down at the bar and started talking to Tom. In New York and Dublin at that time, they used the term "Irish queer." This was not a homosexual, but rather some man who preferred talking to men instead of women when he got drunk. Tom Gannon was no queer, either by Irish or American standards. In fact, he was one of the world's great talkers. When he drank he would talk to anyone as long as it was a man. He even claimed to have gone to Nassau Community College for a term and taken a psychology course. By outlaw standards, this made him a scholar, and he claimed to be an expert on everything in the world, which used to piss the hell out of Sweet William, who used to say that he was nothing but a "goddamn bullshit artist." Having come from a large Irish family where the refrigerator was well stocked with Rheingold for any and all social occasions, Geoff hit it off right away with Gannon.

Then the Gypsy called. He couldn't get his bike started either, and neither could Stevie Hippie. They needed someone to pick them up in Maspeth. Seeing that Geoff had hit it off so well with Tom, and knowing that he was dying to come along, I invited him on the run and we went to get the Gypsy and Stevie. When we got back, I introduced Geoff to Sweet William, who said that it would be no problem if I brought him along. So we all got good and drunk, went back to Davy's house, and crashed on the couch, or the floor, or the backyard.

The next morning we pulled into Rahway, New Jersey, hung over, in a caravan of cars and feeling stupid. For the rest of the weekend, no one mentioned the name New York; they called us "the car club" instead. We pulled out along with the Jersey baggage train and prepared for an uneventful journey to Pennsylvania, where we teamed up with the Bethlehem club and headed for Reading.

The Pennsylvania State Police were trying to orchestrate their first "Pagan Watch." Back in the '60s, electronic communications were still in the Stone Age. But they had identified two large packs of Pagans, one heading southwest along Route 222 from Reading, and the other heading east through the Allegheny Mountains along the Pennsylvania Turnpike, with Lancaster seeming to be the obvious destination. Then, just as every spare state trooper was waiting for them in northern Lancaster County, a third pack crossed the Mason-Dixon Line from Maryland. Twenty minutes later the pack roared into a small Pennsylvania Dutch town in southern Lancaster County called Quarryville. The next morning it was all over the front pages of the Lancaster papers.

"Pagan Invasion Roars Into County," the headlines of the Sunday edition read. "A swastika-wearing, black-leather-jacketed motorcycle gang, known as the Pagan's was under State Police surveillance [sic] early this morning after the group set up camp late Saturday night on a Susquehanna River island near Washington Boro."

"According to the mayor," the group roared into Quarryville where it hoisted a Nazi flag in the town square and terrorized residents. The article went on to report that farther to the north, a small band of about 15 had actually penetrated the Lancaster City limits. Just in case any of the burghers wanted to go out and sniff the streets, the article reported that they "entered by Route 222, turned west on Orange Street and out Route 340 toward Columbia. While in the city, the police kept the group under observation. Other law enforcement agencies lying in the direction of travel were notified of the group's pending arrival."

There was some justification for alarm. After all, the little Dutch town of Quarryville had just been subjected to the largest mounted invasion of Southrons since Jeb Stuart's Virginia Cavaliers crossed the Mason-Dixon line a hundred years earlier and occupied the town of Carlisle, and that had required no less formidable a presence than George Armstrong Custer to dislodge them.

This time the locals didn't have Custer or the Army of the Potomac on their side. Instead they just had over-exalted politicians, under-stimulated reporters, over-excited cops, and under-amused citizens. The truth of the matter was that the Southron clubs had stopped in Quarryville for beer and directions. The swastika raising had been a lark. The brothers actually handed out beer to curious locals and even took some of the local girls for rides. According to the *Lancaster Sunday News*, one enterprising local politician actually came down to see what was going on and reported that they all seemed to be a nice enough bunch of guys who were "actually quite civil and interesting to talk with."

But that didn't matter. The largest threat to local security since the Army of Northern Virginia was now splashed across the headlines of every paper in the area, and by noon the next morning, the banks of the Susquehanna were lined with gawkers and state troopers everywhere, watching as Pagans sat hung-over and strung-out on the island.

We knew that if the cops didn't eventually round us all up and cart us off to the hoosgow, these hicksters might be shooting at us by sunset. So a delegation of the usual diplomats, like Pappy and Satan, was carefully selected and ferried over to the shore, where the prospects who were guarding the bikes reported that a state police observation post had been set up. One member of the delegation was Big John McClure, a new member who had been immediately inducted into the Mother Club and had obviously penetrated the most inner circle of power in the club. Meanwhile, all the drugs were dumped in the river, and the less rational members were disarmed before they wigged and began taking shots at the spectators.

When the delegates came back, they told everyone to start packing. "If we leave now, they said they won't bother us," Pappy told me. "But we don't trust them. Get all your people together on the shore. Don't let anyone leave. We're going out in two groups."

One group was to head south for the Mason-Dixon Line. The other would head north, where it would split into two groups outside of Lancaster: one heading down the Turnpike for Pittsburgh and the Allegheny Mountains, and the other heading down the Lancaster Pike for Reading and points east. We would be heading east. "Whatever you do," Satan warned us, "don't head into Lancaster. They're getting ready to call out the militia there, if they haven't done it already."

We began ferrying everyone across the river, while the state police kept the gawkers at a safe distance. "This'll never work," Sweet William told me. But it did. We began rounding up our people, while a group of Pagans and cops stood around a map spread out on the hood of a police cruiser, planning out the evacuation route with a group of troopers.

Word was starting to get back to us that the troopers really just wanted to get rid of us, and that they wouldn't hassle us as long as we rode out without causing any trouble. However, they constantly emphasized that we were not to go into Lancaster. If we did, all deals were off.

Geoff pulled up with a van. He was now a Pagan prospect. It seemed he had gotten a ride over in the boat the night before with a bunch of guys from the Mother Club. According to him, for some inexplicable reason some goofy hickster decided to stand up in the boat.

"Hey, sit your ass down," was the last thing he remembered hearing someone say, and a moment later they were all in the water swimming. As he sat by a fire trying to dry out he was talking to another shivering victim of the maritime disaster, who happened to be Big Dutch himself. Later Dutch told Sweet William, "I really like that new prospect you have there." According to Tommy Gannon, Sweet William didn't say anything. He just shrugged his shoulders. So according to Gannon, Geoff was now his prospect. Geoff was delighted, but I could think of some people back home who would not be.

When Geoff pulled up with the van, he told me to look in the back. I opened the door and staring back at me were the plump, smiling faces of two 16-year-old Dutch country girls. "Hi, I'm Debbie," one said. "This is my friend Karen. We saw you guys on TV last night and hitchhiked down here to see you this morning."

I slammed the door and turned to Stretch Parker. "This could be real trouble," I said, "even if nothing happens to them."

Then I grabbed the Gypsy and showed him. When he saw them he just said, "Oh shit, jailbait." We weren't sure what could happen to us, whether we could go to jail just for having them with us, or whether we had to try to screw them first. But it didn't look good. Not with all the cops around.

I found a crayon and scrawled, "Property of Stoop," on the back of Debbie's denim jacket with it. Then I wrote "Property of Gypsy" on the back of Karen's.

"Hey, what the fuck do you think you're doing?" the Gypsy asked. "We'll both go to jail."

"Nothing can happen to them," I told him, "or we could be fucked." I told him to stay with them until I got back. If we turned them loose right now, there was no telling what might happen to either them or us.

Finally, everyone was accounted for and we rolled out, as the engines roared and the hinds that were still lining the highway cheered. This is what they came to see, and now they saw it. We headed north toward Lancaster. We were told that the police were going to escort us around the city and then we were on our own. They claimed that they were doing this for everyone's good. Apparently the citizenry had broken out their hunting rifles and were threatening to pick off anyone on a bike.

A bunch of us were crammed in the back of the van. Stretch had a girl-friend who was only 16. He was only 19 himself, but we realized that we could be in more trouble with her than with the two hitchhikers because we had brought her across two state lines. Then she began complaining that she had to piss and couldn't hold it. Stretch had her pull down her pants, held her hands, and told me to open the back doors on the van so he could let her ass out to piss.

At the time they made vans without windows in the back doors, so we couldn't see. I opened the doors and she shoved her ass out the door backwards. Then I saw Stretch's eyes nearly bug out of his head.

"A fuckin' cop cruiser, right behind us," he yelled.

He yanked her back in and I slammed the doors, but she couldn't stop pissing. She pissed down her legs and on her pants and all over the floor. We howled. But the Gypsy, who was riding in the front with Geoff, wanted to know what was going on, so we told him what happened.

"Now we're fucked, thanks to you assholes" he said.

So there we were, waiting to get stopped on the Mann Act for white slavery with three underage girls in the truck. But nothing happened. After a couple of minutes, when we didn't hear any sirens, Tommy Gannon was the first to figure it out.

"They don't give a shit," he said. "They just want to get rid of us."

Sure enough, when we got around Lancaster the police cars left, and we put the two Dutch girls out on Route 30 and told them to hitch a ride back to York, but not before Debbie shoved a piece of paper in my hand with her phone number on it and made me promise to come see her in York, where she could show me to all her friends. I told her: "Sure, real soon."

As I closed the door I heard Gypsy telling Geoff, "You can't in this fuck-ing state on Sunday, they're all closed. We have to wait until we get to Jersey."

I knew they were talking about beer and Pennsylvania's Sunday closing law. We were hung over, it was hot, the van was painted black and soaked up heat like a solar heating unit, and we were parched as we drove through the cornfields all the way to Jersey. No one talked much, not even Tommy Gannon. I got as comfortable as I could and waited until we got to Phillipsburg, New Jersey, where we pulled into the parking lot and rolled out of the truck and into the first open bar. Each of us ordered a pitcher and began chugging the whole thing, and then we stocked up on six-packs. The guy about shit when he saw how much beer he sold in 15 minutes and then we were gone, on our way to New York.

The ritual ceremony had been completed. The whole thing had been a media-spawned event. And it had all been recorded in scripture with ritualistic piety: black leather jackets and black leather boots, chrome chains and lug wrenches, the smell of sweat and grease, pussy and beer—and of course, first and foremost, the ever-present swastika.

The real mystery was not that the Pagans wore swastikas, but the profound and erotic effect that this ancient Teutonic symbol seemed to have on the public imagination: by the time the reporters were done, the police had turned a biker barbecue into a major law-enforcement exercise. Old men who hadn't gotten a hard-on in years were breaking out their hunting rifles and patrolling the streets of America's oldest inland city, while their wives peeked from behind closed curtains., And 16-year-old girls were watching the evening news, beating off in bed, and wandering around the countryside the next morning with their thumbs stuck out on the highways in search of excitement.

It was a civic ritual that was becoming as American as Thanksgiving: black leather barbarians drenched in sweat and beer giving the American popular imagination a ritual fucking on a chrome altar under a black swastika. We were becoming legends and we didn't even know it at the time. We were just hot, tired, thirsty, and driving across New Jersey on a hot and shitty Labor Day Sunday afternoon.

CHAPTER 8

*Christianity was imposed superficially, and by force, on
the ancient Germanic peoples of Northern Europe. For
hundreds of years German mystics tried to express the
ancient pagan beliefs within a framework that would not
bring down the wrath of the religious authorities. It didn't
work in Europe. But in Amerika it exploded into a mystical
folklore that embraced the ancient pagan faith of their
ancestors, along with Christianity, Judaism, Zen, and a
whole bunch of ideas which goes today under the name of
new age theology. According to Pennsylvania Dutch folklore,
God is both male and female. The Schopfer or creator is
masculine, Jesus Christ is the perfect human being, as such
Jesus' personality is both male and female, thus Jesus is
androgynous. The Third person of the Trinity is female: She
is the Jungfrau Sophia, or divine wisdom. . . . When God the
Schopfer created the Earth he held it up in his hand and it
became a mirror in which he saw his own face reflected back
as the image of a woman. This is the Jungfrau Sophia. She
is represented in folk art as the angel you see on tombstones
and barns. She is the Pennsylfaania Heimatland. Her back
is the ridges and the mountains, Her blood the rivers and
streams, and Her soft flesh the valleys and flatlands over
which we ride in Pennsylvania, Maryland, West Virginia
and Western Virginia. She is in the land we farm, the food
we eat, and the water which makes the beer we drink.*

— Pennsylvania Dutch folk legend

And that is what makes *Pennsylfaania,* the old Dutch name that includes western Maryland, West Virginia, and the Shenandoah Valley of Virginia, different from the rest of the country.

The area from New York to Baltimore, down the Shenandoah Valley of Virginia into North Carolina, all the way out to Pittsburgh and into West Virginia, and up to Albany, New York, was settled by Germans, Dutch, and Swedes. The Yankees and the Southrons made no distinction between these groups of non-English speaking Teutons. They simply referred to all of them as "the Dutch," as Robert E. Lee did when he said, "If you took the Dutch away from General Grant, I could whip the Yankees in one afternoon." Thus you had terms like Pennsylvania Dutch, Maryland Dutch, Valley Dutch (Virginia), Jersey Dutch, and even New York Dutch, but the latter descendants of the Holland Dutch were more often referred to as Knickerbockers.

At one point the area was so German that before the Civil War, even free blacks in cities like York, Lancaster, and Gettysburg spoke German as their first language. When they tried to speak English, folks here ended up speaking what the locals called *ferhoodled* English: as in "throw mama from the train, a kiss goodbye," or "the cake is all, but the pie is yet," or "Becky, go in the house and smear Jakie all over with jam, a piece of bread." And back in 1967, you still had locals from out in the *dorflands* who grew up without TV, and they spoke—like almost every guard in the Berks County Prison—fluent Pennsylvania Dutch and *ferhoodled* English.

So here I was, two weeks after the Labor Day run, riding across Jersey into the old Dutch heartland of Pennsylvania with the sun on my back and the bugs blowing in my face. I had gotten real tight with Blackie over the summer, and promised him when we got run off the island in the Susquehanna River that I would be down in a couple of weeks. I had also really gotten to like Pennsylvania—after all, what biker really needs Hempstead Turnpike or Queens Boulevard?

But when I got to Reading, I found out Blackie was in jail. Chuck explained that this was nothing unusual; in fact it happened three or four times a year. Only this time Blackie punched a cop and the judge threw him in jail for three months instead of the usual 30 days.

Chuck was not like Sweet William. He didn't smash glassware, throw people over the bar, and knock things over like some animal that got out of the pen. Chuck was quiet and down-home soft-spoken. His word was his bond, and he would get himself killed rather than go back on it. The flip side was that if you screwed him, he would also get himself killed rather than let people think anyone had gotten the better of him. These were the qualities that impressed the ham-handed German, or Dutch, mentality. The locals admired him; everyone else—cops, crooks, wiseguys—feared him.

The club operated out of Skyline Drive on top of Mount Penn. Chuck had a house right along the road and the garage was in the basement so he could work on his bike all year. Behind his house, there was an old chicken coop or farm storage building that was the clubhouse where the club had meetings and parties. Up a hill in the woods behind the club-house was another small house, and a couple of guys rented this from Chuck's landlord. That's where I lived with Little Joe, Skip, and Rayels. It was also the real clubhouse, because that's where the guys hung out and drank beer most nights.

The landlord also had a daughter who was almost 40 and quite plain, but horny. Big Jim had the foresight to screw her once in a while. So she told the old man that all the stuff he heard and read about us in the papers was a bunch of crap, and we were really a bunch of great guys and model tenants. And as long as Chuck showed up on the first night of every month with a fist full of cash, right down to the last rent penny, on all three places, the old man didn't seem to give a shit about anything else.

There were also two girls that lived with us. Esther was 16 and had rotten, pointed teeth. The story on her was that her parents were "professional nudists"—whatever the hell that was supposed to mean—who traveled around the country visiting various sites of interest to nudists, while they left the kids at home with a pantry full of canned corn and ravioli.

The other girl was about 20 and she had gotten all her teeth pulled out, but the false ones hadn't come in yet, or she didn't have the money to pay for them, or some bullshit like that. And she could never get the knack—as Blackie later explained it after he got all his teeth pulled in prison—of "keeping your gums apart so it doesn't look like you don't

RIDING ON THE EDGE: A MOTORCYCLE OUTLAW'S TALE

have no teeth." On top of no teeth, she also had blonde hair, which she cut short over her ears, and the whole effect made her look like some big blue-eyed tweety bird with no chin. Her name was Marjorie, but everyone called her "Gums."

So there we all lived happily, like one big family, sharing the couch, beds, the women, and our money in the woods on the top of Mount Penn. The only problem was we had to shit in the woods because it seemed the toilet had been plugged for years. Then one day Little Joe came home with an armful of tools and coat hangers.

"What the fuck are you doing, abortions?" I asked him.

"I'm sick of this shit," he said. "I used to work for a plumber."

Then he went in the bathroom, got down on his hands and knees in the shit, so to speak, and he began plunging and cursing and pulling shit out on coat hangers and tossing it out the window. An hour later, he came out and said that everything worked. So now we even had a decent place to shit. What more can an outlaw expect than that?

Skip kept insisting that little Esther had a boyfriend her own age. But Little Joe, who was always with Skip and treated him like a slowwitted son, kept telling him to "shut up" because he didn't know nothing about anything, and it would be a lot better for everyone if he didn't say anything at all anymore.

Only this time it turned out Skip was right. One day a 16-year-old, slowwitted yokel showed up knocking on the front door and asking for Esther. Skip let him in, and Little Joe began goofing on him, acting like he was Esther's father. He asked the yokel why he wanted to speak with Esther and where they were going, and then told him that it just wouldn't work because "we can't have Esther going out and riding around the countryside in a car with some goof all night long." The kid may have been slowwitted, but he was smart enough to realize that we were the Pagans, and when we started running a game, you didn't sit there arguing about the rules. So the kid played along with a big grin on his face. Then the more sinister-looking Rayels came in.

Now when Rayels grinned, he could scare the shit out of the Grim Reaper, and that's all he did besides point at the kid like he was a piece of game someone had brought home for supper. I could see that the kid was genuinely unnerved by the whole situation. At this point it was obvious the kid would agree to anything to get out of the house alive and in one piece, so I saw my opportunity to jump in. I asked the kid if he would mind doing us a tremendous favor.

The kid asked what, and I told him that there was this cranky old man that lived in the house down the end of the road. The miserable old prick was always busting our chops and calling the cops and shit like that, but there was nothing we could do, because if we did something, he would know who it was and call the cops again. But it would be nice if someone he didn't know would walk up to his back door, give it a good kick, and tell the old bastard just what a scumbag he really was.

The kid agreed and we all followed him down to Chuck's house. The guys from Reading were loving it because they would never dream of pulling this on their *fuhrer*, but now they could blame me. Besides there was no telling how Chuck might react. If he had a gun in his hand, he just might shoot the kid in the face right through the door.

As it was, he was eating supper with his wife and little girl in a high chair and, best of all, he was sitting with the back of his head to the door. I saw Sweet Pea look up as the kid walked up to the door, but it was too late. The kid brought back his foot and gave the steel plate in the bottom of the door a mighty kick. Then he cupped his hands over his mouth and shouted right at the back of Chuck's ugly head, "Hey man, you're a scumbag!"

The kid then came prancing back across the grass, grinning at us, and obviously quite pleased with himself, until he heard a crash like the thunder of Ragnarok. Then he turned around and saw Chuck, who had just ripped the screen door off the hinges and was standing on the back porch still holding the door in his hand. The kid then looked at me for some explanation.

"You idiot!" I screamed. "That's the wrong house."

Now Chuck looked at us and his face was oscillating between a grin and a scowl. I could tell that he was trying to decide whether to go after us or the kid.

Finally, Chuck dropped the door on the porch and bolted for the kid. The rest of us followed, and we chased the kid through the cornfields. Now it was a game, but like any beast of prey the kid ran for his life, and because we didn't really give a shit since none of us had a clue what we were going to do if we caught him, the kid easily outdistanced us. Finally, we came to a clearing in the cornfield where we all sat down out of breath and just laughed and howled and smoked cigarets for a couple of minutes. Then Chuck held up his finger, pointed back toward his house and said, "His car. It's still gotta be parked in front of my house. Let's go."

When we got back, Skip wanted to get a sledgehammer and demolish the car, but Chuck said that was stupid because the kid didn't really do anything that was his fault, but we could still have some fun anyhow.

So we sat on the retaining wall in front of the garage door to Chuck's cellar, drinking Reading beer and watching the car. About an hour later a pickup truck arrived with two eagle-headed bald Dutchmen. The guy who was riding shotgun got out, and as he walked over to the car and opened the door, you could see that he was nervous because he was beginning to figure out who we were.

"I don't know what the hell is going on," he mumbled.

Chuck took the cue. "I don't either," he told the guy. "I was just sitting down eating dinner with my wife and kid, and this goddamn *hanswarscht* (which is Dutch slang for a clown or jackass) comes up to my back door and starts kicking the hell out of it and screaming at me."

The old man's face lit up. You could see he was experiencing a revelation. "I knew there was more to it than that bastard told me," the old man thundered as he punched the palm of one hand with the fist of the other. "Wait until I get my hands on him."

He thanked Chuck for straightening him out and not killing his kid, and drove off while Chuck turned around and howled as soon as the guy couldn't see him, because he had been forcing himself not to laugh. A couple of days later, Skip told us that Esther said that when the old man got home he took off his belt and beat the shit out of the kid with it.

We all laughed, but Little Joe thought about and said, "Now, just what kind of a low opinion would you have to have of your own kid to believe that the jackass would do something that stupid, as to walk up to the back door of the leader of the Pagans while he's eating supper right in front of you and start kicking the shit out of it and screaming for no good reason."

But it was precisely this thick-headed and cynical Dutch peasant mentality that made life so much more fun in Reading and dozens of Pennsylvania towns just like it, back in those days when people didn't watch so much TV and weren't as sophisticated as they are now.

Eventually I got the wanderlust, and having never been across the Susquehanna River, I decided to visit that girl Debbie from York who had given me her phone number on Labor Day.

I called her and she told me to go to a place where a friend of hers would meet me and tell me where to go, while she called the girl's house and then came back to tell me where to meet Debbie. It was all a bit confusing, but no more confusing than anything else in my life at the time. So on a bright Sunday morning, I took off down the old Lancaster Pike, past the Dutch farms with their orange pumpkins and ripe cornstalks next to the wooden farm stands selling cider and shoofly pie.

York County is west of the Susquehanna, and to the south it borders the Mason-Dixon Line. Located between the Blue Ridge Mountains and the Susquehanna River, it sits on some of the most fertile farmland in America. The whole area was settled by Pennsylvania Dutch farmers, and there is no difference between the farmers in York County and the farmers in Maryland and Western Virginia. York County is the place where the Pennsylvania Dutch country, Appalachia, and the South all come together. As a result, it has the largest Ku Klux Klan membership outside the Deep South, the most registered handguns of any county in America, and country music is as big there as it is in Nashville or Bakersfield. The last thing that Little Joe had said when I left was, "Watch your ass, it's not Berks County."

So, I met this friend of Debbie's outside of town, and she took me to a house and called Debbie. Debbie told her to bring me to another house where she would meet us in 10 minutes, which she did. But then the phone rang. It was yet another friend. After she talked a minute, Debbie said that we had to leave immediately and go to another house, but we couldn't go there for another half hour, so we had to hang out in an alley behind a third house. The musical chairs continued. We outlaws may not have been geniuses, but we could read our surroundings with the instincts of a coyote, and I didn't like what I was seeing at all.

Here my visit was supposed to be a secret, but it was apparent that every little girl in town seemed to be showing up at some point to take a peek at me. Finally, one of her friends ran up and whispered something in her ear, but loud enough for me to hear the words "father pissed . . . come home . . . call cops."

Not that I had broken any law, but a lone outlaw is always a prime target for advocates of shithead law enforcement, and of course there was always the possibility of the village people turning out in their leather shorts with torches like in the Frankenstein movies.

But what really tipped the balance was a vision rising like the specter of Dark Surt. It was the image of Chuck. Chuck in the front seat of that old low-bellied gas-burning Buick, with a wad of bail money in his shirt pocket and riding down the Lancaster Pike toward the York County Jail. His white knuckles twisted around the steering wheel like he was ready to rip it off, his face all twisted up like a demented elf and frozen like stone, all the way chanting his perverse mantra through clenched teeth: "Leaky cunt, leaky cunt, it's always some fuckin' leaky cunt."

That was simply Chuck's version of what some people call the *cherchez la femme* motif. In Chuck's world, if someone got in a fight in a bar, it was always over "some leaky cunt." If someone got arrested, it was because they couldn't keep their mouth shut and told "some leaky cunt." If two brothers got into it, it was invariably on account of "some leaky cunt." If some brother dropped out of the club it was over "some leaky cunt." And he was usually right.

I did not want to become the latest piece of evidence in his endless litany of examples, so I told her, "Go home. I'm getting out of here." It was obvious that she had about all the excitement she could take for one day, and sensed that her Dutch-Nazi father was about to unleash some sort of blitzkrieg of his own. So she left, and I brought the starter down hard under the sole of my black boot, spun out the back tire, and was off down the road toward Columbia, like Ichabod Crane trying to get across the bridge before the shit hit the fan.

It was getting dark and, as I went down a road shaded with trees, I flicked on the lights. Immediately the engine started breaking up. It sounded like a short in the wiring harness. I turned off the lights and engine purred just fine. Then I turned on the lights again and the engine started to sputter. Now I knew that's what it was.

It would be dark in a matter of minutes. There was no way in hell that I was going to find a gas station on Sunday night out in the sticks with a mechanic on duty who could find the short. And there was no way that I could find it by myself on the side of the road in the dark. The best I could hope for was a gas station with some kid pumping gas who would be scared shitless when I pulled up and more than glad to let me use the shop.

But I didn't even see a gas station that was open. By the time I hit Route 30, it was a pitch black country night, and there was nobody on the road. But then an idea came to me. Richie from the Chicago Outlaws once told me that 90 percent of the people who get killed on a motorcycle get hit from behind by idiots, so all you have to do is keep way ahead of the flow of traffic. I could see the road ahead in the dark. So the trick was to just turn the lights off, crank it up, make sure that nobody's lights came up behind me, and then try to avoid cops for the next two hours and I'd be roaring up Mount Penn and home, scot-free.

I went for it and the idea worked. Soon I was sailing across the Susquehanna bridge from Wrightsville to Columbia, thinking that this thing is going to be a cakewalk. But as I passed Lancaster, I began to think that this thing might work just fine out here in the country with no traffic, but when I got to Reading and had to drive through the city without lights, that could be a problem. So I called Chuck and told him I'd be coming into town in about a half-hour and I had no lights, so could he have someone meet me with a car by Applegate's Harley shop just outside of

Shillington on the Pike. He asked me where I was, and I said someplace called Eeh-frat-ah, and he said "you mean Ef-ra-ta." I said, "Whatever the fuck you want to call it, just meet me in half an hour."

About a half-hour later I pulled into Applegate's parking lot, and there was a carload of people with Little Joe behind the wheel, Skip in the back, and a guy they called Okie riding shotgun. I started explaining to Joe how I was going to follow him through the city and asked him what was the best route to take. But Okie just kept sitting there right between us shouting: "Eeh-frat-ah, Eeh-frat-ah, Haw Haw Hawh." I couldn't hear a word that Joe was saying.

Being from New York, at first I thought that Okie just tried to be a ball-breaking pain in the ass. Then one day Chuck explained to me that he wasn't trying to bust my chops. He was just a Dutch super hickster and that's the way he was around everybody. When they were out in California a couple of years before, the people out there started calling Henry "Okie," because everybody in the state of California thought he was a bigger hick than the real Okies. And that's what everyone had been calling Henry ever since.

We finally got our directions straight over Okie's knee-slapping and howling, and I followed Joe as he pulled out of the parking lot.

They say that neither the deer in the forest, nor the soldier on the battlefield, ever hears the shot that kills him. And they are probably right, because after that I don't remember anything about that night except what Little Joe told me, and here's what he said the next day:

I told Skip: "Just keep looking out that back window and make sure he's behind us." Then I had to sit there listening to Henry's shit. But we hadn't even gone a couple of hundred yards when Skip said: "That's the end of him."

"Now what the fuck are you talking about, Skip?" I asked him. Jesus Christ, I thought, between him and Henry I'm going to go nuts.

And Skip says, "Stoop just wiped out. That big full dress hog that went by made a left turn in front him and the two of them wiped out."

"Shut the fuck up, Skip," I says.

But then Skip starts yelling: "I aint shittin' ya, Stoop just wiped out and he's laying in the road."

*"Fuckin' Skip, You better not be bullshittin' again," I told him. Then I
turned the car around and I really did see two motorcycles lying in the road.
And when we got out there was you layin' in a ditch, and I thought, Oh shit,
he's dead.*

*It really scared the shit out of us because, as we ran up, we saw you layin'
there covered with blood, and all of a sudden you leaped up and jumped
straight in the air, screaming "I'm gonna kill the fucker," and your face was
all red and covered with blood. It was like having some deer carcass jump
up off the butcher table and start kicking.*

*Then we finally got you to sit down and we saw the other guy layin' far-
ther down the road in the ditch, and Skip says that we oughta go kick the
shit out of him and I gotta tell 'im, "Shut the fuck up, Skip."*

*Then people started stopping, someone called the cops, and an ambu-
lance came and took you guys to the hospital, and we followed. Then we
were all in the emergency room and they got a big pair of scissors to cut your
clothes and boots off. But just then Chuck came walking into the room and
he saw what they were going to do.*

"Put them down," he said about the scissors.

*Then the nurses got a little shocked. And he says, "Put 'em down, I said.
You take those boots off him real careful, and then you give them to me.
And then you take that leather jacket and denim vest off real careful, and
you give them to me, too."*

This was back in 1967 when you could still get away with shit like this,
and the ER was full of Pagans. After some initial resistance, they did what
he said. Having done all that, they finally decided that they might as well
take my jeans off, too, and save them since they were the only pair I owned.
Then they put a sheet over me, and a doctor came in to look at my head.
He put his finger on it and I leaped up and conked him with a haymaker.

There I was sitting up on the table, with a bloody sheet over my head
and my bare arms sticking out waving around, screaming that I was
gonna kill someone. And the Pagans were howling, Okie was slapping his
knee and going "Haw, haw, haw," and the nurses were shitting and didn't
think it was funny at all. The doctor staggered over to a chair, plopped
down, and started crying that nobody had ever done that to him before.

Then Chuck walked over, sat down next to him, and explained that obviously I wasn't in my right mind and I didn't mean anything personal by it and maybe there was some way he could try again.

He did. But first he got two guys with Frankenstein straps, and they came in and torqued me down to the table. Then the doctor came over and cut a hole in the sheet. He began poking around and sticking needles in my head, with me cursing and threatening to kill him the whole time. Meanwhile, Pagans were standing there laughing and Chuck was going: "Does it hurt fucker? Good for ya. Remember this is all over *some leaky fuckin' cunt.*"

I do not remember any of it. I woke up the next morning hurting all over and seemed to remember dreaming about looking down and seeing a motorcycle wheel with a green fender in front of my wheel, and then floating through space. Then I looked around and saw the other beds, and I knew that that dream probably had something to do with the reality of me being in a hospital ward.

I ached and I could hardly move. There was a big fuck in the bed next to me, who just laid there and moaned until a nurse came over. She told him that he would be okay and she would see if they could get him something for the pain. Then two minutes after she walked away he started moaning all over again. It was all getting to be a royal pain in the ass.

Then a nurse came in with a tray with orange juice on it and they started giving breakfast to everyone else but me. "Hey where's mine," I yelled.

"You're not allowed to have any. You have a head injury," she said.

Sure enough, there was a sign on the bottom of the bed: "Do Not Feed." *Just like animals in the zoo,* I thought.

I told her to either feed me, or get me my clothes so that I could go find something to eat on my own. Instead, she got the doctor. When I told him that I was leaving, he said, "You can't. We have to do more tests and X-rays and wait for results." Then I told him that I was leaving if I had to tear the whole room apart and him with it. He just turned to a nurse and said, "Get the psychiatrist." And then he walked away.

He was back in about two minutes with a bunch of guys in white suits.

One of them was holding a big long syringe and grinning at me like a fool. *Shit*, I thought, *if they get that fucker in my arm, I'm done.*

"Hold it," I yelled as they began moving toward me, "it's against my religion to get injections." They stopped. But then some wiseass nurse asked me, "And just what is your religion?" I couldn't think of the name of the religion that forbids injections, but I knew there was one, or at least I had them believing there was, so I just told her, "I do not have to tell you what my religion is, all I have to do is tell you that it is against my religion to get injections." This had them stumped and they all just stood still for a minute.

Then I looked at the doctor and told him, "I did not sign myself in here last night and I'm conscious now. I do not want any more treatment from you, and you have no authority to treat me or administer any more medication. I am telling you this in front of all these witnesses; I am being held here against my will and I want to leave now."

It worked. He held up his hand to tell the others to back off. He told me that I could leave, but that I would have to sign a release and it would take a few minutes to send up the paperwork. This sounded reasonable enough, so I waited and listened to the big fuck moaning in the bed next to me. It seemed to take forever, but finally the doctor came back with the release form and two uniformed state troopers.

I knew the game immediately. I said, "You guys are here to arrest me for driving without lights as soon as I sign this, aren't you?" The two troopers nodded their heads seriously, and the doctor just stood there grinning like, *What are you gonna do now, asshole?*

I signed the form, flipped it back at him, and said, "Fuck it, I'd rather go to jail than look at you."

It was high noon on a sundrenched Pennsylvania autumn afternoon as I limped out of the hospital in handcuffs. Fortunately, the cops had gone easy by putting the handcuffs on in front of me, not in back, or I would have fallen on my face. The top of my head was shaved and stitched, and so was the back of my head and the point of my chin. I could not straighten my back, and I had no feeling in my right leg, so I had to drag it behind me like Tommy Gannon did when he had that stupid, shaggy, mummy cast. And on top it all, I had to wear paper sandals because Chuck had taken my boots, along with my leather and colors, for safe keeping.

In those days, the district magistrates still ran courts out of their homes. When we got there, Chuck was sitting in his big-ass old low-bellied Buick, smirking and laughing. Fortunately he had brought my boots, jacket and colors, and the cops let me get dressed in the yard. So I was able to walk into court like a respectable outlaw.

Guilty! Fine! It was over in less than two minutes, and we were back in Chuck's car on the way up to his house on top of Mount Penn, where I sat in his living room drinking Reading Old Dutch beer.

"We got your bike last night," he said. "The gas tank and front end are totaled. Skip has a gas tank you can use, but we gotta find you a pair of forks." Then he inspected my head. "This isn't so bad," he said. "I can take these stitches out for you myself in about eight days, and you said nothing's broken." Then he added, "Shit, you probably could have just laid in that ditch all night and then got up in the morning and walked to a telephone." He seemed quite pleased by this last observation.

After two beers I became so dizzy that I had to stagger over to the stairs and climb up on all fours to the attic, where I collapsed in a bed. When I woke up, it was getting dark and I heard Big Jim and Rayels down in the living room talking to Chuck. Jim was explaining some sort of hassle that was developing, while Rayels was just sitting there, quietly taking it all in and running it around in his head, until he saw me stagger down the stairs with my messed-up head. Then they were howling and telling me that the ass end of a cow was better looking then my head.

I had two beers in about 20 minutes and had to crawl back up the stairs again. This proved a great source of mirth for Big Jim and Rayels, who howled and pointed and made dog noises. By the next morning things were a little better, and I could at least go out in the sun and look over what was left of my bike. Later in the week I was even able to go out with Rayels for a couple of beers. It must have been a roadhouse out on the Lancaster Pike, because on the way back Rayels made a sharp turn onto Wyomissing Avenue and said, "Do you want to meet my kids?"

It was a small bungalow stuck in between some overgrown weeds out in Mohnton, and it looked like something out of Grimm's fairytales. That was strange enough, but when he opened the door, I saw Jane for the first time up close and in the light.

Her eyes were soft and she had reddish brown hair like a horse in the sunshine. It was clean and sleek and hung over her shoulders all soft and bouncy. She was a mother with two kids, but she was only 20 herself, and she looked younger—a perpetual sweet 16, every boy's teenage dream in a booth at the malt shop saying, "Yes, we can go steady, and I'll wear your ring around my neck."

The rules were pretty strict about a brother's old lady. Like everything else, you never knew what the penalty could be. Rayels was my brother. He was righteous and he had a righteous woman. He was also three years older than me. I was only 20, and like Sweet Willie, Flipout, and a lot of the guys in Jersey and New York, we lived with our mothers or grandmothers and had never been married. This way we had the best of both worlds; we could be popping a couple of women in the backseats of cars or on the clubhouse floor, and then after a couple of days, like a tomcat, come home to mama for a hot meal.

We could never understand why these guys outside of the New York and Jersey area would get married and stay home at night like Chuck, when you could go out every night and throw guys around like on TV wrestling, and then screw the shit out of the girls in the audience.

But since I'd been in Reading I had wondered about it, and often thought that the guys like Blackie and Chuck with wives, kids, and clean homes might have it better than Skip, Joe, me, and the guys up in the house on the hill with Gums and Esther. As we sat on the floor playing with his two boys, I had to wonder why anyone would live up at the clubhouse when he had a woman like this at home. Quite frankly if Jane had been a motorcycle, I'd have been down at Applegate's the next morning telling the salesman, "I want the same make, same model, same paint job, same everything as the one you sold to Rayels."

After that night, Rayels started to patch things up with Jane, so he wasn't staying up at the house on the hill that much anymore, but whenever he had to take her and the kids someplace normal, like the doctor or the supermarket, he came and got me so we could sit in the car, drink beer, and bullshit. Since the three of us were spending a lot of time together, I began to see that Jane had the personality to go with looks.

I had pretty much fallen into life in the old Pennsylvania Dutch country, and I was loving every bit of it. But then one day we came back to the house on the hill, and Joe and Skip were rolling around in the dirt out front, cursing and beating the shit out of each other. Rayels and I jumped out of the car so we could watch and cheer, but then we turned around and saw Chuck coming up the hill, wearing the same puss that he had on his face the time he ripped the door off the wall after the kid called him a scumbag.

As he got close, he broke into a trot and ran up to them. He kicked Skip square in the back and then he kicked Joe in the head. "Get in the house," he started screaming. "Get in the fucking house right now!"

When they got up, he kicked Skip in the ass for not moving fast enough. Then he turned to me and Rayels: "Two fuckin' officers, just standing there watching it; I can't fuckin' believe you two idiots sometimes."

Then he went in the house and told us to wait outside, but it didn't matter because through the open window we could see him all the way down at the Sunshine Brewery, clear on the other side of the Schuylkill River, throwing furniture around the room and the night shift could probably hear him screaming, "Over some leaky fuckin' cunt!"

But Chuck's tantrums were like an Allegheny Mountain summer rainstorm: unpredictable, violent, but over as quick as they started. It was simply a matter of finding an overpass to park under until the storm passed—which Rayels and I did. Sure enough, Chuck soon came out the front door with a big grin on his face and said, "Fuck it, let's party." Which is what we did.

The incident was soon forgotten. The next evening Skip showed up with an old pair of forks, and Joe came up with a seat. Soon we had my bike up and running. Of course, it looked like a piece of shit, slapped together with spare parts, but then so did I, with my face and head all scarred and stitched together.

We were heading into October—autumn in Pennsylvania, when it never rains and the sun shines through blazing blue skies. The landscape explodes into gold and yellow and red, and the farm stands on the highway are bursting with ripe apples and pumpkins, jars of pickles and jams, and homemade pies. Every morning Joe and I took a long ride down the Oley Valley, or up the Pottsville Pike to the Blaubarrick, or out toward Kutztown, any place just to feel the wind in our faces. On the way back we rode down Skyline Drive and stopped at the Chinese pagoda on the top of Mount Penn.

That's right, a Chinese pagoda on top of Mount Penn overlooking the city of Reading. Right up until Prohibition, Reading was one of the great beer and party towns in America, and since colonial times it had been known for great food. A string of legendary resorts and restaurants were built on top of Mount Penn, but none of them survived Prohibition. All of them were burned down or torn down, except for the Pagoda, which had probably been inspired by the tower in the Chinese beer garden in Munich. Now it was locked up, except you could still climb the outside stairway to the top and see the whole city laid out in front of you.

So we used to go up there in the afternoon and just hang out, with the whole city and half the county laid out in front of us. The town had begun to grow on me. And seeing Rayels, Chuck, and Blackie all shacked up with their righteous old ladies, who took care of the kids and put up with the grease and the oil and bail bondsman's monthly payments in a never-ending cycle as regular and predictable as dirty diapers, it all made me think that shacking up with a regular old lady and snuggling up with her on the couch every night with some weed and watching *Hee Haw* on the tube wasn't such a bad alternative to nightly barroom fights, backseat romances, and getting chased from one end of Long Island to the other. Because of the accident I had some disability checks from the Lithographers union, and I was thinking about finding an old lady, settling down in Reading, and shacking up for the winter.

But I never got the chance, because one Sunday morning in September, when Little Joe, Chuck, and I pulled up to Chuck's house after a drunken night on the town, Sweet Pea was out the door screaming like the banshee and waving at us all crazy. "Call Geoff! Call Geoff!" she was yelling at me. "Sweet William is dead!"

Well, as it turned out he wasn't dead yet, but he might as well have been. I called Geoff and felt like I was talking with my balls in my throat. He must have been sitting right next to the phone because it hardly started the first ring when he picked it up and began shouting "Hello, Hello, Hello!"

When I told him who I was he started to explain. They had been in a bar in Lindenhurst the night before when some guy pulled up on a Beeser in the rain. When Sweet Willie saw the bike he nearly came in his pants, so he asked the guy if he could take it for a ride. The guy must have been an idiot or scared shitless, because he said yes. And Sweet Willie took off in the rain.

Willie's problem was that he always thought he could ride a bike like a horse and make it do what he wanted by sheer willpower and brute force. He came down on the kick starter with one of his thundering kicks, ripped open the throttle, popped the clutch, and was off with the back tire sliding all over wet asphalt. Then when he shifted, the bike reared up like a horse, spun around in a pirouette, and Sweet William Parker rode off into the scrub brush of the Long Island Pine Barrens on one wheel. Then it was crashing and booming and trees were breaking like the crack of the last doom before Ragnarok, when Dark Surt will lead his legions out of Muspell and over the Rainbow Bridge.

The guys ran like hell down the road, all huffing and puffing and tripping over themselves and each other in big knee-high boots, which were designed for motorcyclists, not sprinters (except for Geoff who always wore black cowboy boots with pointy toes that curled up like little elf shoes). They followed the path of destruction off into the woods where they found the gore from Sweet William's face stuck to a tree and the rest of him lying face-down on the ground in a patch of wet weeds.

As it was, the fucker hung on for almost a week, but it was beyond hope. His brother Stevie just sat in the hospital room all day, slumped in a chair and watching Willie die, a big mass of bandages and no twinkling blue eyes and mischievous smirk, or breaking glass and spraying beer bottles, or bodies flying through the air. Just the dead silence of the descent of the last end, broken only by the squeaking rubber soles of the nurses' shoes when they came in to change the IV bags and bandages.

CHAPTER 9

*There is a little shithole of a Jewish town in Russia, called
Kasrielevky, where the people are so poor and wretched, and
so bored shitless in the Winter, that they rely on the tales
of itinerant rabbis to keep them from falling off the edge of
the world and into the abyss. One of these itinerant scholars
was Rabbi Yudela, who taught folks about the 36 "concealed
saints." Thirty-six saints who on the surface appeared to be
losers, pissbums and utterly worthless fuck-ups, but whose
unknown and unheralded deeds are so righteous in the eyes
of God that it is by their virtue alone that the entire universe
is sustained and kept from falling into the pit of Chaos.*

          — From the tales of Sholom Aleichem

N ow perhaps you already get my point. But for those of you that
don't: I believe that on hot and lazy summer afternoons, when
you are out riding free in the warm breeze, heading for a watering hole
because clouds are gathering and a storm is breaking, and you got your
sweet baby riding behind you, resting her head on your back and softly
humming an old Willie Nelson tune, and the two of you don't have a care
in the whole world, other than that impending storm, that's when you
know that you are one of the last of a dying breed of American aristocrats:
the outlaw biker.

    Well on a day like that, if you look up at the clouds just before the
first clap of thunder breaks, you might see riding out of those clouds and

across the sky an outlaw pack of ghost riders: an outlaw pack of the 36 most outrageous and outlandish of the great American outlaw bikers of the 1960s. The old guys who are still left in the clubs know exactly who I'm talking about—those Sacred 36 of the greatest American fuck-ups of all time, upon whose righteousness the Legend stands and will be sustained for as long as Americans strive to remain free. And in that ghost pack, I guarantee that, among the denim-clad chopper jockeys, you will see one rider on a beat-up, piece-a-shit Beeser wearing tan khakis with his Pagan patches flapping in the breeze on a tattered brown leather vest, because Sweet William Parker would have to be on every short list of inductees into the Outlaw Hall of Fame.

Sweet William, the man who joined an upstart club from Southern Maryland and, in less than a year, did more than anyone to run the Aliens off Long Island and make it a Pagan fiefdom, was laid out in Franklin Square, Long Island. Being that this was New York, where you don't need dinner invitations and whoever happens to be there just sits down and eats along with everyone else, my mother had gotten to know Sweet William quite well. Feeling bad for Mrs. Parker, she stopped by the funeral parlor to pay her respects, not knowing what to expect.

What she found was a bunch of women in their 40s and 50s—Mrs. Parker, Mrs. Bertsch, Mrs. Koharet, Mrs. Fagan—and everyone of them told the same story: *You read about them in the paper and you get sick to your stomach, but then they come to your house and they're all such giants, but they're such nice guys. So polite and so funny, and they eat so much and drink so much beer and have such a great time.* And then my mother told me, she looked around the room at the ladies and thought, *Oh my God, every one of them, they're all just like me, every last one of them.*

Sweet William was buried in Pinelawn National Cemetery with a Marine Corps honor guard. I stood under a tree with Willie's brother Stretch, who was only 18, like some Hofstra freshman, but he had been in more fights, more hassles, and gotten kicked in the ass—and kicked other people in the ass—more than ordinary people do in a lifetime. He was already starting to look like a 30-something-year-old hillbilly, with his crooked teeth and the lines in his cheeks starting to harden like an old hickory tree, and when you looked into his green eyes, you could almost hear the keening of bagpipes.

There the two of us stood, under a tree at the back of the crowd, looking at the Pagans and the marines, the mother and the coffin, and each other. Then we looked over at the fence and saw a woman with beautiful golden hair all pulled up on her head to look respectable, dressed all in black and staring through the wrought iron pickets.

It was Sweet William's girlfriend, Karen. We walked over to the fence and saw that her eye makeup was running down her face in a shower of tears. Neither of us had ever seen her in a dress before, but she always looked great in black, with her snow-white skin and golden Swedish-princess hair.

"You should have come in," Stretch said.

But she just shook her head and said, "I didn't want to cause any problems."

The biggest problem being that she was married to one of the big shits in the Aliens. True, they had broken up, but they had done that before. It seemed that they broke up every six weeks or so, and then got back together a month later. And although they were no longer together and her old man was in another club, we didn't go around hitting on other outlaws' wives in such a situation. The truth was that Willie didn't actually hit on her, or her on him, they just sort of came together. Somehow we all seemed to be attracted to the same women, and the same women seemed to be attracted to us. Like Ragnarok and the Goetterdammerung, these sorts of things just tended to happen without anybody even trying to make them happen.

Like in the case of Crazy Joey Vargas, one of the most outrageous outlaws ever. He was one of the early members of the Mother Club from Prince George's County, and he was the only one in the club who ever called Big Dutch by his real name, Fred. Dutch hated that name, but Joey was crazy so Dutch just let it slide. Meanwhile, whenever he called him Fred, someone would whisper in your ear, "Don't you ever call him that."

Anyhow Joey was crazy, and one day they found him, or what was left of him, floating down the Susquehanna River in an oil drum. He had chains

141

wrapped around his feet. He had been hung over the barrel by his feet, and then his head was caved in with a baseball bat and he was gutted like a deer into the barrel. Then whoever did it dropped him, the bat, and chains into the barrel, welded it shut, and plopped the whole thing in the Susquehanna River, where he floated down to Baltimore like a dead Viking.

Now nobody seemed to know, or even acted like they cared, what happened. Which meant either one of two things: either he had fucked up really bad this time and his own club had done him in, or somebody else did, and his own club had taken care of them—real horrible and real quiet—and now wanted the thing to die, with everyone acting like the club had nothing to do with it and had never even heard of it. In any case, nobody talked about it, and you didn't ask questions in situations like this. But when the shit got bad and you knew something awful might be going down, you could almost smell acetylene gas and burning human flesh in the air, and in your ears you could hear the rattling of chains and the sound of oil drums being plopped in the river.

So like everything else, you never knew what was going to happen tomorrow in cases like this. Some guy drops his wife and some other outlaw starts popping her. One night he might plant a big kiss on the guy's lips to prove that he just don't give a shit, and the next night he could be slashing the guy up with a knife. Either way, it was an appropriate outlaw response.

We didn't vote on a successor to Willie; that's not how it was done. Stretch simply told me that Davy Supermouth was not going to run the club, and Flipout said the same thing. This pretty much meant that I was going to be running it and I wouldn't be going back to Reading. I talked to the hardcore members of the club and told them that I was going to be running it. They agreed. So I walked into the next meeting and announced that I was going to be running things. Nobody said anything. Then I looked at Davy Supermouth. He just shrugged.

My first test was not long in coming. Flipout had found a bunch of guys who were riding up and down Hempstead Turnpike flying colors and one-percenter patches. I told him to tell them they can't. And he said, "I did." Then I asked him if he thought they were the kind of guys who might listen if we tried to explain things to them, or should we just go in with chains and pound the piss out of them and pull their colors. He said the leader seemed like a righteous dude named Bobo. I told him to set up a meeting, and he did at Nathan's hot dog emporium in Oceanside.

The outfit called themselves Hell's Stormtroopers—and they had even gone through the trouble of trying to get it right in German, *Hells Sturmtruppen*. On the night we went to meet them, a contingent of Pagans came over from Jersey, partly as a show of solidarity, but also partly because of a change of style in leadership in the club.

After a glorious summer of sheer insanity and mayhem, the Mother Club was beginning to realize that we were building a rep all right and we had the shit scared out of everyone. But some clubs were just running around like a pack of mad dogs, and if they didn't get some kind of order and stability, there wouldn't be any club left.

So when the Jersey club pulled up, I wasn't surprised to see the Peacemaker riding out in front. We didn't need him to handle Hell's Stormtroopers. It was obvious that Big Dutch had sent him to exert some sort of control over the situation, but Pappy was the supreme diplomat. He never once even hinted that he was there for any reason other than to back us up. So when we walked into Nathan's, I was in charge, but Pappy was right by my side. He patted me on the shoulder and said, "Let's take things slow, see what happens, and not fly off the handle."

When we got inside, we didn't even find a club. What we found instead was only one guy, Bob "Bobo" Dillingham. He was sitting on a bench staring at the door, his back and arms resting on the table behind him, his legs crossed and sticking out in the aisle in front of him, a one-percenter patch on his chest, and big shit-eating grin tattooed across his clean shaven face. His expression did not change one bit as three dozen of us walked up to him.

"Where's your club?" I asked him.

"I told them we had to meet with the Pagans and the lame-ass chicken fuckers said they didn't want to have anything to do with you guys, so I told them "Fuck you, I'll go by myself."

At that point Pappy grabbed me by the arm and looked me in the eye. "This sounds like pretty righteous dude to me," he said.

But that was all unnecessary. From the moment I saw him, the guy reminded me of Sweet William: the curly blonde hair, the mischievous blue eyes, the big smirk on the clean-shaven face, the hulking hillbilly physique—it was all right there, like a ghost, in front of me. I looked over at Bobo, who hadn't moved and was still sprawled out sitting on the bench with his back leaning against the table, and then I looked back at Pappy, who said, "I say we offer to make him a prospect tonight."

"I'll sponsor him," I told him. He squeezed my shoulder and nodded his head in approval. I walked over and sat down next to Bobo.

"Then why are you hanging around with a bunch of assholes, trying to start your own outlaw club?" I said. "It never works. We're the only real club on the East Coast. Did you ever think of riding with us?"

I could see immediately by the guy's face that this was his best possible scenario unfolding. Neither Pappy nor I had ever met the guy, but we both liked him immediately, and Flipout had told us that he was "good people," so I offered to sponsor him as a prospective member of the club. He agreed and Indian Joe handed me the big bone-handled knife he carried in his boot. I cut the Hell's Stormtrooper patches off his back, and Bobo was a Pagan from that night on, until he was cut down in a hail of gunfire 13 years later by two junkie scumbags who tried to rob him.

After that night nobody ever heard of the *Hells Sturmtruppen* again. But Bobo and I got real tight, real quick, which was good because Billy was trying to patch things up with his wife, and Bobby "Flipout" Bertsch was losing it completely in meth heaven. Just as things seemed to be settling back to normal as we headed into winter, I had another problem.

Davy Supermouth came up to me and told me that Joey "the Mortician" Ferry wanted to become a Pagan. Which is like saying that Jane Fonda wants to join the American Legion or Johnny Cash wants to sing coloratura at the Metropolitan Opera.

Now things had been happening rapidly while I was in Reading, which is not unusual in an outlaw club, especially one that is on the skids. The Aliens had been on the skids ever since their big showdown in Elmont in July. Nassau and Queens disintegrated, and the Mortician had quit for real this time. As for Brooklyn, maybe Pinstripe and Wheelchair were drinking beer in the back of a paint shop in Bay Ridge, but no one was about to ride clear across Brooklyn to find out. The Bronx was still the Bronx, and Manhattan was, as usual, a mess—so bad in fact that some of the really righteous people had formed a new Nomad chapter just to get away from them.

I told Davy, "Mortician can't become a Pagan," which is exactly what Dutch told me when I later ran the idea by him. But Davy explained to me that the Mortician was above all else a stone cold outlaw. However much aggravation he had caused us, Davy continued, it was only because he was a good Alien and had always put that club first in his life and he would do the same as a Pagan.

I didn't like it at all. But Davy explained that he had grown up with the Mortician in Queens, and he could be a prick, but so could the rest of us. Davy believed that this time the guy was sincere, and he said that he would stake his own colors on it. Besides, he claimed that the Mortician might bring some sanity and stability to what was becoming known as the wildest and most disorganized chapter in the whole Pagan operation.

I talked to the Mortician and he was actually humble for the only time in his life that I knew of. What's more, I actually believed him. But more important, on a practical level, Davy was usually right more often than me. Besides, I had an ulterior motive for going along with this. Ever since I became the leader, I had been finagling to get Richie "Sleepy" Muzetti back into the club, and the only thing standing in my way was Davy "Supermouth" Kerwin, who had refused to hear about it until now.

So I took the idea over to Jersey one night and laid it out in front of the Mother Club. Dutch laughed in my face and said, "You can't make a Pagan out of Mortician." After Davy and I explained the circumstances, he then said that we just better know what we were getting into. But then J. P. Soul grabbed me by my vest and began shaking me in a corner. He just kept looking me in the eyes and saying, "Stoops, listen to me: You can't make a Pagan out of Mortician." I tried to explain, but he wouldn't listen.

Then in the middle of all the aggravation, I turned around and there was Satan staring at me with his deep blue eyes and mane of jet-black hair. "You're going to check this out real careful, aren't you," he asked.

"Yes, we are. We've been through all this already and we're going to give him a shot."

Then Satan nodded.

"OK," he said. "But we don't want Mortician walking into an Alien clubhouse six months from now waving a set of Pagan colors around his head."

"I know," I told him, "we already considered the possibility and we're not going to let it happen."

"Good," he said. "I know you'll do the right thing."

It was pure Satan. He had a way of inspiring loyalty by letting you know that he was concerned, but that he had confidence in you. I was determined that there was no way I was going to let him down.

I got Sleepy back in and Joey "the Mortician" Ferry became a Pagan, and a good one at that. For me he proved an invaluable asset. As an outlaw brotherhood, we lived together, ate together, shared our money, shared out weed, shared the women we picked up, and generally fucked up together. In the tradition of Sweet William, we rode off to some shit-hole redneck bar, got drunk, got in a fight, wrecked the place, took off, went home, got laid, and woke up with shit-eating grins and wretched hangovers.

Mortician and Davy Supermouth had a different vision of the club. Mortician pointed out that just because we were outlaws didn't mean we had to try to get arrested every weekend, or get drunk and stand up on the seats of our bikes while we blew every red light on Hempstead Turnpike. This was just the sort of shit that had gotten Sweet William killed.

Mortician believed that the club could endure and evolve into a brotherhood of middle-aged men united around a common set of interests that included motorcycles. Men who could have wives and kids and camps and boats, and not throw it all away just for the sake of wrecking some bar. Of course some of the guys, especially Flipout and Bobo, thought that we could just as well rip off our one-percent patches and join an AMA club like the Mercury Riders as take the route Mortician advocated. In fairness it should be said that the Mortician was still around after Flipout was gone, Bobo was dead, and Chuck and I were sitting in a Pennsylvania penitentiary.

Actually, all this was part of a bigger problem the club was having. We were attracting guys who wanted to try to make it something different, a confederation of car thieves, drug dealers, counterfeiters, and credit card thieves, something an outlaw club was not. So we were constantly on our guard against guys like this, who were trying to infiltrate the club. Oddly enough, Davy Supermouth was one of the biggest proponents of this idea. He talked constantly about how we could use our contacts up and down the East Coast to sell guns, drugs, and hot cars. He figured that if we were going to get arrested we ought to at least make a buck out of it and not go to jail for stupid shit "like Bobby Bertsch," as he always called Flipout when he was pissed.

That's how Davy talked *when he was sober*. But come Friday night, give Davy two beers and it was like Dr. Jeckyl and Mr. Hyde. Before you knew it, Davy would be busting heads, swinging bar stools, and rolling around in the busted glass and grease out in the parking lot. All this gangster shit was nothing but talk on his part, just bullshit, because whenever push came to shove, Davy Supermouth Kerwin was always a stone cold outlaw—first, last, and forever.

So the problem was all right out on Long Island. But then we established a Pagan chapter in the East Village, and this caused trouble because it overlapped with the Aliens again. The new guys themselves were not that bad. We liked them and went into the Village to party with them every couple of weeks. But as Sleepy put it:

> There's something weird about the whole place. You have to ride over there on the subway, wearing your colors under your leather jacket so's that you don't look like a fucking idiot hanging on a subway strap with a one-percenter patch on your jacket. And then you're walking everywhere you go, and you're partying in a third floor apartment. How can you be an outlaw, if you can't piss off the back porch or on the floor of the garage, and you can't drink beer on the sidewalk or grill

hamburgers in the lots? And worst of all you gotta keep your bike on Long Island and ride a train to get to it. I mean you gotta have your scooter on hand, in a garage in the alley or two minutes down the block.

And then he added: "Besides, this is going to be trouble. The place is full of hippies and junkies and perverts. Everybody is doing drugs, and buying drugs, and selling drugs. Sooner or later there's going to be trouble in the Village. Mark my words."

CHAPTER 10

We can't all be saints.
— John Dillinger

Actually, who the saints really are depends on how you look at it. John Dillinger is supposed to have given a lot of his earnings back to the poor, and not just dimes like John D. Rockefeller but folding money, and big bills at that. And he never took any money from bank customers; he only robbed the bank's money. One time when he was on the run, he stopped home to see his dad and escaped from 20 federal agents who had the old man's farm staked out. The FBI called the attorney general for the State of Indiana and demanded that the old man be arrested on state charges because, as hard as it is now to believe, at that time there was no federal law against harboring a fugitive. But it seems that the state's attorney general informed the FBI that people like Dillinger, who rob banks, are far better loved in the State of Indiana than the people who own banks. So he was not going to arrest some poor old farmer just because his boy came home for a visit. Now, we weren't exactly in as much trouble as Dillinger, but we had to get mighty cautious.

The Long Island club had pretty much split up into two groups: those living out in Suffolk County, and those like me, Sleepy, the Gypsy, Stevie Hippie, and Freddy Frei, who were living in Maspeth, Ridgewood, and Greenpoint. This was the heart of mob country, where they filmed *The French Connection* and *Donnie Brasco*. The area was teeming with wiseguys, but we didn't take shit. Since just about every young Italian stallion on Knickerbocker Avenue pretended to be connected, we never knew whether or not we were fucking with the real McCoy. So we just beat the shit out of the wiseass fuck and waited to see what happened, which was usually nothing.

Once we really did fuck up somebody important. Fortunately, the Gypsy was working as a bouncer in a club owned by Sonny Franzese, one of the few really flamboyant and swashbuckling mobsters of the '60s. I asked him to check it out, and he told us at the next meeting that Sonny told him that if anyone approached us we were supposed to say: "I have someone to sit down and talk for me." That's it, don't say anything else. Then we were supposed to get back to Gypsy immediately, and he was to go to Sonny and see if we could straighten things out.

But nothing ever happened. We didn't know it until ten years later, when the Philadelphia Pagans shot up the house of the Scarfo mob's underboss, that we had them scared shitless along with everyone else.

I can't say we were becoming paranoid, because paranoid people are people who worry but don't have anything to worry about, and we sure had shit to worry about. So we were a little antsy and we were all carrying guns by now. Some of us were happy with cheap-ass street Berettas. I had managed to come up with a Colt 1911 .45, and Davy was completely over the edge, laying up a supply of grease guns and .357 Magnums. So when we headed out on New Year's Eve, most of us were carrying a loaded gun in one coat pocket and a pint of Jack Daniel's in the other.

The year before, the Pagans had wanted to make an impression, so they rented the hotel in Newark and invited every outlaw club on the East Coast. But this year we wanted something quiet. We were reeling, licking wounds, and we had all the publicity we needed. The word "Pagan" sent shockwaves into motorcycle circles from New York to Pittsburgh to Richmond. All we were looking for was a quiet bar where a couple of clubs could get together and talk over the crazy year in a real "Auld Lang Syne" atmosphere.

We found it in Patterson, New Jersey. Pappy had located a dump out in the asshole of nowhere and had gotten the owner to shut the place down and turn it over to us for the evening. Big Dutch and Apple were coming up from Maryland. Naturally all of New York and Jersey would be there, and Chuck was coming down with a pack from Reading.

Things did not start well. Billy was drunk when we picked him up and he had a bottle of whiskey. He never drank whiskey, but he was beginning to do a lot of strange things he never did before. For one thing, he usually made sense, but he was talking gibberish the whole way and he kept sipping whiskey the whole time. When we got to Jersey, we got lost. While we were riding through the area around Newark with all the big oil storage tanks, somebody innocently said, "I bet this would make a good fire."

Then without warning, Billy rolled down the window, yelled "Watch this!" He pulled out his gun and started shooting at the oil and gas tanks. Nothing happened to the oil or gas tanks, but Davy Supermouth, who was driving, nearly wrecked the car, and Big Jim Fagan, who was riding shotgun, tried to turn around and beat the shit out of him, but he was too big to get around in the seat.

I took the gun away from Billy, but the rest of the trip degenerated into an argument over whether he could have blown half of Jersey to smithereens. Davy Supermouth, almost hysterical, was shouting that he didn't give a shit one way or the other, and that he was going to throw him out of the car.

We arrived without further incident. Chuck was already there, along with Rayels and Blackie, who had just gotten out of Berks County Prison. I may have missed Blackie while I was in Reading that fall, but he was a great talker, and he was determined to bring me up on everything that had happened to him since.

It seems that they let him out of the can the day before Christmas Eve, and being that he was in there for three months, his wife was stone broke. Still, Blackie managed to come up with money to put gas in his big old black Cadillac. He picked up Righteous Fuckin' Elroy, and by the end of the day the two of them had managed to get some toys for his daughter Brenda, as well as a case of beer and some weed. His wife Baby had been directed to the food bank by Frenchy's wife, and she came back with 25 pounds of government surplus spam and a 5-gallon can of instant mashed potatoes. So that took care of the food. Except for his little girl,

Brenda, who just pointed at the spam on the plate and said, "Dirty meat, dirty meat."

After they stuffed themselves on fried spam and instant potatoes, they sat around on Christmas Eve watching the burning log on TV, smoking weed, and drinking beer while they waited for the kid to fall asleep so they could put out the toys.

Somewhere along the line Blackie said what a shame it was that they didn't have no tree to put the toys under. Then Elroy grinned and said, "Did you see all those trees in front of the State Police Barracks with all the lights on them."

Then Blackie just started giggling and smiled at him. He took another hit on the joint and said, "Are you thinking what I'm thinking?"

Elroy just kept grinning.

And then Blackie said, "Let's go."

The two of them put on their leather, and Blackie got a saw out of the closet. His wife asked with some alarm "Where are you two going?"

And Blackie just said, "To get a tree."

The next thing, the two of them were tiptoeing up to the police station in the snow, and Blackie held the tree back while Elroy laid in the cold snow on his belly and sawed off the tree just so some poor little girl wouldn't have to wake up on Christmas morning without one. As Blackie put it, "Didn't even have to decorate it. The lights were already on it. All we had to do was stick the plug in the wall when we got home."

After we got over laughing about Blackie's Christmas tree, we got the big news from Chuck: the Reading club would again be calling themselves the Heathens. Chuck insisted that it didn't make any difference. And he was right. Whenever Pagans went to Reading, they were treated just like Heathens, and whenever Blackie came to New York he was treated just like a Pagan. Heathens in trouble hid out over the border in Delaware with the Wilmington Pagans, and Pagans on the run hid out in Reading. We attended each other's meetings and put our two cents in. No member of any other club could ever have done that.

Chuck's problem was that he was losing members. We didn't know it at the time, but outlaw clubs were going through a transition. Large chapters of two or three dozen members who could ride out on Friday night or Saturday were impressive, but small clubs of less than a dozen members were a lot tighter and that enabled the club to be more like a brotherhood. Chuck wanted to have it both ways, but it wasn't working. He had lost more than half his members. Whether they flew Heathen or Pagan colors, his club members had terrorized and titillated Reading and Berks County. They were local folk heroes, and the old members were saying they would come back as Heathens but not Pagans.

Big Dutch was a true imperialist. He immediately saw Chuck's dilemma and knew that not every component state in an empire needed to be affiliated on the same terms. He told us that not every righteous person and not every good club would always be able to fly Pagan colors, and therefore from time to time special arrangements and exceptions would have to be made.

But it was Pappy, the Peacemaker, who was really at his best that night. He insisted that the whole thing should just be viewed by all concerned as a temporary measure to deal with an immediate but temporary problem. He pointed out that the Reading Pagans had always worn a small Heathen patch over their heart, and now they were just wearing a larger patch on their back. Maybe even something could be worked out where they could wear a small Surt patch over their hearts.

Rayels had brought along Jane. It was unusual for him to bring her this far. They had two young boys, and above all she was a mother first, but he explained that Righteous Fuckin' Elroy and Margie (Gums) were home watching his kids. Some of us questioned this combination baby-sitting duo. But Chuck said that they babysat for him all the time. Elroy was loyal and wouldn't let anything happen to the kids, and whatever he might lack in brains, Margie more than made up for.

I was glad to see Jane and she seemed glad to see me. Now you have to understand here that this does not mean we were carrying torches. It's just that the wives of some members always got along with some members better than with others.

You have to remember that while all Pagans were brothers, some of these brothers were real slobs. Some of them you could work with like

Elroy, who, as Blackie put it, was raised on a farm with an outhouse and you just had to teach him to wipe his feet and put the toilet seat down. Others, like Tommy Gannon, were a lost cause. But the real prize might have been this new prospect from Jersey, who walked around guzzling beer out of a pitcher all night and pissing his pants. Between spilled beer and piss, he was soon soaking wet like a big hairy dog that just come in out of the rain. Then he started walking up to people, slapping them on the back, getting them all wet, and then staring down at his soaking wet dripping crotch and saying in mock amazement, "Somebody just pissed in my pants."

The first time it was funny, but it got old quick. Pappy was trying to explain something to me when the guy came up soaking wet, threw his arms around the both of us, and said, "Somebody just pissed in my pants."

Then, without warning, the Peacemaker lost it. Pappy turned around and started slapping the shit out of the guy while screaming, "Nobody pissed in your pants, you fucking idiot! You pissed in them yourself!" That night was the last time we ever saw the pisspants prospect. But of course every time we saw Pappy after that, we had to ask him how the guy was doing.

Midnight came and the guys were kissing old friends and brothers, except for the guy who pissed himself. Nobody seemed to want to touch him, since there was no telling what the geek might have had in his mouth last.

Rayels was sitting on a barstool next to Jane when I walked past him. He grabbed me by the hair, pulled my head down, and kissed me.

"Happy New Year, Brother."

Then for some reason, out of the clear blue sky, I asked Rayels, "Can I kiss your old lady Happy New Year?"

Now this was not completely unheard of. But Rayels shouted at the top of his lungs "You wanna what? You wanna kiss my old lady? Sure, you can kiss my old lady. Hey everybody, watch this."

Now he had everybody looking at us, and he had just raised the ante. What he was letting me know, without actually saying it, was this:

Since you care enough to ask if you can kiss my old lady, I'll let you kiss her, but you better show her the same care and respect that you would show if you borrowed my motorcycle, which means that you better give her the best kiss that you ever gave any woman in your life, because if I ever catch you kissing any woman better than you kissed her, I am gonna cop a real attitude, Brother.

And what he was letting her know was this:

You wanna kiss my brother, you can, but understand this, Woman, you better give him as good a kiss as you ever gave me, because I don't want him going around telling people that you may be pretty but you sure can't kiss.

So now the two of us were obligated to put on the best show we could. Rayels was standing there with his arms crossed, sneering like *shit, you two ain't shown me nothin' yet.* And everyone else was cheering like they're watching a wrestling match. But the two of us liked each other to start with, and were both twenty and hot to trot anyhow, so there we were, tongue fucking each other in the mouth as hard as we could and grabbing each other and lovin' every second of it. And everyone in the room was watching the exhibition and hootin' and hollerin' and screaming, "Go for it!" except Rayels, who was just standing there like we ain't showing him shit. And neither of us could quit without being booed, so we just kept shoving our tongues around in each other's mouth, until finally one of the more diplomatic brothers—it was either Pappy or Apple—came up, pushed us apart, and said, "That's enough of that." Then it was over and you were never supposed to ask to kiss her or put a hand on her again.

Sometime in the course of the night the party broke up, and Pappy said that there was no place in Jersey big enough to accommodate everyone. They did have two or three crash pads, so each local club should go together to the same place so that nobody would get left behind in the morning. This was a smart move on Pappy's part, because invariably the kind of guy who missed his ride was like the guy in your club who pissed his pants all night. Pappy, Updegraff, and Bucky didn't want to get up with a hangover on New Year's Day and have to contend with the freak show that got left behind when the circus train left town.

So we left the bar and split for Rahway, or Linden, or Union, or wherever in hell it was, because that part of Jersey is all the same, and the only thing that changes from one neighborhood to the next is the color of the peoples' faces and their accents.

The apartment building belonged to Bucky, who actually had a couple of bucks and invested his money, and for this reason some guys found it hard to understand what he was doing in the club. The apartment building had probably been a fashionable middle-class home when it was built around the turn of the century, but now it was divided into three apartments, with some citizen folk living on the first floor, Pappy and his family on the second, and the third floor apartment was rented by the club. There was hardly any furniture in the rooms, and no curtains or rugs. The windows needed to be glazed and rattled like hell in the wind, and the place was heated by old-fashioned cast-iron radiators that clanged and banged all night.

It was impossible to stay warm in the place unless you were drunk. So invariably you woke up freezing and shaking in the middle of the night. Then you would lay down on the bare wood floor in front of a radiator, with your back to it and your hands jammed between your legs, feeling the warmth crawl over your back as you fell asleep. But soon you would wake up again with your back about to catch fire and your front freezing, so you would turn over and try to get comfortable facing the radiator. Eventually the sun would come up with all of us rolling around in front of the radiator, and unable to sleep.

Finally, we ended up at a shithole storefront diner around the corner, huddled together in a booth and drinking coffee out of cracked white mugs trying to warm up. And there I would be staring at Crazy Joey, Domino, and J.P. Soul, the same faces that six months earlier, I had been looking at in the mountains of Pennsylvania under a blazing summer sun. Only back then they had been well-tanned and smiling, but now in the gray winter morning of North Jersey, the faces were just ash gray. We were all tired, and freezing, and starting to look old.

But this was New Year's Eve and we were drunk. When we got back to the apartment we were all sitting around smoking joints and trying to mellow. Against the wall was this brother from Baltimore, Foggy, who was an older guy—about 30. He was a big Irish longshoreman from

Dundalk with a belly almost as big as Pappy's. He ate methamphetamines when he went out to stay wide awake, he dropped a tab or two of acid so that he would have fun, and then he guzzled beer all night like any other Irish longshoreman. And on top of all that, he smoked a little weed just to mellow out.

But tonight he was having trouble mellowing. It was almost dawn, and he was wide awake, incoherent, and drunk all at once. At first nobody paid him much mind, because we were all fucked up and he was just talking gibberish. But since we were all becoming paranoid and could read shit into nothing, we began to notice that every once in a while, he kept saying, "I can see that I'm going to need my gun before this night is over."

Well the night was over, unless he was thinking something we weren't. Then we all heard him say, "I'm going to have to shoot someone before this night is done."

Now we all looked around and realized that there was no one but Pagans and their women around, no other clubs, no citizens and we weren't planning on going out. So the implication was becoming clearer.

We began elbowing each other and saying "Hey, you listenin' to this shit?"

As leader of the Baltimore club, it was German's place to do something. And he said, "Hey, shut your fuckin' mouth. You're talkin' shit."

"I aint talkin' shit," Fog said, "and I aint shuttin' my fuckin' mouth. Like I said, before this night is over, I'm goin' to have to blow someone away."

"And I said you're out of line."

German was pretty emphatic, and Foggy seemed to get the drift. For a while he just sat on the floor against the wall mumbling shit we couldn't understand. But before long, we again heard him say something about needing his gun before the night was over. And German had to shout at him all over again.

You have to understand that unless you were a part of these guys, it is impossible to understand why they did anything the way they did. And if you were a part of it you didn't even try to understand. Under these circumstances, a normal person would have checked to see if he had a gun, taken it away from him, and that would have been the end of it. But these guys were not normal and just didn't do things like that. It was nothing conscious, just a heavily ingrained habit of ignoring danger, like standing up drunk on motorcycle seats, harassing wise guys, or taunting cops.

But one of my guys was sitting there with his new .357 Magnum. He had not been carrying it that long so that it became natural, so he was always conscious of the thing, like he was walking around with a hard-on all the time. And now he whispered to one of the guys in the Mother Club that maybe it would be a good idea to keep an eye on him, meaning: "Maybe I should have my gun out just in case." I don't know how fucked up the guy in the Mother Club was, but he said, "Good idea."

So there was my gun neophyte, sitting there all fucked up himself and holding a .357 Magnum in his lap under a leather jacket, which wasn't so bad in itself, except that he got the hammer cocked back, and his finger inside the loop and sitting on the barometrically sensitive hair-trigger.

Today, people wear ear protection even on outdoor shooting ranges, so unless you have ever heard one of those cannons go off in the room of an old-fashioned apartment with hard plaster walls, no curtains, no rug, and nothing to absorb the sound except your eardrums, you really cannot appreciate the awesome firepower of a high-caliber handgun. Physically, the impact is enough to send you into a temporary state of shock, even if you are not drunk or stoned or hallucinating, which we all were.

The first thing you do is check to make sure you're not shot, and then you look around. Sure enough, there was Foggy holding his gut and bleeding all over the place, and German and another Baltimore brother, kneeling on each side of him. His eyes were open and head moving, so he wasn't dead yet, but probably would be any minute. Then everybody was on their feet and yelling about neighbors calling the cops and we gotta get the fuck outta here. Then everyone was running out the door, up and down the stairs, out into the street, and back into the house.

I was running back up the stairs to see if all my people were out, and I ran head first into Domino on the second floor landing. We grabbed each other by the coats and were shaking each other and shouting some sort of drunken shit at each other, when suddenly the door to the second floor apartment popped open. There was Pappy himself, the Peacemaker, wearing nothing but a pair of blue jeans and standing there in his bare feet with his big Teamster beer belly busting out over the top of his pants and into the hall. And on his face, he had about the most disgusted look I ever saw on anybody.

"What happened now?" he demanded.

"Somebody just shot Foggy with a .357 Magnum," we told him.

Well I only thought his face looked bad before that; now it got even worse.

"Tell everyone not to knock on this door. I'm going inside and I'm locking it. I'm not answering for anyone. I'm getting up tomorrow and watching football, and nobody is opening this door until I go to work Monday morning. Do you understand?"

Then he closed the door and we heard about six bolts clicking.

Now this was the smart thing to do, because whether you are wrecking a bar, or fucking somebody up, or robbing a bank, you got about one minute when your chances of being caught are about 1 percent. Then after one minute your chances of getting caught are still 1 percent, and after two minutes it's 2 percent, and after three minutes it's 3 percent, but by the fourth minute it's 5 percent, and then each minute it goes up to 8 percent, then 13 percent , then 21 percent and then 34 percent. This is called the Fibonacci sequence, and if you hang around for more than 10 minutes, your chances of getting caught are exactly 144 out of 100, which equates to mathematical certainty.

Now I know that Pappy wasn't doing the math in his head, but I also know that he realized that he could not get his boots on, find his car keys, and explain to his wife why he was getting her up at five o'clock in the morning. Then there was getting the two girls up and dressed and letting them go to the toilet, and do all that, without the window of opportunity slamming shut in his face. He would have come out the door with his family right into the face of the police, who would want to know where the fuck they were going at five o'clock in the morning in the middle of winter. And "to the Shore" wouldn't have worked. So Pappy just went back in and shut the door.

Then the Gypsy came flying up the stairs. "We got to get our man back to New York right away!" he shouted.

And he was right. One of our guys had pulled the trigger and that was homicide. But we were only 15 minutes from the Goethals Bridge, and once we crossed the Arthur Kill we would be in New York State, which for the purposes of law enforcement was as good as Canada.

We had been through these quick getaways many times, and this is why the clubs had two officers that, for lack of a better term, were called sergeants at arms, and why they had to be the biggest fucks in the club. I told Gypsy to stand by the cars, count our guys, and throw them in cars as I brought them out of the building. If anybody tried to get out of a car, I told Gypsy to punch him in the head. I then told Big Jim to park his ass up against the building and count the guys as I brought them out, and if anyone tried to get back in, punch him in the mouth. "As soon as I come through the door empty-handed, and you and Gypsy can agree that everybody's out, let's go."

Eventually, I found the last of my guys sleeping in the bathtub with the shower curtain pulled shut.

I jumped in the Gypsy's truck, and I was glad to be on the road because that saved me the problem of having to deal with Foggy. Under the circumstances, if he had died, they might have given him to me and said, "Here, your people did it, now you get rid of him."

I would have had to shanghai Flipout and Bobo, and the three of us would have been out in the South Shore marshes with shovels, in January, in the middle of the night, cursing like hell, and trying to find an unfrozen patch of sand where we could dig a hole big enough to bury the bloated carcass of a large stevedore with a big beer belly. The only advantage we would have enjoyed over Italian wise guys in the same situation would be that we would have been driving the shovels into the ground with big-ass, shit-kicking, Harley-Davidson stomping boots from the Chippewa Boot Company in Milwaukee, and not some cardboard-soled, patent leather, little Italian fairy shoes from Milan.

But as it was, I had just done what I was supposed to, which was to get everybody out and back to New York without being arrested. And if there was a body lying around, well, Pappy, German, and the local police would just have to deal with it the best they could.

As it turned out, Foggy didn't die. But this created another problem. Not that anybody wanted Foggy to die, but German now had to try to save the life of someone who had taken a belly shot. This meant taking him to the emergency room at the local hospital, not that this would have been all that unusual, especially in this part of Jersey. In fact, on New Year's Eve there probably would have been a half-dozen other people, most likely black and Puerto Rican, in the same boat. But the cops would still have wanted to know how it happened, and "cleaning his gun" would not have worked. Then the cops would have wanted to take a look at the gun, and German couldn't very well say that "I didn't know if it was hot, so I threw it in the canal before you fucks could get your hands on it and run a ballistics test."

So instead he ran the usual spiel: "Niggers did it."

Naturally, you might think that they would want a little more than that. But after all, he was from out of town and so upset when it happened that he couldn't remember where it was exactly that it did happen. And as for what they looked like: "How the hell do I know? They all look the same to me."

This is precisely what the cop wanted to hear, because he didn't give a rat's ass about Foggy, or German for that matter. The cop probably figured that, however it happened, the guy probably deserved it, and if it was anything important like a robbery, he would know about it in a couple of minutes anyhow. He knew the guy was lying, but that didn't bother him. What did bother him was the possibility of him having to go out and investigate a bullshit story. But saying "niggers did it" and "I can't tell one from the other" meant that the cop could write down "victim unable to describe attackers." And that meant that there was no point even going out looking for anyone, because the victim just said that even if you caught them he wouldn't be able to identify them. So the cop could close out the report and slam the book on the whole thing before going home to watch football.

As for Foggy, in spite of all the hype about tumbling, and hollow point ammunition, and an exit hole the size of a hubcap, the bullet went in and passed through his beer gut, all fat and muscle, and it never hit bone, gut, or cartilage. The bullet came out through a hole as neat and tight as a worm's ass. And Foggy walked out of the hospital with a bandage and was back home in Baltimore in time to watch University of Southern California beat Indiana 14-3 in the Rose Bowl.

But we didn't know all that yet. So as we rode across Staten Island, my sharpshooter began to wonder what was going to happen to him. That was a good point: What was German going to have to say to Dutch about it the next morning? After all, the guy was all fucked up on acid and he was talking gibberish. But other than that, what had he done? He was just sitting on the floor mumbling. He had not pulled out a gun, he hadn't stood up, he hadn't threatened anyone. He never even moved his hands. Yet we thought one of my guys blew him to Kingdom Come with a .357 Magnum.

That was a problem. But I would deal with it tomorrow. We were back in New York. And as we climbed the ramp on the Verrazano Bridge, I could see the first gray dawn of the New Year breaking out over the primeval darkness of the Atlantic Ocean. We were heading back to Long Island, but I was thinking about Pennsylvania and how nice it would be to find a place out in the country with some little Pennsylvania Dutch angel like Jane, whose warm ass I could crawl up next to in bed when I came home after aggravating nights like this.

CHAPTER 11

Let them call us barbarians,
We are barbarians,
It is an honorable title.
— Joseph Goebbels

When we got back to Maspeth after the aggravation in Jersey, I didn't want to go any place where it would be easy to find me. So I stayed with the Gypsy. He was having trouble with his wife, and he was staying with his mother, who lived in a one-story building on the corner of 59th Place and Maspeth Avenue down in Polack Alley. The place had been a bar, then a store. So there was a large room where the Gypsy kept a couple of couches, chairs, tools, and his motorcycle; behind that there was a small apartment where his mother and uncle lived.

When we got there at dawn it was starting to snow, and we collapsed on the couches. But shortly after that his mother shoved her head in the door and began shouting in a voice loud enough to wake up the dead down the block in Mount Zion Cemetery: "Ant-a-ny, Ant-a-ny, get up and shovel the snow. Come on, get up, the people have to go to church."

For Roman Catholics, New Year's Day used to be a holy day of obligation. I believe that it was called the Feast of the Circumcision, for lack of a better excuse to wake up people with a hangover on the first day of the New Year and make them go to church.

So here was this large Polish woman waking up Tony the Gypsy, sergeant at arms of the Pagans Outlaw Motorcycle Club, on no sleep no less, and telling him to go out in the middle of winter and shovel snow. By the look on her face and the sound of her voice, I knew that the woman was not to be denied. And if I didn't get up and help him, he would never let me hear the end of it. So here it was, New Year's Day and the leader of the Long Island Pagans and his sergeant at arms were out in the cold, shoveling snow and nodding good-morning and trying to smile as we said, "Happy New Year," to a bunch of old Polish women in babushkas and rubber boots as they made their way to St. Stanislaus Kostka Church. The New Year was not starting out well. And it did not get better.

For one thing, the club was splitting more than ever into two antagonistic factions. We had spent a year riding around drunk on motorcycles and getting in fights. We had the mob pissed off, we had the cops pissed off, we had every other biker on Long Island pissed off. Davy Supermouth and the Mortician argued, and somewhat persuasively at that, that this self-destructive behavior could not continue.

Then there was Flipout. He was having a problem with amphetamines. He never slept, and he was constantly getting arrested for chicken shit. His parents kept bailing him out, and they had gotten him a lawyer who postponed court dates. But he knew, and we all knew, that when you added up all this little chicken shit, it was getting bigger than a pile of cow shit. And someday all his shit was going to land on some judge's desk all at once and the guy was going to send him away for a year or so. He didn't give a shit himself. He had been there before, and he said he could do it again.

The problem with Flipout was not just his own behavior, but the people he seemed to attract and bring around. In every case you could be sure of one thing: amphetamines always had something to do with it.

The first was Bobby "the Juice" Martinolich. Actually he was not a bad guy, except for the fact that we thought he was trying too hard to impress. He was always talking about whacking people. Most of the guys thought he was a bullshit artist, but others said that people who knew him warned that you would be better off not calling his bluff. Finally, a couple guys decided to test him.

One of the assholes that Flipout had picked up was a loudmouthed, silly woman in her late 20s named Barb, who seemed willing to do anything for attention, including telling people that she was a narc. Flipout insisted that she wasn't and that she just made it up because it got her attention. I told him to stay away from her because she was obviously nuts, but he wouldn't listen. So we yanked his colors for a month and that seemed to work for a while. But she kept him in a steady supply of speed pills, so he used to see her on the side. Finally, two guys decided to use her to test Bobby the Juice.

They told him that she really was a narc, then they got the two of them together, handed him a cocked handgun, and told him to shoot her. He calmly put the thing up to her head and squeezed the trigger. Nothing happened. He cocked it again and squeezed the trigger. Nothing happened. Then they started laughing at him, and he got pissed off, took the gun, and beat the living shit out of her with it.

The club was now split. Obviously the guy was for real, but half the guys said he was trouble and we should have nothing to do with him, while the other half said that we were becoming lame and this was just the kind of guy we needed. However, the situation soon resolved itself when the Juice got himself in a jam with the law. So he jumped on his scooter one warm morning in late February and just started riding south as fast as he could.

That took care of Bobby the Juice, for a while at least. But Flipout then showed up with a married woman named Mary Jo and her goofy husband. It seemed that they had all gone to high school together. Obviously, Mary Jo was impressed by our act, and if you looked at her husband you could see why. He definitely wasn't outlaw material. It's not that he was a bad guy; in a couple of years he probably would have made a decent suburban breadwinner and Little League coach in beige pants and sneakers. But right now he wasn't what a hot-to-trot, drop-dead good-looking, 20-year-old like Mary Jo was looking for. Invariably she showed up with him on Saturday nights. He just sat there, while she gushed exuberantly. It was obvious that she called the shots in the relationship. And since they bought all the beer, we were glad to let them hang out.

Of course, no one was surprised when, less than a month later, she dumped her husband and moved in with Davy Supermouth. Mary Jo was super good-looking, not just cute in a down-home all-American sort of way like a lot of the girls hanging around us, but actually Playboy-center-fold picture-perfect good-looking. So for a while, Davy was happy as shit. He even started staying home most of the time, which started to worry some of the guys, because as Sleepy put it, "the guy can be a real pain in the ass, but he's one of the best people we got."

But that was not what bothered me. I was worried about Mary Jo. She didn't belong with outlaws any more than her husband did. Davy put property colors on her, and we were obligated to respect that. But Mary Jo did not understand the limits. When he brought her around, she worked the room like she was a TV celebrity at a social event. I don't think the goofy broad even realized that she was flirting. It was just her way of doing things. But I could see by the look in Billy's eyes that his temperature was definitely rising.

So I wasn't surprised when Davy was on the phone one morning, at 8 a.m. no less, with his supermouth going off like the 12 o'clock siren on top of the firehouse.

"She's gone. My old lady's gone."

"So what the fuck do you want me to do about it?"

"She took off with Billy. I want his colors."

"But what did he do, leave his wife and kids?" I had to ask. I knew the guy had a stiff dick and loved to fuck around, but I never thought he would leave his wife and little girls for a piece of ass.

"I already talked to his wife."

Oh, you prick, I thought.

"She's gonna shoot the both of them. And then cut his balls off and stuff them in the bitch's mouth."

And she would. This was a woman who used to wait for him to go to sleep drunk and then beat the shit out of him with a Griswold cast-iron frying pan. But that was his problem. The situation was beyond my control. Once you fucked with a brother's old lady he had a right to pull your colors, and no chapter president, no Mother Club member, not even Big Dutch himself could stop it. Davy was pissed, and there was no telling him that the woman was a fucking cunt, that she had dumped her own husband for him less than a month earlier, and that everybody but him had seen something like this coming down the road a mile away.

He had Billy by the balls. He knew it and was not about to let go.

Later, I got a phone call from Billy. "I fucked up and I know it. I got someone to bring you my colors."

"Wait. Can't I meet you, Brother? Can't we talk?"

"No we can't. I fucked up. I'm out, I know it. And you gotta do what you gotta do. Take care brother."

And that was it. I never saw him or heard about him again. But the next thing, I knew Mary Jo was living at Flipout's house. Only now it was my turn to *flip out*.

"I don't want that cunt around. You hear me?" I told him. "You bring her around and I'll pull your colors."

But Flipout protested. He insisted that it was his mother. She never had a daughter, and she had just adored Mary Jo since she and Bobby were in kindergarten together. And the girl had no place to go, so his mother let her move in the spare bedroom.

I knew that the guy was telling the truth. Like a lot of outlaws he couldn't lie even when he needed to. Of course, Davy Supermouth went off like a bottle rocket when he heard this, but I just laughed and told him to go talk to Mrs. Bertsch about it, knowing damn well that the old German woman would just tell him that it was her goddamn house and she would have anyone she wanted in it.

At this point I needed a break. So I jumped at the invitation when the Gypsy told me that he, Stevie Hippie, and Big Jim Fagan were all going to Reading for a weekend. On Friday night we all piled into the front of Big Jim's truck and headed for Pennsylvania, with four guys sitting on the front seat and one on the floor with his feet stuck under the rest of us. When we got there, things weren't much better than they were in New York. Chuck had not had the big influx of old members he had expected. What's more, Big Jim and Rayels had quit.

Now Billy's fuck-up had hurt, and Big Jim Solley was a surprise. But Rayels! What the fuck was the world coming to when someone like Rayels quits? Bob Rayel was the quintessential outlaw—a tall, lean, bearded, brown-haired Appalachian Mountain Irishman, with one of the most sinister-looking faces you ever saw. He had drifted into town from Harrisburg when he was just a kid. He came down to Reading to build and race stock cars, but then he found a Harley Davidson engine in a peach basket. He built the thing from the ground up, bolt by bolt. And it was not one of those lame-ass home grown choppers that coughed nuts and bolts and pissed oil from one end of town to the other. It was a downright kick-ass, haul-ass outrageous outlaw chopper that handled the curves and could be ridden like hell every day without falling apart.

Then he had found a great old lady in Jane, and he had the kick-ass out-law job to boot. He worked in a scrap yard. This was before anybody ever heard of the word "recycling," when these places were just called "junk-yards." Rayels hauled around scrap iron and bundles of dirty newspapers all day, until his face and hands were one constant glaze of grease and oil and road dirt and dust. And he not only looked the part, he could live up to it too, riding around on a motorcycle for weeks with just the clothes on his back and eating only twice a week. And he wore these big steel-toed boots that practically laced up to his knees, and Skip and Little Joe used to say that one time when he was on the road he didn't undo the laces for an entire month. When he got home, his socks were rotten and there was some kind of worm living in one of his feet.

As strange as all this may sound today, you must remember that this was back in 1968. We were all young, we rode around the East Coast on homemade choppers with just the clothes on our backs, leather jackets, gloves, and our colors. We didn't have toothbrushes or changes of socks. When our drawers got too raunchy, we simply threw them away. We slept on dirt floors in wooden garages and wood floors in dirty apartments. A greasy, smelly moldy old couch with a coil spring worming its way up your ass in a cinderblock clubhouse that used to be a chicken coop was the height of decadence. If you needed a shower in order to enjoy your-self, the outlaw life was not for you. Cleanliness may be next to godliness, but in the outlaw world of Muspell, cleanliness was for candy-asses, and we were cowboys. Perhaps the idea originated with guys returning from Southeast Asia, where they had lived in the jungle for weeks at a time. In any event, Bob Rayel, or Rayels as we called him, epitomized the out-law lifestyle and, like Sweet William Parker, he was one of the all-time great outlaw bikers, the kind of shit from which the Legend was forged in Muspell.

I asked Chuck what the fuck was wrong. And he just said, "I don't know. Rayels had just gotten real strange lately. He stopped coming around, he dropped out of the club, and his old lady told my old lady that he ain't been home much lately and he's been complaining about head-aches all the time."

So that was it for Rayels. And then when I got back to Maspeth, Billy's colors were sitting on my grandmother's table, all clean and neatly folded. Somebody was supposed to give them to me, but somehow the instruc-tions and directions got fucked up, and instead somebody knocked on my grandmother's front door and handed her a set of Pagan colors.

"Wait, let me see if I got this right," Sleepy Muzetti later asked with a big smirk on his face, "some total stranger knocked on the old Oma's door (Oma is Bavarian for grandmother) and out of the clear blue sky he hands her a set of Pagan colors."

"That's right," I said patiently. "Somebody knocked on Oma's front door and just handed her a set of Pagan colors with no explanation."

"Well what the fuck did she do?" He was laughing uncontrollably at this point.

"Oh she knew what they were, all right," I said. "But she decided that they were dirty. So she took them upstairs, put them through the wash machine, and there they were all clean and folded up and laying neatly on the dining room table when I came to visit her this morning."

Well, I only thought he was laughing before that. Now he was rocking back and forth in the chair and screaming. I thought he was about to piss himself. Then he slammed the beer bottle down on the table and slapped me on the shoulder.

"You mean," he said, "that your Oma had a set of Pagan colors hanging out her second floor window on a clothesline in Maspeth."

"That's right," I said, after I thought about it, "I suppose Oma was flying a set of Pagan colors on her wash line." My grandmother, like everyone else in Maspeth at the time, never owned a clothes dryer and this detail, along with the obvious implication, had completely escaped me. But it was just the kind of thing that Sleepy always caught, which is why I was coming to rely on him more and more as my de facto vice president.

So there we sat in the Ridgewood Tavern, under the Forest Avenue El train, sipping bottles of Rheingold beer, two outlaw bikers just patiently waiting out the winter on a dark February night. We didn't say much the rest of the night; we just kind of sat there. But every time we looked at each other, one of us would just start laughing, and then the other, until one of us said something like, "I can't believe that your grandmother washed Billy's colors and hung them out to dry on the wash line."

Finally, Sleepy said he was going home. They didn't call him Sleepy for nothing. We were both working at Austin-Nichols, a wholesale liquor distributor, and we had to be down at the 816 Teamster hall to shape-up by 7:30. I wasn't the one they called Sleepy, so I turned down his offer for a ride home and sat there quietly finishing my beer. I was downing the last sip and I was ready to leave when Nellie walked in the front door.

Nellie was hot, Nellie was Greek, Nellie had just turned 18. She had long black hair down to her waist, milk-white skin, and the classic features of a goddess. Her breasts were more than adequate for any mature woman, and absolutely outrageous on an 18-year-old. She knew this, and she wore tops that let other people know it, too. In another 10 years she would probably be an old hex with a mustache and hips like a cow. But right now she was in her prime.

She was a biker groupie who hung out with the guys in the Rat Pack, but she seemed a little wary of the Pagans. Tonight, though, the bar was dead, and she sat down with me. She told me that she was waiting for a friend to take her back to Astoria. Naturally I ordered another beer. I wasn't about to go anywhere as long as she was there. Her friend was late and I didn't have a car, so the best I could do was keep talking and hope her friend would take her time.

In reality, New York City may be only one subway stop away from Queens or Brooklyn, but in mentality they are galaxies apart. For all intents and purposes, some of the old neighborhoods, like Polack Alley, might as well be tucked in a hollow in West Virginia for all the contact the inhabitants had with the outside world. And like many people from these twentieth century ethnic enclaves of Queens and Brooklyn, Nellie rarely got out of the neighborhood. Leaving Long Island was tantamount to a trip to Australia. But like I said, she was only 18 and bubbling over with exuberance for life in the fast lane. She seemed fascinated with the idea of the Pagans just riding for days out into Pennsylvania, Maryland, and West Virginia. Apparently she had listened to Janis Joplin's "Me and Bobby McGee" once too often, and she was impressed with the way hippies just stuck their thumb out and hitchhiked all over the country.

And soon I thought, *Well fuck, if hippies can do it, an outlaw certainly can.* It might be a little unorthodox, but my bike was down, it was February, and she looked real good and smelled real nice. *Maybe*, I thought, *just maybe, I ought to put the ball in her court and see what she does with it.*

It worked. Soon the two of us walked out the door holding hands like two normal teenagers, on our way to hitch a ride. We didn't have any particular destination in mind, other than "south." But before we could hitch our first ride, we had to take the subway to someplace where there were cars other than taxi cabs. We crossed Seneca Avenue and climbed the steps of the El platform where we bought two tokens, and soon we were on a rinky-dink old wooden subway car, because that's what they used on the Forest Avenue El—the oldest cars in New York City, right out of a Veronica Lake/Humphrey Bogart movie. By now all the German burghers of Ridgewood were sound asleep, so here we were all alone in the car, giggling and laughing and heading for Manhattan, where we picked up the Hudson River Tubes for Newark. Soon we were looking at the opposite side of the New York skyline that we were used to seeing from Ridgewood.

We had to walk across the Pulaski Skyway over the Passaic River and Newark Bay, both of which were nothing more than marshy swamps that stunk like something out of Dante's Inferno in the summer. Since it was winter there was no stench or heat as we mounted the narrow emergency walkway on the skyway, just black, salty, smelly water below us.

The skyway is high enough for oil tankers to sail underneath it, so when you get to the top there is nothing but air between you and the New York City skyline. I don't remember how long we stood there, and at the time we didn't care. Even when you have been looking at it everyday of your life, there is still something magical and romantic about the New York skyline. The thousands of pinpoints of light illuminating the towers against the night sky, the smell of salt water and marshes. And there we stood, on a skinny concrete ramp high above Jersey, silhouetted against the lights of New York City's towers in the middle of the night, hugging each other, rubbing noses, and kissing each other for the first time. Even with her black hair teased up, it barely touched my chin, but it smelled nice, so there we stood for I don't know how long, with rednecks in tractor rigs bouncing over the pot holes and serenading us with their air horns as they whizzed by.

Then we walked down with our arms around each other, and at the bottom I stuck out my thumb. We were ready to go with our feet firmly planted on Continental America and headed into the great web of asphalt that forms one interconnected all-American highway. I had deliberately chosen U.S. 1 South. It was February, and as warm as it was in New York, I was not about to hitchhike into Pennsylvania in the winter. By heading south into the Jersey Pine Barrens and Maryland, I knew it would not get any colder.

As it was, it was a raw and damp around the marshes. Our teeth were chattering and our knees were freezing. We tried to kiss each other to see if we could make our teeth stop chattering. It didn't work, and it made us laugh so hard we couldn't keep our mouths together.

Actually we weren't in such bad shape. This was 1968 and people weren't yet afraid to pick up hitchhikers. I had my colors under my coat, so I was just another 20-year-old kid in a leather jacket with long hair and a beard, and I was with a drop-dead good-looking 18-year-old little Greek girl with patent-leather black hair and skin as white as marble.

We knew the game. I stood there with my arm around her and she stood out in the road with her thumb out. Our first ride was from a cop in a cruiser, who told us, "Jesus Christ, you're never going to get picked up here." So he drove us down U.S. 1 a bit, to where it wasn't so hectic, and cars and trucks could pick us up without worrying about getting rear-ended. Then we stood in the road freezing until a car picked us up. Unless you've been in this situation, you cannot understand the ecstasy of climbing into the front seat of an already warmed up car.

Our rides were short, five or 10 miles at a time, guys going to work in the middle of the night. We ran into problems outside of Philly. It was already light and everyone was in a hurry now, but some black guy in his 40s picked us up. He was genuinely worried that we would never get a ride if he left us in the city, so he drove us clear down to the Delaware County Line, but not before he bought us breakfast. When Nellie told him that we were from New York, he told us that he knew where to get the best bagels in Philadelphia, so now were riding all over West Philly in search of the best bagels west of the Hudson River. Considering how cold and strung out we were, they probably were the best bagels we ever had.

So now fortified by bagels, caffeine, sugar, and the morning sun, we headed through the congestion between Philadelphia and Wilmington. By now it was after the rush hour and rides were coming easy now, and soon we were over the Mason-Dixon Line on the way to Baltimore. But this soon presented a major problem: Prince George's County, Maryland.

Up until now I was just another longhaired young kid with a cute little girl. But unlike the cops in Jersey, New York, and Pennsylvania, the police in Southern Maryland had been dealing with Pagans for years. Colors or no colors, they would pick me out in an instant. And they had a containment policy designed to confine the Pagans to the District of Columbia and Virginia by making their lives as miserable as possible in Prince George's County. I was packing a gun and this could be trouble. So I called Big Dutch from a pay phone at a 7-11 store.

"You did the right thing," he said. "Don't go nowhere, don't do nothing, don't even wait in the store; they might think you're trying to steal something. Wait outside. I'll have someone there right away." And he did. Ten minutes later an old low-slung gas-guzzler pulled up with Big John and Domino in the front seat, and our adventure was over.

I told them we got drunk and hitchhiked down the night before. The first thing Big John did was ask me if I had any money. And then I realized that I didn't. He shoved a $20 bill in my hand and said, "Here, keep it."

They drove us back to Dutch's house, a small one-story bungalow-type house in rural Prince George's County. The girl and I were exhausted, but shit, there was the issue of Southern hospitality, so we sat up drinking beer and smoking weed with Dutch and his wife. With the wife and strange girl in the room, there was no chance of talking club business. So it was just small talk and goofin' on each other. Dutch was not much older than I was, and in the world of outlaw bikers that meant he was extremely young to be running a club the size of the Pagans. But when you got him alone, he was just a good ol' Southern boy with the playful instincts of just another goofy kid.

Finally about noon, Crazy Joey Vargas came over and had a few beers with us, and then he and Dutch had some business to take care of. They took off, and Dutch's wife put us in a sparsely furnished spare bedroom. We peeled off our leather jackets, and I pulled her top over her head. Both of us were strung out, high, and giddy as all hell because we had started drinking again. We were clumsy and had trouble getting off each other's clothes. We got tangled up in the sheets, and at one point they ripped and my ass came burstin' through. When she saw my ass come poppin' out through the white sheet, she started laughing and couldn't stop. Then as we were both getting off, the bed collapsed and one corner was down on the floor. That was the end of it; we couldn't even look at each other without laughing. She started tickling me, I tickled her, and she let out a bloodcurdling scream that nearly took the roof off the house. Then the dogs started barking, which made us laugh even more. Then suddenly after partying for 12 hours and passing through five states, we passed out in each other's arms.

When we woke up, it was already dark. We were still all tangled up with each other in the torn sheets and on a lopsided mattress. We could hear voices in the living room. A lot of voices. It sounded like the whole clan stopped in for a visit.

But first things first. We were rested now and in the dark. We got it on one more time. Real slow and serious with a lot of touching and squeezing and kneading.

When we got out to the living room, it was obvious that the crowd was getting too big for Dutch's house. So Nellie stayed with Dutch's wife at the house and the rest of us moved the party to a roadhouse. The atmosphere relaxed. There were Pagans there, and there were citizens, but it was obvious that they had all grown up together busting Chevy axles in cornfields.

Then Crazy Joey came up to me and whispered in my ear: "Dutch says we can give you a ride home tonight."

This came as a complete surprise. But they were obviously not just giving me a ride back to New York, because in that case we would have all gotten drunk and drove back the next morning, not in the middle of the night.

We rode back in a big old '60s gas-guzzler with a backseat the size of a living room couch—Crazy Joey on one side, me on the other, and Nellie between us. Big Dutch was driving and Big John was riding shotgun. It was obvious they were not on a social visit. They would not be stopping in Maspeth to visit, or in Jersey. Something was up. It was obvious, you could sense the nervousness. It was like being in the locker room with prizefighters while they're waiting to get in the ring. Furthermore, none of them had colors with them. Big Dutch was wearing a tweed cap and a denim prison yard coat. The others too were wearing outfits that would not immediately identify them as bikers. In the Village they could blend.

But I wasn't told anything, and I didn't want to know if anything was even up. That's the way things were. If you didn't need to know, you didn't want to know. You had enough shit of your own to deal with, and you didn't want to go sticking your nose in other people's shit.

When we pulled out of the Holland Tunnel, it was already light. They dropped us off at a subway station. Then I watched them drive downtown toward the Village, and Nellie and I got on the subway and rode back to Ridgewood.

That night I was back in the Ridgewood Tavern drinking with Sleepy.

"Let me see if I got this straight," he said. "You got drunk with Nellie the other night and hitchhiked down to Maryland. Then you went into Big Dutch's house, tore up his bed sheets, and busted up the furniture. Right?"

"Yea."

"Well how many people do you think could have gotten away with that?" he asked. "And then he gives you a ride back to New York after all that."

Well, he found all that pretty funny. But then he got serious. "You know," he said, "they could have been doing anything in Manhattan and it's none of our business. But I don't like this shit. I said it before and I'll say it again. There's something weird about that whole Village scene; I don't like going over there—too many assholes, too many drugs. The shit's going to hit the fan someday, and it ain't going to be good."

He was right. The situation with the Manhattan Aliens continued to fester. Every couple of weeks a bunch of us would ride over to Manhattan and party. Party with the Aliens, party with the Pagans, and we got along with them both. But you could usually feel the friction between the Manhattan Aliens and the Manhattan Pagans, or for that matter, the friction all over the Village at that time. Sleepy was right: too many assholes, too many drugs. It wasn't outlaw territory. We preferred Long Island without the frills, the freaks, and the hippies of Manhattan.

Eventually the shit did hit the fan, just like Sleepy said it would, and good.

I got a phone call one night.

"Don't say nothin'. Just go to a payphone and call me right back at this number." Then he read out the number to me.

I did, and the caller was at another payphone out in Suffolk County.

"Do you have a gun?" he asked.

"Yea, I do."

"Get it. And don't go anywhere without it. Better yet, don't go anywhere at all. And if you do, take someone with you. Tell everybody else to do the same thing."

"Why? What the fuck is going on?"

"Just read The Paper tomorrow morning, you'll see." Back in those days, when a New Yorker said "The Paper," he meant the *New York Daily News* and only the *New York Daily News.* "In the meantime, watch your asses." He hung up.

I called Bobo on the Island and told him not to go out, and then I called Flipout, not that it would do any good in his case, but at least I tried. As for us guys in Ridgewood and Maspeth, this meant don't go out of Polack

Alley or Ridgewood where you know everyone in the neighborhood. At least it was winter, so we had on heavy leather jackets, which meant that it was easy to conceal a gun.

For some reason we had a preference for large caliber weapons, like the Colt .45, which is what I had. They gave us the added option of bludgeoning the guy's head to a bloody pulp instead of shooting him. Besides, there is just something about an outlaw motorcyclist pulling out a cannon like that; it usually stops everything.

That night I slept with the gun under my pillow. And the next morning I walked down to the store for the paper with it stuck in the back of my pants. Now you have to understand that New Yorkers read the *New York Daily News* like an orthodox Jew reading Hebrew, backwards, starting with the sports news on the back page.

This was the first time I ever started at the front. And I didn't have much choice, because there was the answer to all my questions in the headline staring me right in the face on top of the stack of papers standing in front of the newsstand under the Forest Avenue El: "Torture Killing in the East Village"

"Shit," I thought, "this is not good."

Then it got worse. There was a picture under the headlines of a bunch of bikers inside a police station. I recognized the faces; they were Aliens. The caption said that they had been brought in for questioning by police. If they were arresting Aliens, I thought, a Pagan must have been whacked.

I flipped open the paper to page three and began reading as fast as I could:

> Fifteen men and four girls, most of them members of motorcycle gangs, were arrested by police last night and held for questioning in the grisly torture-fire murder of a young man in the lower East Side.

> Police believed the murder was triggered by rivalry between two cycle gangs, the Alien Nomads and the Pagans, and, as the suspects were rounded up, Sgt. Louis Monaco of the E. Fifth Street Station said:

> "One of these groups did him in."

"Who? Who?" I was asking myself as I searched furiously for a name.

The arrests came within hours after firemen found the charred, nude body on the bedroom floor of the 3½ room fifth-floor apartment at 52 E. First Street.

His hands and legs and body were trussed so that, if he struggled, he would choke. The victim had been doused with a volatile liquid and set afire in a pile of rubbish.

From fingerprints, the FBI later identified him as Ray Edward White, 20, of Dayton Ohio.

Shit, I thought, it was Sunshine. He was an Alien. And that meant that the ball was in their court, and we didn't have to do a damn thing but watch our asses.

But Sunshine was one of the most likable of the Aliens—just a young kid who came up from Florida, joined the Aliens, and really believed that all outlaws were brothers. He partied with both Pagans and Aliens and didn't care which club you were in as long as you had a one-percenter patch on the front of your jacket. In some ways, to him, that was more important than the patch on your back. But that's always the kind of guy who gets caught in the crossfire. It never seems to happen to the pricks.

That night the Gypsy, Sleepy, and I sat at a table in Mickey's Sports Lounge, the most Polack of all the bars in Polack Alley, with newspapers spread out in front of us. The place was a shithole. It had once been nice. You could tell that by the pictures on the walls—a bunch of happy Polacks sitting at tables with clean checkered tablecloths eating steaks and kielbasa. You could tell by the clothes on the people that the pictures were taken in the 1940s, and just by looking around you could tell that nothing had been changed in the past 20 years. Nor had the place been cleaned in 20 years. There were black, greasy strands of cobweb hanging from the ceiling and everything reeked of stale beer and piss. The only liquor Mickey stocked behind the bar was the cheapest American vodka available, usually bought in volume from hijacked trucks, and a cheap

American imitation of Polish blackberry brandy called Jezynowka. He sold both in large shot glasses as heavy as Irish crystal for a quarter to illegal Polish immigrants who worked for minimum wage and sent most of their money home. The beer taps had corroded shut about the time the Dodgers left Brooklyn, and he sold cans of Piels beer also for a quarter.

We felt comfortable in places like these. Sleepy and I were the only non-Polacks in the room, and along with Gypsy there were about a half-dozen other American-born Polacks. The rest were all immigrants. If a cop, a reporter, or an outlaw biker tried to come in the place, they would have stood out like a Jewish accountant in niggertown. If anyone did come around the next day asking questions, half the place would forget how to communicate in English and the other half couldn't even if their life depended on it.

So there we sat drinking bottled beer with the papers spread in front of us and Sleepy was nursing a glass of sweet Polish brandy, which he had acquired a taste for. Every once in a while a Polack would come through the door look at us and say, "you crazy cocksuckers you."

Actually we had become somewhat of a local phenomena since we settled in Polack Alley. I cannot remember a Pagan ever having a hassle with a Polack, and the Polacks seemed to be really proud of us. After all, what else did they have besides minimum wage jobs, bars that smelled like piss, and cellar apartments with leaky pipes overhead? When they saw shit like this in the papers, they could point to it at work and proudly say: "You Guineas, you Irish, you think you're tough. But you ain't shit. These guys are real gangsters, real American badasses. And I drink with them every fuckin' night. A bunch of Guinea gangsters or Irish cocksuckers ever come into our bar looking for trouble, these guys would tear the shit out of them. And they're my friends. I say, 'I need a favor,' and Stoop, the leader of the Pagans says to me, 'Janik, what can I do for you, you're my friend.'" And then Janik could walk back to the loading dock in some dirty warehouse with his chest sticking out like he knew somebody really important in America.

We had all the papers spread out in front of us: *The New York Post*, *The*

Daily News, The Long Island Press, and *Newsday.* We even had the German and Polish daily newspapers.

Nothing made sense.

It was obviously Sunshine, an Alien, who got killed. But who did it and why? The papers said that cops said it was the Pagans. But then why were the cops out arresting Aliens, unless the Aliens had whacked one of their own. Now you may ask why didn't we just get on the phone and start asking questions. But that's exactly what you don't do. You don't want to know anything about it and you don't ask questions. That way you're not a part of it, and if someone gets popped, they can't blame you because you didn't know anything.

Although I felt genuinely bad about Sunshine—the world certainly needs more, not less, people like him—there was an upside to publicity like this. It tends to scare people and they leave you alone. This is particularly a big help in neighborhoods where "the white folks are crazier than the *Mulignane,*" as some Italians were fond of putting it.

The Italians did have a point. Shortly after I went to jail, a bunch of Irish, Polish, and German hooligans from Maspeth and Greenpoint began kidnapping Italian wiseguys and holding them for ransom. At one point, they kidnapped the nephew of Carlo Gambino—the real life Godfather—and then killed him *after the ransom was paid,* just to piss off the Guinzos and show them that they weren't shit in their eyes.

So you can see you had to keep your reputation up if you were going to live around guys like them. And like I said before, law enforcement officials may try to make something out of the fact that they consider the Pagans the most violence-prone and baddest of all outlaw clubs, but I maintain that it's just the part of the country that the Pagans come from—Brooklyn, Philly, the rustbelt mill towns and coal patches of Pennsylvania and West Virginia—that spawned people like this.

It's all part of what made being an outlaw great. One night, you're standing high over the world on top of the Newark skyway looking at the city skyline with your arms around some hot little Greek girl with the sweetest black hair you ever smelled. The next thing you know, you're sitting around a stale beer and piss smelly bar, drinking brandy and beer with a bunch of illegal Polacks, while you're reading a stack of newspaper articles about a bunch of pasty-faced NYPD detectives in trench coats traipsing around fifth floor apartments in 100-year-old walk-up tenements, turning over charred corpses on litter-strewn wooden floors.

CHAPTER 12

At the center of the World stands the great ash tree Yggdrasill. It's branches soar and fan out over the world of the Gods, the world of men, the world of the giants, and the world of the dwarfs. One of the roots goes deep into Nifelheim, the world of the dead, where the dragon Nidhogg feasts on corpses. A second root grows down to a well called Urd, the spring of destiny. Here the water flows out, and here sit the Norns, the three Women of the Weird, who weave human lives into The Great Rope of Destiny. Each life is a strand with a beginning and an end. Sometimes strands become tangled together, as individual lives become tangled, and then drift apart. But at times the norns take two strands and tie them together into an intricate Celtic love-knot that bonds indelibly the fate of two people.

— From the ancient eddas of Iceland

But more of that will come later. Right now I was dealing with more mundane problems. I was covered with grease, and I was on my way out the door. The phone was ringing, Bobo was sitting on a chopper out in the street, and I was pissed off. It had all started at a meeting one night in January, when the wind was howling and the snow was flying and the damp cold was seeping right through our leather jackets. Under these circumstances, the Mortician had raised the point that many of our bikes were not currently roadworthy.

"So!" Flipout shouted sarcastically. "Do you think we're going some-place tonight or did your mother drop you on your head when you were little?"

"No," the Mortician said. Then he began explaining patiently that in his experience as the leader of an outlaw club, he noticed that brothers tend to spend the winter fucked up, shacked up, or just plain jerkin' off, while their bike sits in the garage. Then when spring comes, the bikes are fartin' smoke, pissin' oil, and making more noise than a Jewish wife or Italian mother. What he was proposing was that we pick a day, March 1st, on which we all agree to meet at some bar on bikes.

"March 1st," someone moaned.

"Why not?" the Mortician said. "If you're having trouble, tell me now. I'll be over your house tomorrow, and we can go over your bike and see what you need. I'll help you get it. I'll help you fix it."

We all knew that he was right, so we agreed on March 1st. But sure enough, we spent the winter drunk and fucked up. Bobo shacked up with his wife in Oyster Bay and I was pounding a little jailbait girl from Brent-wood that I had picked up in a bar. She was only 16, but she had quit school and gotten a job wrapping meat in a supermarket. Her old man was a real Italian *heinekaplotz*, right off the boat as they used to say, so he could understand that. But when she stopped coming home at night, he had a shit hemorrhage, which at this point must have been running down his legs, all over his socks, and into his shoes, because somehow he got the number at Davy Supermouth's house, and he used to call up screaming in half Italian and half English.

Billy and Davy shit and said that she was going to get us all arrested. Big Jim Fagan and Tom Gannon used to try to lay a line of Irish malarkey on him. But when the old man went off on Sleepy Muzetti in his Italian version of *ferhoodled* English, Sleepy would just shout, "*Bah fongool,* you crazy Guinea bastard," and then slam down the phone. Meanwhile, I just kept pounding her at night in the back of Davy Kerwin's house, in the back rooms of bars, and on the front seat of her car in broad daylight.

So here it was, March 1st, and Bobo and I thought we had just made it. We were supposed to ride together to a bar in Bethpage, where we were all supposed to get together. But when he came for me, he found me sitting on the garage floor covered with grease, cursing and swearing in three languages—German, English, and Italian—and again struggling with the esoteric mysteries of a Lucas electrical system.

Together we got the problem worked out, and it actually wasn't Lucas' fault this time. There was a bare wire in the harness and we taped it. But we were now late. I ran into the house to get my colors and didn't even bother to wash my hands. Then as I was slipping on my colors and running down the stairs, the phone rang. I ran back up stairs and grabbed it.

"Hello. Stoop?" It was a woman's voice.

"Who the fuck is this?" I asked.

"Margie." It was fuckin' Gums.

"How the fuck did you get this number?" I asked.

"I snuck into Chuck's house and went through his stuff."

Now I was more amused than pissed. The crazy bitch had burglarized Chuck's house. I always knew she had balls, but Chuck Ginder's house? I wouldn't have burglarized Chuck's house, the Mafia wouldn't burglarize Chuck's house, even Crazy Joey Vargas wouldn't burglarize Chuck's house. But here she was, waiting for him to go out so she could climb through a window and rummage through his stuff looking for phone numbers.

Although this explained *how* she had gotten my number, it raised the question of *why* she had gone through so much trouble to get that phone number—my mother's number at that. But just about the time I was wondering all this, she said the words that made my heart jump up into my throat.

"Jane's here. She wants to say 'hello.'"

At first, it was just "Hi" and "How are you," and "glad to talk to you again." But then she made it a point to tell me that Rayels and her were no longer together. She retold the story about how Rayels began getting headaches and acting strange, and then one night he just walked down the road, handed Chuck his colors, and announced that he was out. Two days later, he and his wife were done. All of this still did not make any sense.

After Sweet William died and I went back to New York, Skip had knocked up some 16-year-old Dutch girl and got married. Little Joe took his old lady north to the Blaubarrick and wintered over in Hamburg. That left Rayels all alone in the little house in the woods on the hill, but it was bigger than the bungalow he had for his wife in Mohnton. So he gave the bungalow to Blackie, and moved Jane and the kids into the house on the hill behind Chuck.

Now Rayels was gone, and Jane was all alone in the house in the woods and scared. So she moved Margie in to keep her company. The two of them were sitting around talking like women do, and the next thing you know, Gums was sneaking down the hill and burglarizing Chuck's house so they could call me.

I kept talking, and she kept talking. The subject came up about it being spring and how she had a good time last year with the club, and how she would miss seeing us guys. And I told her that I would miss her this year, too.

Then she told me that I could come see her when I was in Reading. She would really like that. She might be staying with her mother, so she gave me that address and phone number. And then I gave her my grand-mother's phone number, and Gypsy's phone number, and Sleepy's grandmother's phone number, and the number of Tessie's Bar and Grill in Maspeth. In fact I gave her the number of every place she might reach me except the county jail.

She asked me if she could write me a letter, and I said sure and gave her my address. She promised to write, and I promised to get down to see her real soon. When we hung up, I went downstairs and Bobo took one look at me and said, "What the fuck is a matter with you?"

"Nothing," I said. But of course, I was lying.

Ferhexed and *ferhoodled* the Pennsylvania Dutch call it: bewitched and confused. I had never gotten over that midnight kiss on New Year's Eve. And for a year, I had wanted a real live-in old lady just like Jane. Now, suddenly, here she was, alone and free, but 150 miles away.

Two days later, a letter came in the mail. It was long and she was pour-ing out a lot of feelings. I wrote back immediately and told her that I wanted to see her. Meanwhile, I couldn't think about anything else. Again, she wrote back immediately and told me that Rayels was back in the house on the hill, living up there by himself like Howard Hughes and not talking to anyone. Jane had taken the kids and was staying at her mother's. Margie would be there on Friday night, and after they put the kids to bed, they would come out for a while and hang out.

I wrote back and told her that I would be there. Now I needed a car that come rain, shine, or snow would get me to Reading on Friday night. The question was who I could turn to with such an asinine scheme, and the answer was obviously Bobby Flipout.

He thought the idea was absolutely wonderful and he assured me that, "you can count on me brother. Just be ready to go at five-thirty."

By the way he said it, I knew that he meant it. So there I was, sitting in the living room with my leather jacket over my colors, and sure enough at 5:45 p.m. Bobby pulled into the driveway in a brand-new powder-blue sedan.

"Now where did he get that?" my sister asked.

"I don't know," I said on the way out the door.

But the first thing I asked when I got in was, "where the fuck did you get this?"

"Mary Jo," he said. "She's scared to death of you and thinks that you want to kill her over that shit with Billy. So I've been telling her all week that you do, but that if she did you this favor, she would be your friend forever."

"Nice work," I said as I sat back for the ride.

He had a case of beer in the backseat and bunch of joints rolled on the dashboard. He backed out the driveway, peeled rubber all the way down the block, and soon we were on Southern State Parkway heading for the Verrazano Bridge, with Bobby hootin' and hollerin' and cacklin' with a joint hanging out of his mouth as he passed every car on the road.

For the first time I realized how utterly he had changed. Last summer he was just another big ass-kickin', beer-drinkin' German kid, like one million others on Long Island, but now he had lost about 50 pounds and his face was all sunken-in, making him look like some sort of deranged dwarf. Of course, all this had affected his brain as much as his body.

"Did you bring your gun?" he asked.

"No." I said.

"Well I did."

It was then that he began explaining how Chuck and his people might try to kill us. Of course it made no sense. But Bobby had been speeding for days, months, almost a year now. And the rest of us were all paranoid too. You have to realize that growing up, we were always in trouble at home, at school, everywhere. We were the kids who made mothers say: "Oh shit" when we showed up in their back yards. So we just assumed that everything we did was going to bring the shit down on our head.

I hadn't done anything wrong. Rayels was out of the club, and he had dumped his wife. She was free. But then again I hadn't run it by anyone but Bobby. And why?

You have to consider the social environment we were operating in by the spring of '68. Drugs had devastated blue-collar America like hard liquor once devastated the American Indians. On top of that, you had incidents like Sunshine going up in flames in the East Village. That didn't help. Neither did Crazy Joey getting welded into a barrel. Then there were other incidents, even more bizarre.

Like Little Joey "Sir Lancelot" Anastasia (that's right, Anastasia—his uncle was Big Albert, who was gunned down in the barber's chair). But Joey was nothing like his uncle; he was just a nice kid like Sunshine, who got along great with everyone from the first day he came around to join. Well, Joey had an old lady called Suzy "Creamcheese," and he and Creamcheese were sitting in the backseat of a big old car one day without a worry in the world. Meanwhile, the guy in the front seat riding shotgun was tripping on acid and speeding. He suddenly decided that Joey was now the Antichrist, so he turned around and shot both Lancelot and Creamcheese right through the head, causing the driver to wreck the car.

As you can see, people were starting to get real weird, and there was no telling anymore how they might react to any given situation. Some people might say that we marched to the beat of different drummer, but in reality we were no longer marching, nor did we even have our feet on the ground, for that matter. We were now flying through life like screaming banshees dancing to the tune of screeching bagpipes. So by the time we got halfway across Jersey, Bobby had me convinced that we might really be taking our lives in our hands simply by going to Reading to see these two goofy chicks.

"They're gonna shoot our asses, they're gonna shoot our asses," he kept saying over and over again, and then laughing like one of those phony voices in the Coney Island funhouse.

It was dark by the time we got to Reading and drove down Wyomissing Avenue. The mother's house was the last one in a row and we parked under a bunch of trees a little down the road. While it wasn't exactly in front of the house, it wasn't the height of privacy either. Of course, this didn't deter Bobby from popping Margie right on the front seat. He would have done the same in broad daylight in front of his own mother's house.

But Jane was coy and rightfully apprehensive, so we just curled up in the backseat. I listened to her tell me how much nicer it would be the first time when we could be all alone and take our time and do it right like people do on a honeymoon. If the guys could have heard me listening to this, they would have laughed me out of the club. Fortunately, Bobby was the kind of guy who, in spite of all his faults and problems with speed, would never say a word. As for me, I was loving every minute of it, completely *ferhexed* and *ferhoodled* by this auburn-haired little Dutch girl with the fairytale imagination. And so I wasn't paying much attention to Bobby as we drove through Reading on the way home.

He was pointing out the fact that it wasn't even one o'clock yet and they were probably still partying up at the clubhouse, but by the time we got back to New York, it would be four o'clock and all the bars would be closed. He had a point, and the next thing I knew we were tearing up the road to Mount Penn.

We parked down on the road and walked up behind Chuck's house to the clubhouse, and sure enough they were partying. When I walked in Chuck was sitting in a swivel chair with his back toward me, and everyone else was looking at me. Then Chuck spun around in the chair. He was holding a large caliber revolver and it was pointed right at my gut.

"I'm sick of your shit," he said as he fired the gun.

The whole room shook, my ears rang. I couldn't feel anything. I looked down and didn't see any blood.

Then Chuck started laughing, and everybody else started laughing. And as soon as he figured out what happened—or didn't happen, I should say—Flipout started laughing. Under ordinary circumstances Flipout had an extremely loud, exaggerated, and obnoxious laugh that he practiced just to piss people off, but now he was really overdoing it deliberately as a way of telling me: *It's a joke, laugh, you fuckin' idiot, before they figure out something is supposed to be wrong.*

I don't think I ever laughed. I think I just grinned. Then Chuck jumped up and gave me a big hug and a kiss.

The others told us that someone seen us coming, ran in the clubhouse, and told Chuck that we were coming up the road. They had been fucking around with blanks, so Chuck just sat in the chair, turned his back to the door, and said, "Everybody watch this." And they did. Years later we talked about it one winter night in jail, and Chuck explained that he had no idea that I was seeing Jane at the time.

And after I told my story he said, "You mean you had just come from seeing her?"

"That's right."

"So then you thought? . . . "

"That's right."

"So if you were gonna die, that's exactly the look you would'a had on your face?"

"I guess so. What did it look like?"

"Nothing. You didn't look scared at all."

Maybe I didn't have time, but I sure remember thinking that I was about to avoid the *strohtodt* and die with my boots on.

In any event, the incident sure loosened things up. Now I was in the mood to party. The word was that the mass return of old Heathens that Chuck had anticipated never materialized, but some of the guys were telling us that it was only a matter of time until they would be back flying Pagan colors. One of the old guys that did come back was a big, loud, gregarious character called Frenchy, and he even wore a beret to complete his act. Both his legs were shot from motorcycle wrecks and he hobbled around on a cane, which, when he was not trying to walk, he waved around his head to emphasize various points he was trying to make. Flipout and I took to the guy immediately and we were talking to him, when one of the brothers shoved his head in the door and screamed, "Somebody's stealing a bike!"

This is the outlaw equivalent of "Mayday!" Everyone dropped whatever they had in their hand, unless it was a weapon, and we ran out the door and down the road. The thieves heard us coming. A car raced away. Two other guys were trying to shove a Triumph in the back of a station wagon. When they saw us they dropped the bike and tried to run away. They didn't make it. They had the living shit beat out of them, and then Chuck told them while they were half-conscious to get in the car and never come back.

Then we went back to partying. But finally Bobby told me that he promised to have the car back by 10 in the morning so we had to go. Since it was obvious that I might need it again, I didn't think that this was a bad idea. Meanwhile sometime during the course of the night, Blackie had announced that he was coming back to New York with us, so the three of us started walking down the dark road with Skip and Frenchy.

As we got near the car I heard Bobby whispering, "What the fuuuuuuuuck?"

Then I looked, and I saw that there was no glass where the windshield in the car was supposed to be. When we got up to the car, I saw the windshield shattered all over the front seat.

Then I heard Frenchy shout, "Oh fuck, I'm sorry, I'm sorry!" He had his beret off and was twisting it up in both hands screaming, "I'm sorry, I'm sorry, I didn't know it was your car!" all the while spinning around like a top about to fall over. "I didn't know it was your car! When those guys were stealing the bike, I saw a strange car so I figured it was theirs."

Then Bobby started screaming: "I can't believe that somebody did this to me! This is the kind of shit that I do to other people! I can't believe that somebody actually did it to me for once!"

Meanwhile, Frenchy was still yelling, "I'm sorry! My legs are too fucked up to kick the guys, so I figured I'd bust their windshield instead!"

Bobby grabbed his head with both hands yanked it towards him and planted a big kiss on his lips: "I can't believe that you did this to me. I love you brother." At this point Frenchy's bad legs gave out, and they both tumbled to the ground where they were just laughing and screaming, "I love you brother!"

Then we cleaned off the seat as best we could, got in a car without a windshield, in the middle of the night in March, and started driving back to New York with a 70-mile-an-hour wind in our face.

A cold spring rain started falling before we got to Allentown. By the time we got to Jersey, we were soaked. And there we sat, Bobby behind the wheel, me by the window, and Blackie in the middle, our arms folded, our teeth chattering, a raw, cold, wet wind in our face. A few hours earlier I had been lying in that woman's arms not wanting it to end, and now here I was with these two guys, freezing to death without a windshield in the middle of the night, in the middle of Jersey, in the middle of March.

CHAPTER 13

The proper function of man is to live, not exist.
I shall not waste my days in trying to prolong them.
— Jack London

Blackie wanted to see "the City," which is what people from Brooklyn, Queens, and Long Island call Manhattan. At seven o'clock on a Saturday morning, who knows what he expected to find. But to these guys from out of town, the City was like the Grand Canyon, impressive at any hour of the day or night. So there we sat, in Yorkville in a coffee shop on East 86th Street, with a car with no windshield parked outside, eating strudel, drinking coffee, and just trying to get warm. Our ears were starting to thaw and they stung like all hell. Blackie had sobered up and was now beginning to wonder just what made us show up at the Reading clubhouse in the middle of the night. We told him that we had business in New Jersey.

The sun was now up. We had been up all night and our blood sugar had been depleted by three hours of chattering teeth. So Flipout drove us back to Maspeth, and then he took off for the Island. When we asked him what he was going to say about the windshield, he said that he would think of something. As it turned out, it was a real speed gem. Only he never told me, someone else did.

About six months later, I was sitting in a bar in Bethpage, and Mary Jo, the car's owner, came up to me and said, "That was real righteous, Stoop, the way you stabbed that nigger."

"What?" I shouted.

"The way you stabbed that nigger. In Hempstead."

I didn't say anything. I just let her talk.

"Bobby told me how when that nigger threw the brick through the windshield, you jumped out of the car and chased him for three blocks and stabbed him, and how you woulda killed him if he hadn't stopped you."

"Oh, that nigger," I said.

It was the oldest excuse in the book: "Niggers did it." But if he was going to make up bullshit stories about me, the least he could have done was tell me about it. It didn't matter really; he needed to come up with something and he had done me a favor. Actually, the fact that I didn't remember something as vivid as a stabbing should have told her something in the first place, but it didn't. She had the whole thing firmly planted in her head and apparently wanted to believe it. So I let her. As for the plausibility of the whole thing, that was another story all together.

Not that there was anything suspicious about us riding through niggertown in the middle of the night. We were capable of showing up anywhere at any hour, especially Flipout, and we did sometimes hang out in black clubs. Back in the '60s, black folks tended to be more tolerant than white folks, and nobody bothered us as long as we didn't bother them. But the image of some black kid throwing a brick through our window was another thing. This was 1968, and the only other white people with beards and long hair were hippies. We didn't look anything like them with our greasy pushed back hair and trimmed beards, not to mention the leather, the earrings, and tattoos. No, there was something different about us—greaser, redneck, and violent different—just the sort of thing that any kid would try to avoid tangling with. Kids are not stupid, if they are going to toss a brick through a windshield, they get a good look at the occupant first.

And of course, this doesn't even begin to explore the possibility of how a 210-pound white man, in knee-high motorcycle boots, managed to catch a black kid, in sneakers, in his own neighborhood, with a head start at that. But not all the girls we attracted were as bright as Margie. If Mary Jo wanted to walk around spreading the story that I ran through a black neighborhood after one of their own and then stood on a sidewalk plunging a knife into him while the rest of the neighborhood stood idly by gawking in terror, let her do it. After all, half the shit about Davy Crockett and William Tell was made up, too.

The next night, we dropped off Blackie at the Port Authority Bus Terminal so he could catch a bus to get him back in time for work Monday morning. But as my head was going through the Queens Midtown Tunnel with Tony the Gypsy on the way back to Maspeth, I realized that my heart was on the bus back to Reading with Blackie. I couldn't think about anything else but Jane, and I no longer cared about anything else but Jane. My whole life revolved around Jane. I wrote her a letter every day, and as soon as I got home I reached in the mailbox and ripped open her letters. This went on for about a week, and then we simply decided that she was coming to New York along with Gums.

Now Gums saw a ticket out of Reading to the Big Apple, and she was not about to miss the bus. So she kept Jane from changing her mind, and pretty soon it was all set. Bobby and I would be going to get them on Friday night. I was between jobs, but I had been working as a lithographer and had just gotten a fat income tax return check because I had worked a bunch of overtime the year before. All I needed was a car with a windshield, and Mary Jo was kind of out of the question.

I bought a black '56 Pontiac. Back in the '50s, before John DeLorean and the GTO, Pontiacs were nondescript, indestructible tanks that your grandfather bought once every 10 years. They even steered like tanks, and you would have had trouble putting a dent in one with a sledgehammer. This one stalled out a lot and had no muffler, which made it sound like the Concorde taking off, but it only cost me 10 bucks. So on Friday night, I picked up Bobby and we were on our way with nothing more than a roll of bills, a case of wide-mouth Rheingold bottles, and this monster of a black Frankenstein car.

Jane and Gums had reserved the honeymoon suite at Kline's Motel just outside Reading. They were going to grab a cab after dinner and wait for us there. Bobby, Gums, and the two boys were going to sleep in the front room, and Jane and I were going to have the back room all to ourselves.

Jane was excited about that, and so was I—so excited in fact that I screwed up as soon as we got to Jersey.

I made a wrong turn just below the Newark Airport, and we ended up heading south on an eight-lane divided highway with an island of concrete in the middle. At the time, it was impossible to turn around in New Jersey. You got off one highway and found yourself on another headed someplace else. You simply had to wait until you got to Pennsylvania, Delaware, or the shore to turn around.

I decided not to even fool with the system. So I got all the way over into the far left lane, cut the wheel hard, and tried to jump over the island without breaking something. It worked, but the car came down like a tank with a thud on the other side. When I went to goose the accelerator, it stalled out and flooded—right in the middle of the highway, sideways and blocking the middle two lanes of traffic.

The car was black and it was getting dark; it was overcast and a fine mist was coming down. I tried to start the engine, but it wouldn't start and soon the lights went dim. The battery was low, so I had to shut the lights off to keep the starter cranking. Flipout was laughing his demented ass off, like he always did in situations like this. He was also looking out the passenger window, and I realized that he was thinking the same thing that I was: there were no cars immediately upon us, but there was a large pack of headlights in the distance, covering all four lanes. As long as the engine cranked, we would be out of there. But the headlights of the cars in the distance were coming on fast, so it had better crank soon. It didn't.

The headlights were getting closer and no one was showing any sign of slowing down. We were about to be broadsided by a pack of cars, old-fashioned heavy '50s- and '60s-style tank cars. It would be the ultimate outlaw disgrace, getting wiped out in a stalled car while sitting still in Jersey.

"Just be cool," I told Flipout.

"Hurry the fuck up," he whispered.

I could see that he was getting antsy. After all, he was sitting in the seat closest to them, and the situation was out of his hands. I tried again, but it wouldn't start. The headlights were bearing down on us, and nobody was slowing down. Then they all seemed to start honking their horns at once.

"Be cool, be cool," I whispered to Bobby, as I turned the key one more time.

But finally Bobby just threw the door open and screamed "Bail out," as he jumped out the door and scrambled for the concrete divider island.

Now I could see the headlights coming at me through the open door. They were not slowing down. I had only seconds to either start the car and get out of the way, or abandon it to almost certain annihilation. I cranked it again. It was really getting slow. I threw the headlights on for whatever good that might do now and jumped out the door not a minute too soon. I ran up on the traffic island with Bobby and got ready to watch what I was certain would be the mother of all wrecks.

This was northeast Jersey, which meant that for all intents and purposes, these people were typical New York drivers: go like a bat out of hell and expect everything to clear out of your way. And if it don't, start honking your horn while you practically stand on your brake pedal and curse like all hell. Which is exactly what they did.

At the last minute, a chorus of screeching brakes joined the orchestra of horns. The two cars in the middle lanes swerved right and left, respectively, to avoid slamming into my car, but as they did, they were both hit on the side and spun around. The next two cars managed to swerve into the outside lanes without a collision, and the third set of cars managed to stop, but got rear-ended by the cars behind them. We now heard the sound of crunching metal and busting glass going all the way down the highway as cars started piling up. In a matter of seconds, it was all over—all over the highway. I could see lights reflecting in the green water from busted radiators, and little speckles of red, white, and yellow glass glistened on the wet road. But the big black Pontiac was untouched. The ancient gods of northern Europe tend reward balls rather than humility. Car doors were slamming, and people were getting out and cursing.

"Fuck it," I yelled. "Let's go!"

We ran for the car. I got in, shut off the lights, and turned the key. And the beast started right up.

"We are out of here!" I screamed, as I gunned the motor, cut the wheel, and pulled out to the sound of screeching rubber.

The incident kept us howling all the way to Allentown.

"You lucky motherfucker," Bobby howled as he cracked the tops on two wide-mouth bottles of Rheingold and handed one to me. He was right. It was woven into the rope of destiny. I would sleep in Jane's arms tonight. Nothing could stop me.

Kline's Motel was a typical post–World War II Pennsylvania Dutch tourist motel, complete with hex signs, flower boxes, and loads of red and yellow gingerbread. Inside, it was sparsely but comfortably furnished and cleaner than most New York City hospital rooms.

Gums was hopping up and down in the parking lot with the two kids when she recognized the two bearded faces in the car. Jane was standing in the doorway, silhouetted against the light like a little Dutch farm girl in her bare feet. She was never able to hide her feelings well, so you could see joy and happiness radiating out all over her face.

I ran up and gave her a big hug, grabbing her by the ass with one hand and lifting her off the ground and spinning her around. Then after I said hello to Gums and the kids, we took each other by the hand and led each other into the back room.

The next morning, I woke up with her head on my shoulder. She had an arm and a leg wrapped around me and I could feel her breathing. It felt good, and it wasn't just sex. There was something about her. As I watched her getting dressed, I wanted to get out of Pennsylvania as soon as possible so that nothing could go wrong to keep her and I out of each others arms when it was time to go to bed again.

The ancient Germanic poets of northern Europe believed that there was something so sacred about the bond between a man and a woman that their marriage vows were carved into the spear of Woden, the All-Father. And Richard Wagner celebrated the love between a man and a woman as the most powerful force in the universe. Let cynics say what they want, but there is something mystical about it. Lying there with Jane's head on my shoulder felt better than anything I could remember, better than riding a motorcycle with the wind blowing through my hair. It even felt better than fighting.

But the kids had to eat. So we stopped at a hole-in-the-wall Pennsylvania

Dutch diner, the kind of place that always smells like freshly brewed coffee. The kids had pancakes, the girls English muffins and coffee. New York Germans are fascinated by Pennsylvania Dutch cuisine—that's all they want to eat in the area—so Bobby and I had deep-fried *panhass* (that's the old Dutch word for scrapple) swimming in molasses and a thick slice of warm shoofly pie all covered with whipped cream.

Bobby was nervous. Chances were slim that anyone we knew would walk in, but he had a point. If anyone saw me and him there with Gums, Jane, and Rayels' two kids, the situation would demand some sort of explanation. The only plausible one was the truth, which I didn't want to have to deal with yet.

So after breakfast we piled into the car, emanating that warm super-charged feeling that comes from having eaten deep-fried *panhass*, molasses, shoofly pie, and whipped cream with about six cups of coffee with real cream and sugar. Soon we were across the Delaware River and flying through the Jersey Meadowlands. Bobby kept fiddling with the radio, trying to find the oldies station, which he did, just about the time the girls got their first glimpse of the New York skyline. Soon we were whizzing across Staten Island in this beat-up piece of black metal with no muffler. Jane was scrunched up against me with her hand resting on the inside of my leg. Bobby was riding shotgun and slapping his hands on the dashboard, beating out the rhythm to Tommy Roe on the radio singing "Sweet Little Sheila." And Gums was in the backseat with the two kids pointing excitedly at the skyline.

We dropped Bobby off in Massapequa, and I knew that after a couple of speed hits, the news of our arrival would be all over Long Island. So I just started driving east, out into the Suffolk County Pine Barrens, past Lindenhurst, past Ronkonkoma, past Northport. Then out past Patchogue and the Polack potato farms, and the duck and strawberry farms, almost to Riverhead. We finally stopped somewhere off Montauk Highway at a motel surrounded by nothing but sand and dead weeds and pine trees. It was nothing at all like the Dutch farmlands of Berks County, and to Jane and Gums, it might as well have been the moon.

As for myself, I just wanted a day to sort things out and think, which was impossible with Bobby around, since he was always trying to do something to get your full attention back to him, even if it was throwing a brick through the window of a closed store to make the alarm go off.

We let the kids run around in the sand and the weeds for a while. Then we found an old log cabin bar that served German food and imported Dinkelacker beer from Stuttgart. As soon as the kids fell asleep, we took off our clothes and got into bed. Gums sat up on the other bed where the two kids were sleeping and watched TV, while Jane and I just laid there as close as we could get and talked to each other in whispers until we fell asleep.

The next day we drove to Freeport, an old seaport on the western end of the Great South Bay on the southern shore of Long Island. I was familiar with Freeport from back in the days when I was a sparring partner for Bobby Stallings. Stallings was handled by Johnny O'Rourke, an old-fashioned Irish fight manager who wore a Humphrey Bogart hat and top coat, and who wouldn't dream of going out for a pack of cigarettes without putting on a tie. O'Rourke had a gym in Freeport, which was a town in transition. The old part was working-class blacks, but along the channels that feed into the bay, that area was prime real estate. But one of the best-kept secrets on Long Island was that off-season the motel rates were ridiculously cheap.

The Freeport Motor Inn and Marina was located on one of the channels that fed into the bay. We got a second-floor room for 35 bucks a week, with no questions asked. You could walk out the door, stand on a deck, and stare out across the bay at Jones Beach, and there were two boats tied up to the dock right below the deck. In another two months, the rates would soar through the roof, but right now it was the perfect hideout for me and two Dutch girls from Pennsylvania.

After we got settled in, I drove up to Hicksville with Jane and the two kids to meet my family. I suppose I could have prepared them better. But in true outlaw style, I had told them nothing. I hadn't even told them that I had a girlfriend, a nice girl who I really liked and who, in their language, I was serious about, much less that I would be bringing her down from Pennsylvania along with two little boys and a friend with no teeth. But we were only 20 and convinced that we had found the love of our lives.

They took it in typical German style, nonplussed. They said hello and my mother rummaged around until she found enough for everyone

200

to eat. Then, while we ate, she found an old hot plate and started filling shopping bags with cans and boxes of food. "I'm worried that those boys aren't going to get enough to eat," she said.

When we got back to the motel, Jane pulled a box out of the bag. "How do you make rice?" she asked. At the time the Pennsylvania Dutch were still all noodles, dumplings, and potatoes. Rice was considered a foreign food.

Monday morning I was out early. It was now time to deal with club business. A heavy storm had blown in off the Atlantic Ocean, which would at least make it easier to find people. The first one I found was Bobo. An outlaw club can get itself in a jam in about as much time as it takes to squeeze a trigger or render a bar to splinters. Since no one had seen Bobby or me since Wednesday, naturally Bobo had been worried.

Fortunately nothing had gone down, but when he heard what I had done, he insisted that Rayels was probably on his way down to shoot me. So he made me go and get my gun, which was stashed in Maspeth, but I had to see the Gypsy anyhow. Apartments were tough to come by in Polack Alley. They were usually only rented to relatives, so you needed an in. I told the Gypsy to start looking because I would have to be out of the marina in a couple of weeks.

I drove Bobo back to Oyster Bay. He was in a couple of real tight jams, and he explained that he might be taking off on the lam for Florida until it all blew over. Naturally, he was nervous every time we saw a cop car. In those days they might still stop you for a loud muffler, and he didn't want to be checked out. The cops also had been coming around asking questions about me. Up to now it had been a joke, and it probably was just chicken shit. But suddenly I got this unfamiliar feeling in my stomach, as I asked myself what would happen to Jane if I went to jail, even if it was only for a couple of days. Who the hell would take care of her? I couldn't afford to go to jail. I didn't want to go to jail. For the first time in my life I cared, even if it was for someone else's sake.

I thought about this all the way back to Freeport. I couldn't run the club in my usual style if I had to be afraid of getting busted. This seemed like a fatal flaw for the leader of an outlaw club. On the other hand, I didn't want to let down Jane.

I got over it as soon as I got back to the marina. Gums had the kids down on the dock looking at the boats. That gave Jane and me a few moments to ourselves in the daytime. We just lay on the bed, and I could feel her soft auburn brown hair on my cheek as I smelled the marshy salt-water from the channel drifting in through the open window. Spring was in the air and my life was going uphill.

As it turned out, Gums had even found a dress factory down the road and gotten a job while I was out. She was not fooling around. She was determined to make it in New York.

That night Jane and I went out by ourselves. Behind the marina there was a small bar on the channel. It was one of the few hole-in-the-wall places still left that catered to the local wharf rats. Most of them weren't real sailors, but they were guys who had spent their lives around boats or at least around saltwater. And they dressed the part: sailor hats, shirts with red stripes running sideways, white denim pants, and canvas sneakers.

There were a few of these guys at the bar, smoking cigarettes and drinking beer. Past the bar was a backroom with a pool table. It had started to rain and there was another storm coming in. The pool table took up half the backroom and the other half was under about six inches of saltwater. The water was actually moving in waves and splashing up against the wall. No one but Jane and I seemed to be impressed.

"Does this happen often?" I asked the bartender.

"Only when there's a storm," he said, without even taking the cigarette out of his mouth.

I looked at the walls and saw that the varnish on the wainscoting had been eaten away by saltwater. We shot pool by ourselves and drank pitchers of beer, watching the waves crash against the wall and giving each other big, dramatic passionate kisses between shots.

By the time we left, we were so trashed we fell trying to climb the stairs behind the marina and just sat there on the steps laughing at ourselves in the pouring rain. We started kissing and I started pulling her blouse off.

"Let's get inside," she said.

As we lay under the sheets naked with our wet hair on the pillow, I could smell the bay and hear the rain. I knew that in a week or so I would be down at the Amalgamated Lithographers union hall looking for work.

The Gypsy still was looking for apartments in Polack Alley. He had remembered a guy who owned a grocery store with an apartment on the second floor. He said that the guy was constantly afraid of getting robbed and maybe he could be convinced that nobody would dare rob a store if you had one of those guys you read about in the paper living upstairs.

A couple of days later Bobby Flipout was arrested again. He had been caught by a cop taking a piss in the parking lot at Nathan's. When push came to shove, the cop made a big deal out of it, and Bobby was sitting in the can. By now Mrs. Bertsch usually took his altercations with the law in stride, but this time she was going off like Davy Supermouth went off the time his old lady ran off with Billy.

"Lew-ed-ness, lew-ed-ness!" she shouted into the phone at me. "Can you believe that? He was arrested for 'pub-lick lew-ed-ness!'" Making it sound like he was waving it around in a schoolyard full of kids. She was actually more upset about this "publick lewedness," as she pronounced it, than she was about all his assault and drug charges.

In the end, we found a girl who had been with him in the parking lot, and she convinced his mother that it was dark and he was behind a bunch of cars. The cop was hiding and just waiting to bust someone for anything. In other words *the cops were picking on him again.* So Mrs. Bertsch calmed down and bailed him out again.

Meanwhile, Bobo gave me a stiff lecture on the welfare system. I wasn't interested, but he insisted that I listen anyhow. "It ain't just for niggers and Puerto Ricans," he said. "White folks got the same fuckin' rights in this country as niggers and Puerto Ricans do. We work and pay taxes and it's as much our money as theirs. In fact they got a list of essential shit like beds, couches, tables, chairs, and dishes. And they have to buy it for you. Furthermore, they got to find you an apartment in 48 hours or else they gotta start pickin' up the tab on the motel."

"But I don't want to live in niggertown," I told him.

"You won't have to," he said. "They'll find you a place in Maspeth or Ridgewood. I'm telling you, they'll cut her a check right on the spot."

He had me thinking. Law enforcement authorities, such as retired police detectives and professors of criminal justice, made a good living by

RIDING ON THE EDGE: A MOTORCYCLE OUTLAW'S TALE

going to seminars and lecturing people on how we rake in bales of money selling drugs, stealing cars, and peddling pussy. But it was all lies to scam the public and make a buck for themselves. We were outlaws, not crooks and pimps. In fact we were stone broke most of the time. So I decided, "what the fuck, give it a try," and I took Jane down to the welfare office.

Jamaica, Queens. It's a shithole today, and it was already a shithole back then. I had sent Jane and the two kids into the welfare office, and I was sitting in the car, because there was no place to go. The few white bars that were left had names like the Lakes of Killarney or the Rose of Tralee, but like everything else in Jamaica, they were shitholes, too. They were dark and smelled of stale beer. The only people in them during the day were retired Irish pricks with their white hair and shitty skin with melanomas the size of dried prunes. World War II veterans who thought everyone with long hair and a beard was a Communist. They hated people who wore swastikas almost as much as they hated the niggers, who they thought were ruining their precious shithole of a neighborhood. So rather than risk a fight I couldn't afford right now, I just sat in the car.

As it turned out, Bobo was dead wrong. Jane had to spend half the day in an un-air-conditioned office, sitting wedged between two smelly lard-fed welfare sows with a pack of unruly pickaninnies running all over the place. When she finally got her turn, a large ham-faced white woman, probably from Jackson Heights, told her that she had no business in New York and that they would get her and her kids bus tickets back to Pennsylvania.

In other words, the old woman had lied. Had Jane been black or Puerto Rican, the ham-headed pasty-faced Nazi from Jackson Heights would have been scared to death by her. There is no way in hell she would have said, *We're going to give you a ticket back to San Juan or Georgia.* But here this middle-aged, middle-class white woman had to sit in her office doling out taxpayer money to blacks and Puerto Ricans all day long, and she hated every minute of it. So when she got the chance to bring down the hammer on some poor little white girl from Pennsylvania, she brought it down hard. Bobo, the outlaw, obviously had too much faith in straight America and its political system.

When we got back to the motel Jane was feeling pretty sad, so she called her mother for the first time in a week. That turned out to be a mistake. About 15 minutes later, Bob Rayels called to talk to her.

I heard her saying, "No, no, I can't. I don't want to." Then she handed the phone to me and said, "He wants to talk to you."

"How is she?" he wanted to know.

"Fine."

"And how are the boys?"

"I'll take good car of them," I promised. Then it began to get messy.

"Can you send her home?"

"She's gotta make up her own mind," I said.

"I really love her," he said.

This is exactly what I didn't want to hear. We were passionate, we were temperamental. Let him come after me with a shotgun and I could handle it. Rage, anger, bring it on. I could even shoot the bastard to protect myself, but that didn't mean that I still didn't really like the guy. We had lived up on the hill together and shared every penny we had. We'd gotten in fights together and protected each other's backs. It was just a matter of fate that we also shared a remarkably similar taste in women. Throughout it all, I had allowed myself to believe that he couldn't really still like her, because I didn't even want to think about the possibility of it coming down to a mess like this. And now here he was telling me that he still loved her. What could I do?

"So do I, brother," was all I could say because my voice was about to crack and there were tears in my eyes, and he sounded the same way.

Those were the last words we ever spoke to one another.

CHAPTER 14

In a Christian Society the true Puritan worships the Devil.
— George Bernard Shaw on Diavolonian Ethics, paraphrased from his introductory essay to the play *Devil's Disciple*

The next day I was on a high. I talked to a lithographer, and he told me that things were really hoppin' down at the union hall; there were plenty of short-time gigs to fill in for guys on vacation. That meant I could work for a week or two and then take time off if I needed it. Or I could always shape up with the Teamsters one day at a time. Flipout was also out of the can. Gypsy had a lead on another apartment, but wanted to talk to the guy first to calm him down and assure him that I wouldn't be bringing more trouble than I was worth. Also, right after I got done talking to Rayels, I called Big Dutch and told him I had Rayels' old lady up in New York with me.

"That sounds like a personal problem," he said, and that pretty well settled matters as far as the club was concerned.

I was coming back to Freeport late that afternoon. Without thinking, or looking, I pulled into the motel parking lot, and only then did I see two state police cruisers sitting right under the window of our room. If I had looked, I would have seen them, because there was only one other guest in the motel and the parking lot was almost empty. I was getting careless—real careless.

Now I could not, even in my wildest imagination, think of why the cops would want to talk to Jane or Gums, but I could easily think of a half-dozen reasons why they might want to talk to me. I drove the car down to the end of the motel by the dock, figuring that it was safer than letting them see me fly out of the parking lot. Then I got out and walked out on the dock by the weeds, figuring I could wander off into the marsh if they came out.

The thing that had me confused was the fact that they were state cop cars. Our official club business was usually conducted through the Nassau County Police or the NYPD. But as I was trying to figure this all out, the motel door opened and two cops came out along with Jane and the two kids. Then out came a middle-aged black-haired woman and a man about her age, and then another woman in her 20s and then Bob Rayels. *Oh shit,* I thought, *did they ever pull a fast one on us.*

Jane and the kids left in two cars with Pennsylvania plates, and the two police cruisers left with them. I had been so preoccupied with the two police cruisers that I didn't notice the cars with Pennsylvania plates, or it might have all started to make sense. When I got upstairs to the room, Gums was sitting on the bed, a mixture of terror and shock smeared across her toothless face. But when she saw that I wasn't going to throw a tantrum and smash up her or the room, she relaxed.

"The first thing Jane said was 'I'm not going back,'" she explained, "But then her mother said, 'You can sit in this motel with your boyfriend until you die, but *we're* here to take *those two kids* back to Pennsylvania.'"

Now it was all a crock of shit. She was their mother and she had every right to be in New York with her kids. But she was only a kid herself, and when she saw her mother with the two cops, she figured that the old woman had the full weight of the law behind her. And she probably did, because in those days, cops could still pretty much do whatever they wanted to fuck with people, just like the lady from Jackson Heights at the welfare office had done the previous day. So Jane thought she had no choice but to go with her kids like any decent mother would do.

While Gums was explaining this, the phone rang and she picked it up. It was the desk clerk telling us that we had to get out immediately because we had brought the cops down on the place. Of course we hadn't done anything, and the clerk didn't volunteer to refund our money for the rest of the week. It was all part of the Jackson Heights–welfare–police syndrome. But at this point I no longer cared. Gums and I were going back to Pennsylvania.

But not in any great hurry. Even though we were out of the motel in about five minutes, we sat in rush-hour traffic for hours. When we finally did get to Jersey, we headed for North Bergen. They had just formed a Pagan chapter up there, and we liked the guys a lot. They reminded us of the Bronx Aliens. They had all grown up together and most of them had known each other since kindergarten.

I stopped in a bar where they hung out. One of the guys got on the phone, and pretty soon everyone was coming in just to say hello. I told them what I was up to, and they asked me what kind of heat I was carrying. I told them about my 1911 Colt. One of the guys went out to his car and came back in the bar with a loaded shotgun.

"Here take this," he said. "They're going to shoot you up there."

Now just who was going to shoot me and why, we never got into. And actually the whole thing seemed pretty ludicrous. Here I was drinking beer in some shithole in Jersey with a 10-gauge shotgun sitting in front of me on the bar. And what was it supposed to be for? To shoot Chuck? Blackie? Elroy? Little Joe?

While I was sitting at the bar getting wasted and getting lectured on how to watch my ass, the Beaute came in. He was a tall lanky guy with a beard and hair like Jesus Christ. He always wore big white plastic sunglasses and he talked like he was stoned, drunk, and tripping at the same time. "He wasn't always this way," the guys said, and they once told me that when they were eight years old, they were sledding in the street and Beaute got run over and nearly killed by a car. He was never right after that. But like with Elroy and other guys who weren't 100 percent right, the club always took care of its own.

The Beaute started hitting on Gums, and I called her over and asked her if she would do me a favor and take Beaute out in his car. The two of them walked out and the rest of us sat drinking. When they did not return for a couple of hours, one of the Jersey guys went out to see what happened to them. He came back in shaking his head and muttering. It seems they were sitting in the front seat of Beaute's van and Gums was wearing a cut-off denim vest that said "Property of Beaute" on the back.

"No!" I yelled. "I need her! He can't do that to me."

"I'll go out and talk to him," the Jersey president said. He explained to me that the Beaute had gotten a set of property colors made up even though he didn't have an old lady to put them on. But he carried them around everywhere he went, hoping that he would find one, and on more than one occasion, a brother had to walk up to some drunken slut in a bar and lift them off her. "Don't worry," he told me, he would take care of it.

As it was they didn't have to. Gums had anticipated the problem and had it all worked out. She explained that she had told Beaute that she had to go back to Pennsylvania with me to get Jane, and she would stay with me for as long as that took. She had promised. But then, after we got Jane, she was coming back to live with Beaute and his mom and two sisters. Never mind that she had never met his mom and two sisters. Life has a way of taking care of things, and we had a history of ignoring important details, such as what Beaute's mom and two sisters might say when their eccentric son and brother came home with a girl with no teeth who he met in a bar, like she was some stray kitten he found in the street.

Gums looked wonderful. I had never seen a woman's face as radiant and beautiful as Margie's when she walked back in the bar with her new property colors. She had been around the club and looking for her own set of property colors longer than the Beaute had been riding around looking for someone to put a set on. In her eyes right now, that raggedy denim vest was better than a diamond ring, a fur coat, or a villa in France.

She was leaning with both hands on my knees and looking up at me with big blue eyes that were saying, *Please don't make me give them back.*

And what could I do? I was as *ferhexed* and *ferhoodled* as anyone at the time. If I couldn't sympathize with her, no one could.

Actually, as I began to ponder the implications of the situation, it looked like a tremendous stroke of luck. Gums would be traveling with me to Reading, to Norristown, and who knows where else. I could have started a war between two clubs over one woman, and it would be extremely awkward for me to show up with yet another woman and claim that she was under my protection and off limits to the rest of the club. And if I did end up having any dealings with the Heathens, there was no way I could pull this off, especially with Gums.

But by showing up with *Property of Beaute* on her back, the matter was out of my hands. I was now escorting a brother's old lady, and by all outlaw standards, I was honor-bound to shoot if necessary to protect a brother's property that had been left in my care. I could not have wished for a better development.

We left Jersey in the middle of the night, drunk, and drove onto a dirt road in a cornfield between Kutztown and Reading. We pulled into a patch of trees and brush, shut the lights off, and sat there for about 20 minutes, sucking Rheingold beer out of wide-mouth bottles from a six-pack the Jersey brothers had given us so that we wouldn't get thirsty. After we were convinced that nobody had seen us and was going to follow us or call the cops, we went to sleep with the loaded shotgun in my lap.

It was April in rural Pennsylvania, we were drunk, and we soon fell asleep. But we woke up in the dark, shaking and freezing. The heater in the car didn't work, and Gums said that we were stupid for not grabbing a couple of blankets from the motel. We ended up snuggled against each other, shivering and with our teeth chattering. We might have been better off if we'd started fooling around and got each other all worked up. But that was out of the question. She was now Beaute's old lady, and like I said, on some things like loyalty, we were more rigid than the Mennonites.

Finally about dawn, we decided to drive around and hope the car would warm up. We drove all over Berks County and ended up on a rural back road in a rundown shanty of a diner, eating grilled cinnamon sticky buns and drinking coffee next to a cast-iron radiator that hissed and blew steam. Between the sugar, caffeine, and the radiator, we were soon feeling a lot better, and we started talking about what we were going to do next.

We realized that we had no clue what sort of reception we might get from the Heathens. And there was no point in even trying to get in touch with any member other than Chuck to find out, because Chuck would be calling the shots. The others wouldn't know anything, anyway, but they would be able to tell Chuck that I was in town. As for confronting Chuck, I wasn't ready for that yet, and a lot of it had to do with the fact that I was simply embarrassed. We were two leaders of local clubs and we were supposed to keep other members from pulling shit like this, as Chuck would say, "over some leaky cunt." And what could I say? *That I was in love?*

Gums explained that there was no way Jane was going to be back up the hill with Rayels, so the only place she could be was at her mother's place in Shillington. This could be a big problem she said. Gums knew the whole family. The mother was a real piece of work.

Gums tried to call. It didn't work. The family knew that she had been in New York with Jane. So the sister just told her she went home with Rayels and the two of them had a lot to work out. Then we went to a friend's house and had her call. She got the same answer that Gums did. They were taking no chances. I suggested that maybe they were telling the truth. But Gums was Jane's best friend, and she insisted that there was no way she was back with Rayels. She insisted that we try riding past the house. We did and she saw one of the boys looking out the window.

"They're lying, they're lying," she said. "There's no way that she would leave those two kids."

So now we knew what we were up against. The woman was under virtual house arrest. There was little we could do but ride around or drink beer. We stopped in a roadhouse. The Old Dutch tasted great, but we soon realized that we were exhausted, from excitement, from sitting up in the cold all night, and from being hung over. We needed sleep. Gums suggested that we go to her granny's.

As it turned out, the old woman lived by herself like a hex in the middle of a cornfield, in a trailer that was one of those original silver bullet jobs that were really designed to be pulled behind a car. It was not much larger than a porta-potty, but she was delighted to have company. She was so much a part of a lost rural world that she would not have known who the

Pagans were, or even understood if Margie had tried to explain. She just assumed that I must be Margie's boyfriend, and she sat in a chair talking a mile a minute while we sat at the table trying not to fall asleep. Finally, the old woman fell asleep in the chair, like she always did, while Margie slept in her bed and I slept on the floor under the table.

The next day we drove down to Norristown, where I explained my predicament to Jerry and Dirty Hombre. It was never quite clear which of them was running the club, and they seemed to like it that way. Jerry immediately saw it as more than a personal problem.

"If anything happens to you while you're up there," he said, "I'm the one who is going to have to go down there and straighten it out. I'm the one who's going to have to explain it to Dutch and your people in New York when they call." He thought it would be a good idea to call Chuck and just ask "what's going on" and "where do your people stand on this issue."

Chapter president or not, I was in his town and I took orders from him just like anyone else in the club. So Gums and I headed up to Ozark's place in Lansdale. The New York and Jersey people were big by any standards, and that was simply because we tended to attract barroom brawlers. But the Norristown brothers were relatively small guys. That didn't mean they were afraid to rumble, they were just relatively small guys. But Ozark was the exception. He, along with a guy they called "Herc," stood out like two Harley-Davidsons at a Honda rally. Ozark was big, Ozark was bad, Ozark was a brawler. He lived by himself in a little white house in the middle of a cemetery in Lansdale off the Northeast Extension of the Pennsylvania Turnpike.

When we got there the place was empty, but there was beer in the refrigerator. We were both asleep before we finished half a bottle. I woke up when I heard Ozark coming in. He was a big hillbilly and made more noise than Sweet William used to. He had heard we were going to be there, so he had gone to scrounge up more beer, and had made a couple of phone calls. People started showing up, like Satan, which meant that we spent the afternoon cracking on each other with everyone trying to outdo Satan.

The next morning I went to see Jerry. He had talked to Chuck, and

Chuck had told him that, as far as he was concerned, it was a bunch of personal shit "over some leaky cunt." And that was it. He wasn't too happy with the example I was setting, but as always, I was more than welcome.

I drove up to the clubhouse on Mount Penn with Gums. Chuck didn't say anything about Gums, but being a Dutchman you could read the emotions on his face like it was a message on a roadside billboard. It was obvious that he wasn't exactly sure how, but he knew damn well that she was somehow implicated in my skullduggery. And he didn't like it. But when he saw her wearing a denim vest with Beaute's property colors, he lightened up and cracked a smile. Like everyone else, he liked Beaute and his property colors would be respected in Reading.

He was glad to have the resources of another chapter president, and he began by sitting me down and running club problems by me like he used to do with Rayels. Also, because I wasn't working and he was, he could use me to run around town during the day taking care of business.

One of the first things we had to deal with was Peanut Butter. Chuck wanted to bring Peanut Butter around as a prospective member. The problem was that, according to Blackie, Peanut Butter's mother was Pennsylvania Dutch, but his father was a black Puerto Rican.

Chuck brought it up at a meeting in his usual style. He said that he wanted to bring Peanut Butter around, and if anyone had a problem with that, he wanted to hear about it right now. If nobody said nothing Peanut Butter would be down at the next meeting as a prospect and he never wanted to hear nothing about it again. Nobody had a problem, but one guy did raise a legitimate question. He said that he didn't see the club having any problem with Peanut Butter, but he said that Peanut Butter had to understand that if we ever have a hassle with blacks, they ain't his brothers, we are, and he's going to have to stomp their asses.

At this point Blackie interrupted. He said that it wouldn't be a problem because Peanut Butter once told him, "White people don't think I'm white, and black people don't think I'm black, and the Puerto Ricans tell me I ain't a real Puerto Rican because I can't speak a lick a Spanish. And that's what's been causing me most of my problems since I popped out of my mother's hole."

That did it. This was just the sort of guy that made the Pagans as tight as the medieval brotherhood of Teutonic Knights. In a room full of whites, he was a Pagan and didn't have to give a shit about what a bunch of white rednecks thought. Among blacks, he was a Pagan and didn't have to give a shit about what some crazy niggers thought either. As for the spics, they could go chicken-fuck themselves, too. Peanut Butter went on to become a brother, and a good one at that.

The next problem was a bit more complicated. A new chapter was prospecting in Lancaster County, and as it was, they eventually turned out to be what Sleepy used to call "a bunch of real rubberholes." They were getting no respect in Lancaster, and Satan was soon on the horn going ballistic over the club being embarrassed in his hometown. Chuck was ordered to take over direct control of the club. He made them come to Reading on Sunday afternoons for their meetings, where they explained that the problem was a bunch of guys who spent their afternoons hanging out in a diner. It seemed that they were the ones who were badmouthing them, and that's why they got no respect.

Chuck pulled me aside and explained, "If I go down there, I have to take a day off work. So can you ride down and check these guys out for me?" I told him I would, and he told the guys from Lancaster to come and pick me up on Tuesday morning.

Three of them came and got me and we rode down to Lancaster. We pulled up to the diner in a car without wearing our colors, and they explained to me that I would find the three biggest wiseacres all sitting in the same booth toward the end of the counter. I had been through this before. Go in and walk through the diner, right past them, but without making eye contact, just like you're minding your own business and only going to take a piss.

As it was, the restrooms really were at that end of the diner, and since we had been drinking beer I really had to piss. As I stood over the urinal, I could feel an adrenaline rush like you get before you enter the ring or get out on a wrestling mat. When I got done, I wet my hands and pushed my hair back. I looked in the mirror and knew what I had to do.

I came out, walked over to the booth and grabbed the guy with his back toward me by the back of his collar and the seat of his pants. I pulled him right out of the seat and threw him over the counter and onto the stove. That spooked the cook and he ran away. Then as the guy in the opposite seat started to stand up, I hit him square on the jaw with an overhand right and he dropped face down on the table. The third guy tried to climb under the table and I kicked the shit out of him with my boot until I hit my leg on the table and gave myself a charley horse. Meanwhile, the guys from Lancaster had gotten out of the car and were watching the whole thing through the window with their mouths hanging wide open.

They had obviously never seen anything like that before, and they squealed about it all the way back to Reading. But when we got back to the clubhouse, Chuck just sat and listened with this cold, icy, iron-faced stare.

"I'll see you guys next week," he told them when they got done.

Then, when they left, he turned to me and smiled: "I suppose they couldn't have done that by themselves."

"That's exactly what I was thinking all the way back," I said. "But I wanted to let you make that decision yourself."

The next week the prospective chapter was dissolved.

Over the next couple of weeks, things settled into a routine. I was back up on Mount Penn and things were like old times, except without Rayels, and of course I would have preferred to be with Jane.

Gums had found out through a series of phone calls that Jane was pretty much under house arrest at her mother's. Rayels was coming over every night and sleeping on the couch. Having been confronted with the prospect of Jane living in New York, the family had decided to make a pact with the demon from Reading in order to thwart the designs of the demon from Long Island.

With the whole family working on her, and Rayels coming over every night, it was obvious that things were not going our way. Even Gums had pointed out that if Jane wanted to run away again, she would have found a way to do it by now. And even if she did, we were about broke and would have a real hump of it with the two kids. Then one Saturday, a bunch of guys from Jersey showed up. The Beaute was with them, and he and Gums were as obviously *ferhexed* and *ferhoodled* as I was. I could tell that Gums wanted to go back with them and was trying to figure out how to break the news to me, so finally I just told her that she might as well go, because things were not working out for us.

Margie left. Now with her gone, I had only the Heathens. Not only weren't they sympathetic, but I also had to pretend around them that I didn't give a damn about the whole thing. They were obviously sick of the whole affair, and they seemed to be getting the feeling that Jane had something to do with Rayels dropping his colors. If they saw that she had *ferhexed* yet another brother—well, these guys were not part of the twentieth century and their thinking would have been like that of the Middle Ages, when people believed in witchcraft. Which brings us to another interesting point.

As I sat there on cold rainy nights drinking White Lightning and beer, guys like Skip, Elroy, and Little Joe often made references to something called *pow-wow*. And when they did, they always looked at me askance. It seems at first they thought that being a New Yorker, I might laugh at them. But finally, after some prodding, I got it out of them. *Pow-wow* is Pennsylvania Dutch witchcraft, a hybrid of Old World folklore and American Indian beliefs. Every one of them had a story about some old woman who claimed that when she was a girl she got a love potion from an "herb granny," mixed it with her menstrual blood, and slipped it to some young man at a dance. A week later he proposed, and now they've been married for 50 years. Then there were stories about how someone put a hex on someone and a week later the person died, or broke their leg, or their barn burned down, or some other terrible thing happened to them. It seemed that these otherwise fearless outlaws had a great awe for this thing they called *pow-wow*, so one day I asked Chuck about it.

He simply said that he didn't believe in it himself, but that when you got out of town and into the country, he knew many people—people that he respected, "people like you and me," he said—who put a great deal of stock in it. "So my attitude is, why fuck with something you don't understand if you don't have to."

So there I spent the better part of a month, drinking White Lightning and Old Overholt, and listening to *pow-wow* stories at night, and during the day, I just sat around staring into the cold spring rain, feeling *ferhexed* and *ferhoodled*, and wondering if there was anything to *pow-wow* and love potions.

CHAPTER 15

The day-to-day realities of being an outlaw motorcyclist in California are not easily transplantable. Bikes are a sunshine thing; they are dangerous and uncomfortable in rain and snow.

— Hunter S. Thompson

No shit, Hunter.

In the Appalachian Mountains of Pennsylvania, the temperatures drop to 20 below in January and February. Sometimes it doesn't go above zero for weeks at a time. Then the last week in February, or the first week in March, the sun comes out and the temperature goes up to 50 for a couple of days. The wiseacres start to say, "Spring is here." Then the sun goes away, and a cold rain falls every day, sometimes until between Memorial Day and Fourth of July. Even in the summer, you never go anywhere without your leather jacket, a pair of gloves, and a flannel shirt, and at any time you can be caught under a bridge, waiting out a storm. September and October are gorgeous—nothing but sunshine, clear blue skies, and gold and red autumn foliage. But even then, the temperatures seem to drop 20 degrees as soon as the shadows of the mountains fall across the roads in the twilight. Then comes Halloween; the leaves are gone and the snowflakes again begin to fly. In other words, you have to be nuts to own a motorcycle in Pennsylvania.

Nevertheless, Pennsylvanians stubbornly persist in maintaining the second highest motorcycle registration in the country, higher than New York, or even sunshine states like Texas and Florida. Take away Philadelphia, and rural Pennsylvania may have more motorcycles per capita than the whole state of California. On a Sunday afternoon in the Pennsylvania mountains, you can see more American bikes than cars on the road.

Picture a dilapidated old shanty or a run-down trailer in the Appalachian or Blue Ridge Mountains, with a beat-up old four-wheel-drive pickup truck parked in the mud outside. Inside, you'll find a wood-burning stove and a couple of hunting rifles and handguns, and outside a couple of barking dogs and a steel shed. And if you pop open the doors on that shed, you're likely to find a big American V-Twin motorcycle worth more than everything else on the property put together. No, motorcycle riding in Pennsylvania is not an activity for sunshine boys.

And here I was in rainy April, sleeping on a damp couch in the clubhouse, smoking unfiltered Camel cigarettes, and drinking Pennsylvania White Lightning to numb the cold, until Blackie felt sorry for me. He brought me home, where I slept on a dry couch with a cat named Spooky. But even then, we ran out of oil and froze all night.

Finally, a day rolled around when the first breath of spring air blew in off the Blaubarrick. Skip and Tom came up and said, "We're riding tonight and you're comin." They were heading down the Oley Valley to the Pleasantville Hotel.

"It's the closest thing we got to New York," Blackie said. "It's a bunch of hicks, but they got a band and a real go-go dancer."

The brothers began pulling up to the clubhouse about seven o'clock: first Blackie, dressed all in black on his black hog, and then Skip and Tom and Grizzly. It was the first decent riding weather of the season and they were pumped. They drank everything they could find in the clubhouse. Then they turned on Chuck and drank up the six-pack he had in the refrigerator. While we were drinking it, Chuck told us not to make plans for Saturday night because there was going to be a big party at the clubhouse.

We were out in his yard wrestling and grab-assing, and trying to set each other on fire, until finally Eggy pulled up. At 32, Eggy was completely bald on top, and this was a problem. Buzzed heads were definitely not in style back then, since every Dutchman over 60 seemed to have one. When Eggy tried to grow his hair long, it didn't make him look like a badass, it only made him look like a deranged scientist. So he finally found the solution to his problem, by giving himself a Mohawk—well, half a Mohawk anyhow—down the back of his head. He was delighted with it and was prancing around the yard showing it off. He had also found an 18-year-old girlfriend, whom he kept calling his teenybopper. Actually he was crazy about her. He had to be. He was the only one who brought a wife or girlfriend that night.

So about six of us got on our bikes and rode down Mount Penn, racing and wheelieing all the way down the Oley Valley toward Pleasantville. The Oley Valley is one of those pockets where the locals still speak a bastardized form of German. The farms have been in families for centuries, and the mortgages were paid off by selling rye whiskey to George Washington's army. The locals were well-fed and prosperous; maybe not athletic enough to run a race, but big enough to throw around bales of hay like they were pillows.

The Pleasantville Hotel was an old wood-frame building, originally designed to house itinerant farm workers, but now it was primarily a Dutch redneck roadhouse featuring honky-tonk music and cold beer. Inside, little had changed since the depression. There was a wood floor, an ornate back bar, and tin ceilings, as well as two rooms: a front room with the bar, bandstand, and dance floor and a back room with chairs and tables and a go-go girl so skinny and flat-chested that everyone called her "Broomstick."

When we walked in, I noticed a bouncer sitting on a stool by the door. It was Big Jim Solley, Chuck's old sergeant at arms. I hadn't seen him in months since he quit the club, so I said hello and he acted genuinely glad to see us, although he did seem to have an *oh shit, why did they have to pick this place* look on his face.

The bar was loaded with corn-fed Pennsylvania Dutch farmers. The band was playing the usual rockabilly and country covers, like Kitty Wells' "It Wasn't God Who Made Honky Tonk Angels." Most of the girls looked the part of the song, but there was one that stood out. And she was hot. She was wearing her hair straight and natural, like most of the girls were now wearing it in New York and Philly. But in those days, it took style changes, like bell-bottom pants, a year or two to filter down from New

York and Philly to places like the Oley Valley. She was also wearing a simple white dress with spaghetti straps and no bra. In New York she would have been lost in the crowd, but here in rural Berks County she stood out like Pamela Anderson at an Amish wedding.

The six of us got a table, sat down, and grabbed a couple of pitchers of Old Dutch beer. Blackie picked up on the girl immediately and began commenting on how she looked more like she was from New York than Berks County. Tom—Reading Tom that is, not New York Tom—said that he thought he knew her and that she was from Reading. Skip said that he was right. Then they began arguing over whether she was the girl that used to fuck someone they knew.

Meanwhile, Blackie and I watched her. She was standing at the bar with the farmers, paying particular attention to one guy who looked like a hog in a too-tight cowboy shirt. But like everybody else in the place, she noticed us and kept looking curiously over at our table. Finally, she made a trip to the bathroom. On the way back, Tom grabbed her arm and pulled her down in the chair next to him.

"Didn't you used to. . . ." he started.

It turned out she wasn't fucking the guy he thought, but they had some other mutual friend. So he started talking to her. It was obvious that she wanted to stay with us, but it was just as obvious that the guy at the bar didn't like her sitting with us.

Her name was Nancy, and the guy at the bar in the too-tight shirt was Sammy. She had been talking to Sammy that night, and now he thought she was his girl. So he just stood at the bar glaring at us. We didn't care. But she did, and she kept running over to him every 15 minutes or so to talk to him for a few seconds, hoping that would make him feel better.

It didn't. She kept on coming back to our table. And I could see it, smeared all over his face, that he was pissed. He kept staring over at us, trying to look mean. I decided to jerk the hog's chain, and jerk it good. I began pawing her to death. My hands were all over her, and she didn't seem to mind it at all. But the hickster was sure looking pissed. Then I dragged her out on the dance floor and began throwing her around.

And for a while that's how it went. She was enjoying it, I was enjoying it, but the hickster was not. I began grinning at him. He began punching the palm of his hand every time I looked at him. Then one of the white spaghetti straps fell down and the girl's tit popped out. Without missing a beat, she calmly stuffed it back in her dress and kept right on dancing. The brothers were standing around us, stomping their feet and clapping their hands. But the hickster's face was now as purple as the pickled eggs in beet juice on the bar.

Then the guy who was leading the band called out: "Last dance of the night," and the band broke into "Jailhouse Rock." I started throwing the girl around and grabbing her all over the dance floor.

We were drunk. It was wild, and I even forgot about the hickster . . . until I felt something like a large slab of bacon being placed on my shoulder, only it had fingers the size of bratwursts, and they were moving, tightening, digging into my skin, and turning me around. I saw the farmer's face, and next to his face I saw a fist coming at me. He was about to deliver a hay-maker. But like I said, I had been in the ring with pros. A quick snap of the head and I took it on the forehead instead of the button. Then I began lacing into him with counter punches. The other farmers and the guys I was with jumped in, and soon the whole room was one big donnybrook.

Tables were getting knocked over, beer was spilling, and glass was breaking. Suddenly we were yanked apart. I looked around and saw that a couple of the farmers had their shirts off, and Big Jim Solley was standing over two guys lying on the floor and pushing hicks away from them. Then the owner of the place came running out in the middle of the floor, holding his head in his hands and shouting, "Stop it! Stop it! You're wrecking my bar!"

I saw that most of the farmers had taken their shirts off, and I realized that Sammy punching me on the dance floor was not spontaneous. The whole thing was a setup. Then one of the half-naked Dutch hogs stuck a meaty finger in the owner's face and said, "You said that you wanted someone to get rid of these bums for you, and now we're doing it. So shut up."

I thought, *Oh shit, here it comes*, I looked around quickly. The only friendly face I saw was Blackie with his hair all messed up. Then I looked down at the floor and saw two sets of patches staring me in the face, with their owner's faces down on the floor. I went over and grabbed Skip and Tom by the collars and pulled them up. I was the only heavyweight we had, and after me, Blackie was the biggest guy at about 150 pounds. Meanwhile, the opposition was bigger than the offensive line of most college football teams. It was obvious that we were about to take a beating if we hung around.

Big Jim Solley was holding off about a half-dozen of the hicks, with his right hand cocked back, telling them that they would have to deal with him if they didn't stop. They were huffing and puffing and yelling at him. But it seemed like they were looking for an excuse to take a breather, so I turned to Blackie and said, "Find everyone. We're getting out of here."

We rounded up the guys and did a quick head count. Big Jim looked at me and said, "Go ahead and get them out of here. I'll take care of these guys."

Skip didn't like the idea. He was arguing: "No let's stay and fight. Fuck these guys, they ain't shit." Meanwhile, Eggy, the stocky little Dutchman, had him around the waist and was dragging him out the door backwards, and Little Joe was in front of him, pushing him in the chest and shouting, "Shut up Skip, you fuckin' idiot!" Between the two of them, they had him going out the door and didn't need any help. Meanwhile, Blackie was telling me that everyone else was out. So I started to go, but then I saw the girl with the white spaghetti-strap dress. I grabbed her by the arm and said, "Come on, let's go."

I put the girl on the back of my bike, short dress and all. We roared through Oley, down the Friedensburg Road, and back up the winding road on Mount Penn. Back at the clubhouse, the mood was a lot different than it had been a few hours earlier when we left. The guys were pissed and drunk, the testosterone fuel-injected. They were talking about burning the hotel down with everyone inside. We had no beer, no pot. The guys were getting nasty; eventually their attention turned to the girl in the white dress. Some of the guys had the idea—and it wasn't completely out of hand—that since they had all gotten into a fight over her, she ought to belong to all of them. Meanwhile, the girl was completely drunk and going around flirting with all of them. She didn't have a clue what she was getting into. These weren't Oley Valley farm boys.

She was cute, she was young, and she thought it was all harmless, but I knew better. The guys were drunk and getting into a berserker rage over the fight at the hotel. There was nothing they could do about it tonight, and as soon as they figured that out, they would turn their attention someplace else. I waited until no one was looking, then I pulled her by the arm out the door.

"Where are we going?" she asked.

"Just shut up and come with me," I said.

I took her home. She lived in a second-floor room, down by the old railroad yards in northeast Reading. When we got upstairs the two of us pulled off each other's clothes. Then we fell into bed and got right into it. We were both quite drunk and soon passed out.

When we woke up, I could see blazing sunshine outside and I knew it was about noon. I was hung over and horny. I looked over at the girl, closely and soberly for the first time. She was young, about my age. She had a pretty face and long clean brown hair lying on her shoulders. She had that Alpine kind of skin that looks tan all year. The Dutch get that from their Swiss ancestors. And she was Dutch, so she was not skinny, but she had a nice shape, firm shoulders, nice lines in her back that curved into a dimple at the end of her spine, and her butt, rising like two firm melons. And I could see her tits oozing out on her side.

I had to piss like hell, but instead I rolled her over and began banging the shit out of her. She was as hung over as I was, but she shared my favorite hangover cure. Soon she was screaming and pulling at me. She was strong and the two of us were wrestling. She put her legs up around my back and tried to crush me in a leg scissors. I tried to drive her through the bed into the floor. Soon we were both drenched with sweat.

She laid there, her arms and legs spread out, panting and sweating. Meanwhile I got up to piss out the window. As bad as I had to go it seemed to take forever coming out, and when it did it was like a racehorse. I was back in my element, but would have much rather been someplace else. As I left, she asked me about the party that night, and I told her to forget about it.

When I got back up Mount Penn, Chuck had a pickup truck and

wanted me to take a ride to pick up a couple of kegs of Reading Old Dutch beer. He had made some phone calls, so guys were coming from Jersey and Norristown. When we got back, Blackie and Little Joe were standing around the clubhouse with three guys who blew in early from Jersey. We tapped the keg on the back of the truck. Someone had brought a pile of ground beef and we soon had the grill going.

Then a Hog pulled up with a guy on it the size of a refrigerator. It was Big Ski Marcinkowski, one of the more interesting characters who Chuck had recently recruited. In the army he had been a guard on the Southeast Asian football team, until he blew out his knee. Then he went out for the army boxing team and won the heavyweight position. He was an amiable Polack, but right now he was pissed as hell that he had missed the night before in Pleasantville. Needless to say, we could have used him.

Bikes and pickup trucks began rolling in from Jersey, Norristown, and Lancaster. It was the largest gathering of the clan since the New Year's Eve party in Jersey. Some of these guys had not seen each other since the Labor Day run, and here it was only two weeks from Memorial Day.

Soon it was dark, and it was just like old times, a bunch of longhaired unshaven outlaws in the dark and nothing but barbecue smoke, beef, beer, bulging biceps, tattoos, chain belts, black leather, and blue denim. Yes, it was just like old times except for one thing: drugs. They were becoming more of a problem than ever.

First, there were the downers, heroin, and little yellow capsules called "yellow jackets." The powder was emptied into a spoon filled with water and boiled over a cigarette lighter, then sucked up into a syringe and injected intravenously, rendering the taker a zombie in about 0.2 seconds. Last fall, we watched Muskrat nearly die on the stuff. There he was, in a field in New Jersey, turning colors, dying right in front of us, until Big John McClure came running up screaming. He threw Muskrat in the creek, jumped in after him, and stood there up to his waist, shoving Muskrat's head in and out of the water like he was John the Baptist.

"Speed, speed!" he yelled. "Get me some speed!" Then he kept dunking Muskrat, only now he was slapping his face, too. "Speed, speed!" he kept yelling. "Get me some meth!"

Finally, someone yelled back: "We got some!"

"Quick!" he yelled "cook it up and get it in a syringe as fast as you can!" Meanwhile, he kept alternately slapping Muskrat across the face and dunking his head under water.

Finally, someone yelled, "We got it!" Big John dragged Muskrat out of the creek and pulled him up on shore. He ripped a bandanna off his neck, wrapped it around Muskrats arm, and tightened it in his fist, until the veins popped out of Muskrat's forearms. Then he shoved the needle into the vein, pushed the plunger, and pulled it back until he saw blood. After that, he shot the cooked meth straight into his veins.

He yelled for help in dragging Muskrat to his feet. When he had him up, Muskrat's eyes opened, and Big John breathed a sigh of relief. He then put Muskrat's arms around the shoulders of two brothers and told them to keep walking with him and not to let him go to sleep for the next couple of hours.

But this experience didn't do any good. It only reinforced a general attitude that we were invincible, that we could not only cheat the Reaper with guns and motorcycles, but now with drugs, too. In fact, the only thing to come out of the incident was that Muskrat was forever renamed "Suicide."

Then there were the hallucinogens. Acid, mescaline, and PCP—a drug that veterinarians invented to tranquilize large animals like horses and hippopotamuses. But then one day someone must have tried it on a gorilla and found that it didn't work on primates. Instead of tranquilizing them, it only made them hallucinate and sent them into muscle spasms. The shit could be sprinkled on marijuana and smoked, and the effect on humans was the same as on gorillas.

Drugs were obviously becoming a problem for outlaws, just like they were becoming a problem for the rest of America at this time. Blackie and I didn't do drugs—we didn't need them. We just drank and drank, and the more we drank, the crazier we got, we also never seemed to fall asleep, no matter how drunk we got, which was not always a good thing.

And we were both already drunk now as it started to get dark. That's when Blackie and I took a walk down the driveway to the end of the road in order to clear our heads. We were standing there smoking cigarets when one of the prospects for the Reading club pulled up on a bike, and

227

behind him he had the girl from the night before. Only she wasn't wearing the white dress; now she had on knee-high boots, Levi's, and a leather jacket, but she still looked hot. She hopped off and ran right over to me.

I said to the prospect, "What the hell did you bring her for?"

"Because she called me up and said she was your girlfriend and needed a ride up here."

Blackie just laughed and said, "Now you're fucked. Wait'll Chuck sees her."

I asked her how she found the prospect. She said that she knew some people who knew people who knew Pagans, so she just started making phone calls until she got someone to give her a ride when I didn't show up to get her. I told her she had to leave, and I called the prospect over and told him that it was all a mistake, so he had to take her back. But she said that she wasn't leaving. I told her to suit herself.

I later found out that she was Chuck's cousin, but he hated her because she was a flirt. Two of his guys once nearly got in a knife fight over her, Since then, she was one of the main foundation stones underpinning his "leaky cunt" theory.

As we all walked up the road toward the clubhouse, I saw Chuck, who just scowled at me, pointed at the girl, and said, "Get her out of here."

"Now you're fucked," Blackie said.

But there was nothing I could do; she refused to leave. I didn't have property colors, and she wasn't my wife or girlfriend, so there was no way I could offer her any protection. All I could do was hope that she stayed by my side and kept her mouth shut.

The party was only beginning and everybody was fucked up on something. Pappy was running around yelling that nobody was allowed to leave the party under any circumstances. All the trucks from Jersey were parked in a circle around the bikes. Then Pappy demanded the keys.

"What's this shit?" I heard somebody asking.

"Chuck and I don't want anyone driving out of here all fucked up and getting arrested," Pappy said. "None of my guys are leaving and Chuck says none of his are, too."

Some of the brothers were bitching, but if you thought about it, it wasn't a bad idea. A year earlier, guys like Sweet William would have gotten all fucked up and led a pack down the mountain to descend on some shithole of a roadhouse. Then they'd get in a fight, and the next morning everyone would be looking for bail money. But hell, that's kind of how Sweet William got himself killed. True, he was a legend, but legends tend to die, and if the club was going to survive it needed guys like Pappy to keep things in line.

While we were standing by the trucks, Skip came up and asked Blackie, "Are we going back to wreck that bar tonight?"

"Nobody said nothing to me," Blackie said.

"Well, some of the guys from Jersey and Norristown were asking, and I said I don't know."

The talk persisted, but those days were supposed to be over. Smashing up bars was too costly, not just in terms of bail money and legal fees, but it also brought too much heat in the form of newspaper publicity and police attention—just the kind of shit that the clubs were trying to avoid this year.

But as the night wore on, people kept talking about it, asking questions like, "When the hell are we going to do it?"

Finally, I heard Pappy screaming at one of his people, "Nobody's going any fuckin' place until tomorrow morning!"

But it was no use. People kept asking, and finally Pappy had to ask Chuck, "What's this about wrecking some fucking bar tonight?"

Chuck said he didn't know nothing about it.

"But your people," Pappy said, "keep telling my people that we're going to do it."

Now Chuck was good and pissed, in addition to being drunk. One thing he couldn't stand was his people doing anything without his approval. Just then, someone handed him a joint the size of a Churchill cigar. He took a couple of hits on it and gave it to me. I gave it to Pappy, who took a couple of hits, and we passed it back and forth. Then Pappy started to talk while trying not to let the smoke out of his lungs.

He thought that some sort of retaliation might not be a bad idea. But if you are going to do it, you don't go bursting through the front door all fucked-up and drunk, swinging pipes and chains. You find out who did it and you get them quietly, sober and alone, so that they know who did it but can't prove anything to the police or reporters.

Then Chuck said that this kind of shit always has to start over some leaky cunt. Pappy said that any shit that starts over a cunt without property colors ought to be personal business and not involve the club. Bucky agreed and he and Pappy said that if we did go they didn't want any of the Jersey people going. Then Jerry and Dirty Hombre said that they thought it was stupid too, but if any of their people wanted to go they wouldn't stop them.

Then Blackie said that we ought to fuck the whole bar up and fuck it up good as a warning, because that's the way outlaws are supposed to do things and not worry about jail or the cops. Chuck told Blackie that he was just being stupid and drunk and that's why he spent more time in jail than on the street.

Then Pappy turned and appealed to me as the leader of the New York club. He asked me if I didn't think that was stupid. But I had to tell them that since I was the one that started the whole thing, I had to go along with Blackie and retaliate, since he had gotten his ass beat for me. Pappy told me that I was no fuckin' help.

Then I heard Grizzly telling Chuck that Blackie was right. I could see that Chuck was getting pissed. He told Grizzly and Blackie that they were both fucking assholes. But then Skip told Chuck that Blackie was right, and that set Chuck off.

"All right, fuck it!" he shouted. Then he reached into the breast pocket of his leather and pulled out a .38 caliber revolver. He fired it into the air three times. Everyone froze and a dead silence descended over the party. Now that he had everybody's attention he shouted, "I want all of my fucking people up on the hill, behind the clubhouse, for a meeting, right now!"

Pappy hollered that the Jersey people were supposed to stay out of it. But I heard some of the Reading people telling some Norristown people that their man had said that it was all right if they got involved. So the entire Reading club followed Chuck up the hill, with a few people from Norristown tagging along. When we got there, I could see the light from the fire flickering across Chuck's face, making him look downright satanic. *Was he ever pissed.*

"This is the most fucked up thing I ever heard," he said. "If we go back tonight looking for trouble, we're only going to get our asses arrested. But all I keep hearing all night is you guys saying that you're going to wreck the fuckin' place. But the talk is over right now. I'm going to let you guys do something I never did before: I'm going to let you vote on it. I say it's fucked up and I vote no."

But Blackie voted to fuck the place up and so did Skip. Then Chuck turned to me hoping for some common sense, but I had to go along with Skip and Blackie. Eggy said wreck the place and Grizzly said wreck the place. Chuck turned to Big Ski, who now saw the chance to rectify his absence the night before. "Wreck the fuckin' place!" he screamed.

Finally, Chuck threw both his hands up in the air. He had the revolver in one of them pointing straight up at the North Star. "Then let's go wreck the fuckin' place!" he screamed, firing the pistol two more times into the air by way of emphasis.

That set everyone off in a berserker rage. We went charging down the hill, yelling and screaming, hootin' and hollerin'. Truck and motorcycle engines were starting, headlights were going on, brothers were grabbing chains and tire irons and anything else that could be used for a weapon. Pappy was still yelling that it was stupid, but it was no use. They had smelled blood. The berserker brotherhood was on the loose, and like a rolling summer thunder, there was no stopping it now. I saw Grizzly take a pistol out of his pocket and pull back the slide to chamber a round. He then shoved it back in his pocket, turned to me and said, "Let's go."

We were off in a caravan of bikes and pickup trucks, down Skyline Drive, across Lower Alsace Township, and down the pike to Oley.

As we pulled up across the street from the hotel, I could feel the place rockin'. The front door was open to let out the body heat, and I could hear the noise from the band through the screen door out in the street. There were cars and trucks parked all over the place, and I could see through the screen door that the place was packed.

Big Ski was the first to hit the ground running. On his feet the guy was as light as an elf, but he was as strong as a bull. He sprinted across the street, threw his arms up in front of him, like he was about to take out a linebacker, and blew the screen door right off its hinges. That sent it flying out onto the dance floor, which was probably the first hint the folks inside had that the legions of Muspell were coming through the door.

After Big Ski, the next two brothers through the door were Herc and Ozark, the twin hillbilly towers from Norristown. Before I even got across the street, I could see through the door that Big Ski was already into the back room, punching people left and right and knocking them out as they tried to get up from the tables and run away. When I got to the door, I bumped into a six-foot-six giant from Norristown named Tom Thumb.

Later, the editors of the *Reading Eagle* heard that three off-duty Reading police officers were sitting at the bar. When they saw Big Ski coming through the front door at the head of the leather-clad phalanx, they dropped their drinks and ran out the back door as fast as they could. The next week reporter Joe Farrell was down at the courthouse trying to find out why these three people—who called themselves full-time *peace officers* whenever it was time to negotiate a salary contract—dropped their drinks and ran away when the shit hit the fan.

By the time I got in, the place was already a shambles. The band leader later testified in court that he didn't see much because he was knocked down and run over by his own musicians. Someone also later told me that the go-go girl Broomstick picked up a barstool and was swinging it around until someone decked her. Blackie jumped on big Sammy, who started the whole thing, and only because he had a 100-pound weight advantage did Sammy start getting the better of him. That was, until Chuck pulled out his revolver and smashed Sammy in the skull with it three times. People were running all over the place. If they were lucky they got out; if not, they got knocked out. When the place cleared out and there were no more standing people to hit, the brothers started smashing glasses and bottles and tables and chairs and mirrors. I picked up a barstool, swung it around my head and managed to take out the whole liquor shelf and a mirror to boot.

Then I heard Chuck yelling, "Out! Out! Let's go!"

When I got outside I could see Righteous Fuckin' Elroy running around the building punching out the windows, his hands soaked with his own blood.

"Get that fuckin' nut!" someone yelled.

I went and got him. But as we both ran across the street, we heard someone screaming and roaring like a bull. I looked over in the direction of the building where it was coming from. I saw Sammy standing in the doorway where the screen door wasn't anymore. His had ripped his shirt off again, and his head, face, and chest were covered with blood. But there he was, a bloody mess standing in the doorway, challenging us to come back and fight some more. Then I saw someone pull out a handgun, prop his arm on the hood of a truck, and start emptying it in the direction of loudmouth Sammy. The guy flew back into the building so fast, I thought he was shot.

When we got back, it suddenly occurred to me, Chuck, and everyone else, that we didn't have a clue as to what had happened. We had been in and out in less than five minutes and left the place in a shambles of broken glass, with furniture and limp bodies on the floor. No one claimed to have killed or maimed anyone. But everyone had heard gunshots and there was no way of knowing if someone was lying on the floor with a knife in their gut or a hole in their head. Hell, we couldn't even be sure we had gotten all our people back in one piece, since nobody even knew who went. We would just have to wait and see.

Pappy was horrified. This was just the sort of shit that we had decided we were going to avoid. That's why we had the party out in the woods. That's why the bikes had been put in a circle and surrounded by trucks and cars. That's why nobody was supposed to leave until the next morning. We were just supposed to get fucked up and have a good time. But now we had just assaulted a whole damn honky-tonk dance hall full of citizens in berserker fashion, and nobody had any idea if the cops were down there at this minute investigating a homicide.

"We got to get out of here," Pappy said. "I'm all right to drive."

Bucky said that he was too. They decided to get the bikes in trucks and clear the hell out for Jersey rather than stick around waiting for the cops to show up. But then Pappy asked where the hell everyone was, and someone told him that they were up the hill "fuckin' that goofy cunt."

Clearing out proved to be a problem. Outlaws had a habit of bugging the shit out of other outlaws who crashed at parties, usually by setting them on fire. So when you knew you were about to pass out, you crawled off into the bushes and found a secure place to sleep. Besides, no one was expecting to have to leave in the middle of the night so no one really bothered to get a head count.

But Pappy's instincts told him to get out. He and Bucky decided that it would be better to just pull out and leave a few guys behind, who could be picked up later, rather than have the whole club hang around so that they could all get carted away in school busses like they did at the New Year's Eve party in Newark.

Jerry and Dirty Hombre also decided that it would be better to get on down the road to Norristown, since it was only an hour away, and Chuck told them that it would be no problem because he would see that any stragglers got driven home the next morning, by "one of the fuckin' assholes whose idea it was to wreck that hotel in the first place."

Then just as we had all this worked out, Sweet Pea came out of the house and ran up to Chuck. Her eye makeup had been washed down her face in a shower of tears.

"Rayels is dead," she sobbed. She went on to explain that Jane had called Grizzly's wife, and she had called Sweet Pea. It seems Rayels had gotten one of those wicked headaches he had been getting lately. He went upstairs to lie down and soon started yelling. They called an ambulance, but he was dead by the time he got to the hospital. Some vein or something just blew like a radiator hose inside of his head.

That kind of put a bummer on everything. The party was clearing out, and we were all in a post-adrenaline letdown. And now this hit us like getting rear-ended by a coal truck while sitting on a motorcycle at a stoplight.

Chuck and I went back into the clubhouse. I poured us both a beer.

"Did they say what caused it?" I asked as I handed one to him.

We did not know the difference between an aneurysm and a hemorrhoid. All we knew is that if you stuck needles in your arm, you could die. If you drank too much, you could die. If you rode a bike too fast, you could die. And if you rode too slow, you could still die if you got hit in the ass by a car. Anyway you looked at it, you were fucked. And even if you didn't die, you could still go to jail.

We were superstitious and fatalistic. Normal 24-year-old people did not have to worry about dying or going to jail. Outlaws did. And it was usually due to something that we did to bring it on ourselves. In Rayels' case it seemed obvious that he had aggravated himself into a seizure over his wife running off with me—even if the doctor said otherwise. Or as Chuck put it, "All this aggravation certainly didn't help it any."

He wasn't so much accusing me of causing anything. I certainly couldn't have known ahead, and we never second-guessed ourselves or each other. Things either worked out, or they did not, that was all. If I had anything to do with it at all, it was an accident, like I had loaned him a motorcycle that he wrecked, or I had given him drugs that I didn't know were bad, or he took a bullet that was meant for me. It was just Chuck's way of affirming that in our superstitious and fatalistic instincts, we were always right about how the axle of life was greased, in spite of what the doctor had to say with all his education and book learning.

So there we sat contemplating the death of another brother, this time by something we couldn't understand. Veins and other shit inside your head were not supposed to just pop while you were sitting on the couch watching television. At least not when you were only 24 years old. Hell, we had enough ways of killing ourselves without having to worry that something could just blow at any time like a radiator hose inside your head.

As we sat in the clubhouse pondering this, I looked over at Chuck. He was slouched in the chair next to me, and I saw a tear running down his cheek.

CHAPTER 16

Pennsylvania Dutch folklore has it that when their ancestors started moving to America, the Evil One didn't like it. So he went to a place where the Rhine River flows into a deep dark cave. There he reached into a pool of water and grabbed a handful of mud that contained the mingled ashes of tortured souls—slain warriors, highwaymen, and drowned children; people burned for witchcraft and heresy; unfortunate pilgrims and prostitutes. From this he forged a ghost and smuggled it into a chest bound for Pennsylfaania, where he hoped it would wreck havoc and make folks miserable. But the ghost fooled the Evil One. It was neither good nor evil. Rather it was unpredictable and mischievous. Sometimes bringing good fortune, sometimes bad. It was a factor in everyone's life to be respected and reckoned with. The Native Americans soon recognized him as a trickster, but the Dutch called him Eilenspickel.

— Union County Dutch folktale

I t was a Sunday morning in late May 1968. The Memorial Day run was less than two weeks away. Last year we were ticklin' our carburetors, goosin' our throttles, kneadin' our clutches, rockin' back and forth in our saddles, and just waitin' for good things to happen. This year the whole thing seemed more like a hassle sandwiched between all the shit that was coming down. I hadn't seen Jane for almost a month. I'd been pretty much out of touch with my chapter and didn't seem to care. One thing for sure, Rayels was no longer a factor, but that didn't tell me much either. Nothing seemed to matter. I didn't seem to even care much if we got arrested for the night before. At least that would make something happen to jump-start my life all over again.

Then as I was walking around outside the clubhouse with a strong spring sun shining down on my face, I heard Sweet Pea in front of Chuck's house saying, "Baby's here with Jane." And my knees turned to rubber, like I'd been sucker-punched with a hard overhand right.

Jane came walking around the corner of the house. Like I said, it was almost a month since I had seen her, but her walk, her soft brown hair bouncing on her shoulders in the sunshine, her shape, it all still made my stomach kick and sputter like a V-Twin engine on a cold morning. Only her face was no longer that of a coy little teen-angel at the ice cream parlor. She now looked like a woman who had been run over by a coal truck and made up by a cheap undertaker from Scranton.

We sat down under a tree, and she started to talk. "The doctor said it had nothing to do with anything we did. It was something he was born with."

Nether of us believed a word of it. We knew better: the "women of the weird" who spin the rope of destiny had simply cut the string on Rayels for some reason we simply couldn't yet figure out. But if we could, regardless of what the doctor said, we'd see that it was all connected somehow, like the ashes mingled in the muck at the bottom of the pool that spawned the Eilenspickel.

Then as we sat there quietly she turned to me and said, "You know, Rayels and I were almost back together."

She said it as if it might upset me, and I suppose she had good reason to think that it would. But it didn't. I had already figured that out. With us, it wasn't so much sex that attracted us to each other, that was the easy part. It was what came next, just lying next to each other and feeling good. We both just always felt good around each other. There was no rational explanation why. It was an animal thing: we were simply bonded like two Minnesota timber wolves scavenging through life on a stripped out, frozen iron mine in the dead of winter.

While we were sitting there quietly pondering the implications of Rayels' sudden demise, the party girl staggered out barefoot with a blanket wrapped around her. Skip came out, grabbed her by the hair, and pulled her back inside. "I figured you didn't need her just then," he later told me. Say what you want, we always took care of our own.

Jane couldn't stay long. She had told her mother that she needed to get some of Rayels' stuff out of the house for the funeral, and her mother agreed to watch the kids while Baby drove her up. I watched her walk away. Her auburn brown hair on her shoulders in the sun, her hips, her bare legs in shorts. That's all I wanted. Give me her and I would ride full throttle through life and into the mouth of Hell in a hailstorm.

That night I went back over to Blackie's in Mohnton. He was living in the same house where Rayels and Jane used to live. I had been staying over there occasionally, since it wasn't as damp as the clubhouse and there was coffee in the morning. Besides, Blackie and I now shared a common interest besides motorcycles. My money was running out, and we both needed jobs.

Getting a job, like everything else in Blackie's world, was not something to be taken lightly. You didn't just walk up to a construction site and say, "Got any work?" No, that would never do. Getting a job was a problem like a carburetor you were trying to rebuild. You laid all the parts out on the kitchen table and subjected it to microscopic scrutiny so that you didn't waste your time chasing jobs that either you wouldn't get or wouldn't pay you enough. "The work was too hard." "They only paid $1.50 an hour." "They didn't like people with beards," Blackie complained. Between a Sicilian suspicion of eternal conspiracy and a Teutonic sense of the impending Goetterdammerung, in Blackie's world there was no reason to even plan on getting up and going out the next morning. But we did, real late the next morning, almost noon. Blackie had a big old '56 Cadillac. And naturally it was black, like everything else he owned, except for his underwear, and that was only because they didn't make black underwear yet. At least not the kind men would wear.

He had made a big thing about letting Baby know that we were going out to look for work that day. Actually we were really going out to see if we could find out where to find someone who, according to him, could tell us where to find a good paying job. That necessitated several social calls and long-winded conversations. If the person had beer, so much the better.

We quickly forgot about jobs; all anyone wanted to talk about was the rumble at the Pleasantville Hotel. It was on the front page of the *Reading Eagle*, where it was described as a "barroom brawl right out of the Old West." "The place had been demolished in a matter of minutes." "The State Police and Oley Township Police were investigating."

Apparently no one was seriously hurt. But Blackie latched on to the words "state police" like a dog with a bone. If it was just the Oley Police, it would have been a joke. But he insisted that the state police don't get involved unless it's serious. And this time the Dutch-Sicilian doomsayer had a valid point. We found a couple of brothers and talked about going to Delaware until the shit blew over, but nobody ever did anything in Reading without asking Chuck first.

So we went back to Mohnton, where Baby was all excited when we got there.

"I talked to Skeet's wife today," she said, "You guys have been on the radio all day. She said the state police were down in Oley digging bullets out of the wall."

That was all Blackie needed to hear. He was spooked. "That's it. We're going to Delaware," he said.

I was from New York, where if you get two blocks away from the scene of the Donnybrook, the cops would never find you. So I couldn't believe that it was serious. Besides, I wanted to be there for Jane if she needed me. But I couldn't say that, because it would just have confirmed that I was *ferhexed* and *ferhoodled* like everyone already suspected. Besides Blackie was determined to go to Delaware—obsessed, actually. Then suddenly it all became quite clear to me. If we went to Delaware, we wouldn't have to look for a job all week. In the meantime we could lie back and party on Dirty Louie's farm. With a motive like that, there was no arguing with him.

So, after supper we began making serious plans about going to Delaware. Blackie didn't have a phone, so he told Baby to go to the neighbor's every couple of days and call Skeet's wife. She would know where we were and when it was safe to come back. Then I sat in the living room watching TV with his little girl, Brenda, while Blackie was saying good-bye to Baby in the bedroom.

Suddenly there was a pounding on the front door. *Shit,* I thought, *now we get arrested because he had to knock off of a piece of the old lady's ass before we left.*

But it was Chuck, bursting into the room and pissed as all hell. "What's this shit about Delaware I keep hearing?" he demanded.

Blackie came into the kitchen wearing just a pair of Levi's.

"Where the fuck do you think you're going?" Chuck demanded.

"To Delaware," Blackie said as he was trying to zip up the fly of his pants. "We can't take no chances. If this thing blows over we can come back in a few days. Meanwhile we can party down at Dirty Louie's."

"That's great for you guys," Chuck said, "but what about the rest of us with jobs? We can't just go taking off for a week. And if any of us gets busted, who's going to bail us out? Whatever we do, we are going to do it as a club. If we're going to split, then we're all going to split together. If not, then we're all going to stick around and deal with this problem together."

The way Chuck looked at it, we didn't even know what was coming down. No one had been seriously injured. Or if they had, they had not shown up at the hospital for treatment. In spite of all the publicity, it was still just a barroom fight. In the long run they would need real witnesses to point the finger at real people and say, "He was there and I saw him break a glass." And what was that? Disorderly conduct? True, the place was trashed, but they certainly couldn't blame that on any one person. Besides, after the fact, the police had a miserable record of coming into court with witnesses who were willing to point their fingers at Pagans.

But Blackie pointed out that the state police wouldn't have gotten involved unless it was serious. Chuck disagreed. The local cops knew there were no outlaw bikers in Oley. There was no point in even looking. So they turned the problem over to the state police, who probably didn't even give a damn and only told the papers that they were investigating so that the concerned public didn't think they were sitting around jerking off.

He had a point. The Oley Township Police would have gotten lost if they tried to drive into Reading, and if they asked questions half the people wouldn't understand them with their Dutch accents. Besides, it was all a bullshit charge anyhow. Nobody gave a shit about some honky-tonk shithole, especially when the state police probably had found out by now that the owner had instigated the fight himself the night before.

So we stayed in town. Unfortunately, as it turned out Chuck had been wrong, but for all the right reasons. It was only a barroom brawl, and back then these were normal occurrences. Our fight probably had been just one of about six in Berks County that weekend. But we had no way of knowing just what State Police Detective Harley Smith had found lying on his desk that morning.

As it turned out, the cops had never showed up at the clubhouse on Skyline Drive because they didn't need to talk to us. And that's because when Oley Township Police Chief, Russell Wren, was dragged out of bed and down to the hotel in the middle of the night, he had found a witness who knew all of us not merely as Chuck, Big Ski, Skip, Eggy, Grizzly, Stoop, Blackie, and Righteous Fuckin' Elroy, but a witness who knew all of us by name: Charles Ginder, Robert Marcinkowski, Charles Dorman, John Kline, Gerald Freeze, John Hall, Roger Smith, and Leroy Stoltzfus Jr. In other words, a witness who could give him the names that matched the names on our driver's licenses and social security cards. Big Jim Solley had rolled over on us.

The following morning, Police Chief Wren had a list of these names on his desk as he began the formidable task of reading the entire corpus of Purdon's Pennsylvania Criminal Statutes. He started with A for Arson, which he didn't think applied, but probably would have if a Pagan or Heathen had left a cigaret burning in an ashtray. Then he continued reading through B, C, and D, where he found disorderly conduct. But he didn't stop there. He continued reading until he got to R, and there he struck a motherlode when he came across two peculiar statutes. One of these was Riot, which defined it as "any sort of disturbance that involves more than two people." And the statute went on to state that "any person who is present at the scene of a riot is guilty of riot, even if there is no evidence that that person actually participated in the riot." Now that certainly seemed to him like it might work in this case.

That statute was followed by another statute called Riotous Destruction of Property. If any property is destroyed in a riot (see above), whether intentional or not, that constitutes Riotous Destruction of Property, and anyone who participated in the riot is guilty of Riotous Destruction of Property, whether or not they actually destroyed the property. So as you can see, just being in the hotel made us all guilty, but more important was the fact that both these statutes were not mere chicken-shit eatin' misdemeanors, but big-ass, shit-kickin' felonies.

Berks County lawyers had never even heard of these statutes up until then. Barroom fights were usually Disorderly Conduct, Disturbing the Peace, Assault, Malicious Mischief. The lawyers had trouble defending a case like this because they couldn't even find a precedent where anyone had ever been charged with these statutes before. Eventually, they ascertained that the statutes had been written in the nineteenth century when an Irish gang called the Molly Maguires had been terrorizing the southern half of the anthracite coal region. At the time, the Pennsylvania and West Virginia state legislatures were agents of Standard Oil, the Pennsylvania Railroad, and the mining and steel cartels, so the riot statutes were passed in order to bust unions and protect the property of millionaires. As late as 1933, private mine and steel mill police were still allowed to machine-gun miners and steelworkers in Pennsylvania and get away with it. But if the workers tried to fight back, they could be tossed in Graterford State Penitentiary for seven years on *riot* charges.

Eventually the Democratic Party, which was still trying to recover from the disastrous impact of the Civil War in Pennsylvania, realized that there were more Irish miners—not to mention Italian, Russian, Slovak, Polish, Dutch, and Hungarian miners—than there were mine owners, so they made sure that the laws were never enforced. The Molly Maguires went on to become the United Mine Workers of America, and by World War II, it was said that its leader, John L. Lewis, had the president of the United States by the balls.

Meanwhile, the riot statutes were shit-canned and forgotten until Sunday morning, May 21, 1968, when Oley Township Police Chief Russell Wren endeavored to enter the *Guinness Book of World Records* as the only person to ever read Purdon's Pennsylvania Criminal Statutes from

"A" for "Admiralty" to "Z" for "Zoning" in one sitting. But that stubborn Dutch persistence had paid off, because by that afternoon Russell Wren had done something that no other Pennsylvania law enforcement officer had ever been able to do. He had felony warrants issued in the names of the core membership of the Heathens and Pagans motorcycle clubs.

So when Harley Smith walked into the state police barracks on Monday morning, that's what he found lying on his desk: warrants already issued by another law enforcement official for the Heathens and Pagans motorcycle clubs. He didn't have to send any state cops up to Skyline Drive to talk to us, because he didn't have to send state cops to talk to anyone. The work was already done. All he had to do was pick us up to get his name in the paper. Never mind that the charges were bullshit. He didn't file them, the Oley Township Police Chief had, and he would not be embarrassed if the district attorney or a magistrate laughed and tossed them out of court.

By the next morning he would be ready. In the meantime, we later heard, he had called the Kuhn Funeral Home in West Reading and terrorized the undertaker by telling him that he had heard from reliable sources that the Pagans and Heathens were on their way down to hijack the body of Robert Rayel so they could give him a decent outlaw funeral. He then suggested that they might be deterred by a couple of plain-clothes cops posing as funeral directors. The undertaker immediately agreed and even offered to loan them suits that he kept on hand for the stiffs if they needed them.

Now any idiot knows that if you want to deter people, you send uniformed policemen, not plain-clothes cops. This was obviously a surveillance operation, with probably the whole barracks standing by in case we showed up at the funeral. It's not that Harley Smith thought that we were stupid, he knew better than that. But he also knew that we were the most arrogant bastards that he had ever seen in the Berks County underworld. And walking through the front door of a funeral parlor as the head of the entire club, all decked out in swastikas and colors while the cops were running all over the county with warrants for our arrest, was just the sort of stunt that Chuck, or any old-time '60s outlaw for that matter, would have loved to pull. All publicity, but no payoff.

But it never happened, and the next morning, Blackie and I left the house at the usual time, between 11 and 12 o'clock. This time we didn't have to say that we were looking for jobs. He just told his wife that it would be better if we weren't around if the cops came knocking on doors. So we were just going to slip over the county line into Lancaster, where we could take it easy and hang out and shoot pool for a day.

We had just left the house and were coming down Lakeview Drive, when Blackie yelled, "Oh shit!" There was a car coming toward us with two middle-aged Dutchmen in the front seat.

"So what?" I said. "It's just a fuckin' car." I was from New York. You didn't even notice shit like this up there.

Blackie swerved sharply and made the next right-hand turn.

"You're fuckin' nuts," I said. "We'll never get anywhere if you turn around every time you see a car."

"I'm telling you, this is a small neighborhood," he said. "You gotta be suspicious of strange cars and strange people." He was now visibly annoyed and continued yelling at me. "If I let you drive, we'd be arrested already."

We continued arguing and were coming up to the top of a hill, when another large black car appeared coming the other way. It swerved around, blocking the entire road. Blackie hit the brakes and had to drive off the side of the road to avoid slamming into it.

Then the first car that we had seen pulled up behind us. Two men jumped out of each car. One of them was Harley Smith. They had their snub-nose .38s pointed straight up in the air.

That's right, straight up in the air, not at our heads with both hands on the gun and their legs spread like they were about to shit their pants. These were the days when cops could still be recruited for purely subjective reasons, like being just as tough, crazy, and careless as the people they had to arrest.

Harley Smith told us to put our hands on the dashboard where he could see them. Then they surrounded the car and told us to get out. They patted us down, read us our Miranda rights, and handcuffed us—in front, not in back, like they would do today. And they didn't have us lying in the road on our bellies for half an hour, like today's cops would do while they got on their radios and called the marines for backup.

Blackie explained that he only lived around the corner, and he asked if he could take the car back to his wife so that she would have something to drive. Then Harley Smith did something else that would be unheard of today: he said that he didn't see anything wrong with it. So they handcuffed me and put me in one of the cop cars, while they let Blackie drive his car home. Then after the cops and I watched him give his wife the keys and a kiss goodbye, before they handcuffed him and put him in the back seat with me. Harley Smith sat in the front seat riding shotgun and looking back over the top of the seat at us. He said that the whole idea of riot charges for a bar fight seemed ridiculous to him, but that we were really in trouble because the district attorney was taking the matter as seriously as the Oley police chief. Then, after some idle bullshit talk, he casually asked, "So, which one of you guys got the blow job under the table Friday night?"

Blackie and I looked at each other. This was news to us. If it had happened we would have known about it since all of us were sitting at the same table Friday night. We could see that Harley Smith was proud of himself for having turned up a detail like this. He was actually getting pissed when he thought that we were jerking him off by denying any knowledge of it, as if we were so lame as to think he might try to arrest us for something like this.

Someone probably told them that he saw it happening and actually believed it himself. The public perception of our lives was always so much better than the reality. To them it was all a cold beer, a round of blowjobs under the table, and beating the fuck out of anyone we pleased with impunity. They never knew about the freezing nights on the cold floors next the radiators, or driving across Jersey in the winter without a windshield, or eating slabs of fried spam that the kid called "dirty meat."

Finally, Blackie convinced him: "It didn't happen, Harley. We were there, and I wouldn't bullshit you if it did."

He looked a little disappointed, and even pissed at the fact that he had been jerked off by witnesses. But he soon got over it.

Some things were not any different back then than they are now. Even then, you didn't just throw people in the can. There was a mountain of forms, fingerprints, and mug shots, and you could tell that they considered it all a royal pain in the ass. They didn't get any bonus for hurrying. Anyway, what were you going to say? "Hurry up and get me to jail before my friends decide to leave"?

So there we sat on a bench, handcuffed and waiting, when two more plain-clothes cops came through the front door with Chuck Ginder in handcuffs. He was all cool and grinning. Chuck only got pissed and excited when there was something he could do about a situation. When it was out of his control, he sat back like everyone else and just went with the flow.

Chuck was working up on a roof someplace; only his boss knew where. It's amazing how good the women were at transferring information back in those days before cell phones and beepers. Sweet Pea managed to get the boss' wife, and she and the boss knew all about Chuck, like everyone else in Berks County. Actually they seemed to enjoy not only knowing such a celebrity, but also being privy to such important goings-on in his life. Chuck had the message in 20 minutes.

He knew the shit was up to his waist, so he told the boss he needed off and he didn't know for how long. Then he drove home, where he called the bail bondsman, Joe Biancone, whom everyone called "Gibraltar Joe."

Gibraltar Joe was about 400 pounds, so he was as conspicuous on the street as a hippopotamus. He was another one of those local characters who made Reading an interesting place back in the '60s. All he seemed to do was ride around in a brand-new Cadillac all day. When he got too big to fit behind the wheel, he got a chauffeur. He carried his money in a wad of bills the size of a Campbell's soup can, and he kept the wad in the front pocket of a pair of pants that looked like they had been cut out of a tent.

Bail bonding was not his only business. He had his hands in a lot of shit, but nobody knew exactly what. He was constantly in one jam after another and spent as much time as his clients in the Berks County Prison, where he was installed in the kitchen as *chef de cuisine*, so to speak. Thus, the food went overnight from Pennsylvania Dutch to Italian and back again depending on whether or not Joe was there. Eventually they lifted his license to bail people out, but then he just got a bonding license for his mother. He used to ride around in the car with the chauffeur in the front seat, and his tiny little mother in the back. He still took care of everything, only the mother now signed the paperwork.

Because he dwelt in the *Schattenlands* between law and crime, he served as a liaison between the police and the outlaws. Both sides trusted him and knew that he would not betray them. This meant that Chuck could meet him to find out what was happening and know that the cops would not show up.

When Chuck got Gibraltar Joe on the phone, he told Chuck that it was a probably a crock-a-shit, but if he had been there too, it was best that he didn't go walking in the front door of the courthouse, because chances were that he'd be coming out the back door in handcuffs. Harley Smith had been careful not to let the whole county know that he was holding felony warrants for us, so even Joe thought it was just the regular $50 bullshit. Joe told Chuck to meet him at the Italian Club, but Chuck never made it to his meeting with Joe. He was pulled over and arrested on Skyline drive as he was coming down off Mount Penn. And he was now sitting next to us on a wooden bench in the state police barracks.

When they finally got done processing us, we were taken to the Berks County Prison, where the prison authorities now had to process us all over again. Then we were sent to the barbershop, where there was a brawny Dutch guard waiting to see that we were shorn like sheep. Chuck was first, then me, and while we sat there laughing at each other and waiting for Blackie to come out, we saw Eggy being led through the barred gate. Later that afternoon they brought in Skip, who was trying to act pissed off.

"They pulled me and my wife over right on Penn Street while we were driving to the store," he fumed. "How the fuck did they even know it was my car?"

Eggy just laughed. "Maybe the fact that you have the only car in Berks County with a swastika spray-painted on the roof had something to do with it." And then we all laughed.

The next day they brought in Big Ski, and Elroy was picked up on his father's farm in Lancaster. Thirty years later, it would take over 200 state and federal agents, complete with flak jackets and assault rifles, to arrest the Pagans on Long Island. Yet back in those days, it took only a half-dozen Dutch detectives with sport jackets and snub-nose .38s to arrest all of us in just two days. Either outlaws are getting badder or cops are becoming weenies.

One good thing in those days was that they still gave you real prison blues, not day-glow orange or purple jump suits. So we sat with our new haircuts, in washed-out denim shirts and baggy dungarees, eating ham pot pie with plenty of raw spring onions and fresh-baked white bread.

Back then the Berks County Prison was still a Dutch club. Out of 250 inmates, there were about 30 blacks and maybe a dozen Puerto Ricans. Italians and Polacks were the minorities. Other than that, the nameplates in the cellblocks read like the membership book in a Lutheran church: Weaver, Weber, Wagner, Smith, Kline, Eckart, Miller, Dietrich, Nonnemacher, Hostetler, and Stolzfuss. All of them seemed to know each other since they were kids, and all the guards were Dutch country bumpkins, who still spoke *ferhoodled* English like just-off-the-boat *dorflanders* from *Schwabenland*, even though their families had been in America for 200 years.

Therefore, the whole place was run like a Dutch inn, with Dutch respect for cleanliness, courtesy, quiet, and privacy. No one dared run around jiving, and grab-assing and screaming, because it would have brought an icy stare of warning from one of the elders of the Dutch Mafia, like Eggy's brother Jim Kline, a professional criminal who was in there for robbing a whorehouse at gunpoint. The guards let the inmates take care of their own problems and liked it this way.

Almost half the inmates worked on the farm, which the warden and guards ran with the same pride as any other Dutch farmers would, and since many of the inmates were farmers too, the food was great. Every morning you got either *panhass*, sausage or bacon, and French toast, pancakes or waffles, and there was always scrambled eggs, coffee, and fresh bread. For dinner (which is what the Dutch call the big midday meal, as opposed to a lighter meal at suppertime), you got baked chicken or ham or pork chops with some kind of corn and vegetables, along with fresh baked bread and green onions. Then for supper you got chicken or ham pot pie, or corn pie, or corn fritters with more fresh bread and onions.

Between the order, the camaraderie, and good food the whole place was permeated with a general air of *gemuetlichkeit* that made it one of the few county jails that were better than state pens.

The next morning a guard took us to the weave shop, or *veef* shop as he called it, where we pulled rags—that's right, pulled rags. Not the sort of rags you could wipe grease off your hands with. Rather they were long strands, dozens of yards long, and skinny and curled up like the kind of rags you used to put on one of those little frames in kindergarten to make potholders for Mother's Day. They were brought in from the mills in bundles the size of large bales of hay and dumped in a pile on the floor. When you cut them open, they about tripled in size.

Then we sat around the pile on three benches. We grabbed a rag anyplace, cut it with scissors, and started pulling an end. We pulled and pulled and piled it on the floor, until it was hopelessly knotted. When we couldn't pull any more, we cut it and wrapped the whole strand around a card. The cards were then taken to the back of the shop, where they were put on spools, which were set on rods in a rack so that they could be fed onto the large spools that went on the looms. The work was boring, but what isn't in jail, and you could joke and laugh the whole time. Nobody pushed us and we could take a cigaret break whenever we wanted.

Once while I was standing by the window, smoking a cigaret and staring aimlessly into the yard, I saw the gate to the yard open and three guards came out with a shackled inmate. He was about average height and build, with brown hair. The guards took the shackles off his legs and let him walk around.

"That's McCarthy," the guy standing next to me said. "He's crazy, so they keep him in the hole and bring him out to exercise a half hour each day."

I took a drag on my cigaret and looked at the guy who had just spoken to me. He elaborated. "They say he picked up a hooker on Penn Street, took her up to her room, and began kicking the shit out of her. By the time someone heard her scream and got upstairs, he had busted up her whole face and even chewed off one of her nipples."

I was fascinated. Here was one of those characters right out of a Jean Genet novel, the kind that most folks only read about in supermarket tabloids. I stood there smoking my cigaret and wondering what made a guy like him tick. Then as he was walking around the yard, he saw me and walked over to the open window.

"You got a cigaret?" he asked.

I took one out, lit it off mine, and handed it to him.

"Thanks," he said.

We talked a minute, about the usual prison bullshit, while I stared into his sad brown eyes. I was looking for something—anything—that might make him seem different from the rest of us. But I saw nothing: nothing scary, nothing bad, nothing that seemed to make him different than anyone else. Then he thanked me for the cigaret and walked back over to the gate, where the two guards shackled him and took him back to the hole.

I went back to pulling the rags. This went on for a day or two. Then one of the guards came up one afternoon and asked me and Chuck to come with him. He took us to the back of the weave shop, where they loaded the strands of rags onto the spools for the looms. Here, about 50 small spools of rags were attached to one of the large spools that went on the looms, and they needed to be loaded on to that large spool by cranking a wooden handle about four feet long. It started easy, but the more you cranked, the more torque you needed to apply to move the handle. By the end you were pulling hard enough to bust the lug nut off an 18-wheel truck.

Say what you want about Germans being smart cookies. When it comes to work we are just dumb Dutchmen, perhaps the dumbest race on the face of the earth, for we seem to take great pride in performing work that other races consider fit only for horses, oxen, mules, donkeys, elephants, camels, and jackasses.

The guards had our number. One of them would come up after lunch and say, "I need two strong boys," and he would point at two of us Pagans, usually either me, Chuck, or Ski. Then we would go to the back of the shop by an open window, strip to the waist and take turns cranking. As the spool got fat and the work hard, we would start cursing each other.

"My old lady can do better than that," Chuck used to yell at me.

"You ain't shit without your club to back you up," I used to tell him.

And of course, Ski, being Polish, was just as easily sucked into the game as any Dutchman. Maybe he was even worse, because he started kicking us in the ass when we didn't crank fast enough. Then Eggy, Blackie, Elroy, and Skip got insulted because the guards weren't picking them, so in the end we were all back there cranking spools and cursing and kicking each other in the ass. The guards loved it. They kept shouting with their country accents that we weren't so tough after all and that we wouldn't last a week on their father's farm. Everyone loved it, and we all had a good time. And it built up an appetite for all the Dutch food we were getting. One day, some old Italian guy said that we were crazy and should just say we had a bad back. But we would have sooner said that our dicks didn't work.

So there we sat like we were having the time of our lives. Memorial Day weekend was coming up, the first anniversary of our triumphal coming out parade on Penn Street, when we were drinking beer, getting laid all over the place, and terrorizing the hinds. And now, here we were a year later, sitting in the can, eating corn pie, and pulling rags, pulling the crank, pulling our pricks, and entertaining a bunch of Dutch country bumpkins, while Rayels was lying dead and buried in Laureldale Cemetery at the foot of Neversink Mountain. The Goetterdammerung was descending all around us, and the Fat Lady had begun to sing.

But we couldn't hear shit.

CHAPTER 17

As through this world I've wandered, I've seen some funny men;
Some will rob you with a six gun, some with a fountain pen.
And as through your life you travel,
As through your life you roam,
You will never see an outlaw drive a family from their home.
　　　　— Woody Guthrie, "The Ballad of Pretty Boy Floyd"

T he wheels of justice now grind slowly. Gone are the days when you could be arrested and shackled in the afternoon, and then swinging from the old oak tree before the sun rose the next morning.

We had been charged with felonies, so our bail was high. But it was still a barroom fight, and our case was causing a lot of lively debate across the county and even in the courthouse. The question was not whether we were guilty of felonies, because to most people it was obvious that we were not. It was whether the felony charges, although bogus, should be used as a technicality to send us "up the river," as the saying generally goes, but more accurately in this case down the Schuylkill River, to Graterford Penitentiary.

Many of the folks in Berks County considered us local characters who added some spice to an otherwise bland diet of life, and who offered no real threat to the average Reading burgher or Berks County *bauer*. But then there were the more timid souls, the *sesselfurzers* who sat reading the *Reading Eagle* and hallucinating on their own gases, with images floating around their heads of leather-clad, swastika-wearing, roadkill-eating bar-barians bursting in their front door and skull-fucking their plump little Dutch wives and daughters right before their very eyes.

However, these people were in the minority. Back in 1967 most red-blooded American men, and women too, felt that it was downright un-American to put people in jail for having been in a fair fight.

Our story was all over the newspapers, and people talked about it for weeks like it was the Gunfight at the O.K. Corral. By now, everyone knew that we did not come crashing through the front door out of the clear night sky. The Dutch hicksters had picked a fight the night before and most folks believed they deserved the thumping they got. The owner of the bar had instigated the fight, and if his bar was wrecked, he too had it coming.

But there was a problem in the person of the Berks County District Attorney Robert Van Hoove. He was a big guy from Texas, more belly than beef, but he nevertheless sucked in his gut and stuck out his chest and jaw in an attempt to present a more formidable appearance. He had been stationed in Pennsylvania during the World War II, married a Dutch girl, stuck around, and went to law school. He really was a law-and-order, red-blooded redneck from Texas, and his blood pressure was jacked through the roof of the Berks County Courthouse over two other items.

About the same time that we were wrecking the bar, the students over at Albright College were protesting the war and wrecking the campus, and downtown there had been race riots during which several stores were looted and torched. Now, while the average Dutch country burgher or *bauer* may have thought at that time that it was un-American to put bikers and farmers in jail for fighting, they also felt that college kids who protested the war should be taken out and shot, along with crazy niggers who burned and looted stores.

But because of the social and political climate at the time, there was very little that Van Hoove could do to bring down the hammer on either students or blacks. As a result, the Dutch hardasses felt that this big tough Texan was acting like a little liberal pussy. Therefore, between the college kids and the race-rioters, the district attorney walked around like he had two large corncobs wedged up his ass. His head turned bright purple, and the sour expression on his face made him look like the poster child for irritable bowel syndrome.

So now when he saw our case, his bowels began to rumble, and he began to feel like he had finally found a way to blow out those twin corncobs, clear his bung, and restore his redneck credentials by prosecuting a band of infamous outlaws, who were becoming legends all over southeastern Pennsylvania. After all, he did not file the charges against us, the Oley Township Police Chief had, so Van Hoove would only be doing his job by presenting those charges to a jury.

He also enjoyed a considerable home-field advantage in the Berks County Courthouse. This advantage is illustrated by an old Pennsylvania Dutch farmer's tale, in which a farmer from Womelsdorf dies and goes to Heaven, where Saint Peter merely says, "How ya doin Jakie? Come on in, find yourself a seat, and make yourself at home." The following day the farmer hears a brass band, and when he goes out to investigate, he sees Jesus Christ himself walking arm-in-arm through the gates with a guy he recognizes as a local lawyer. When he asks why he didn't get this treatment, Saint Peter merely tells him, "Jakie, this place is full of Berks County rednecks, just like you, but this is the first time *any* Berks County lawyer ever made it through those gates."

That pretty well describes the judicial system in Berks County—hellish, corrupt, and stinking like a shithouse in August. And there we were, about to be thrown smack into the middle of the Berks County Courthouse with Judge Hess, the *Ferdamnte Hess*, presiding. In other words, we were fucked, but we didn't know it yet.

Meanwhile, Blackie had found us a lawyer that his mother knew from the Sons of Italy club. His name was Fred Giorgi, and he had a reputation for being able to help people who were obviously guilty and who lacked political connections. He looked the part too. Although he was pushing 40, he was almost a dead ringer for Blackie, tall and lean with a thick mane of slicked-back black hair. If he walked onto a Hollywood set, Martin Scorsese would have cast him as a mob lawyer in a heartbeat.

Giorgi knew that we didn't have a nickel in our pockets, but he had known and liked Blackie since he was a kid. Also, like a lot of people who had been around the block in Reading, he knew that the felony charges were bullshit and saw us as colorful local celebrities. Then there was the fact that anyone who knew Chuck Ginder tended to admire him for his integrity and straightforwardness. So we rode in a sheriff's car to our hearing before the Oley Township District Magistrate, expecting Fred Giorgi to grind these farmers into sausage meat before our very eyes. We had a lot to learn.

For starters, when we got there, Giorgi didn't show. Instead he sent a smirking young kid who smoked a pipe and wore a tweed jacket. His name was Bill Bernhart, and he was Giorgi's associate. Needless to say, we found the pipe and tweeds far less impressive than Fred Giorgi's slick mannerisms and Italian suits.

Chuck immediately started grumbling that we had paid for Giorgi, not this twerp, but Blackie thought that we should give the kid a chance. He insisted that Giorgi wouldn't send an idiot down to defend us, and he reminded us that we were out in the country, where we would probably do better with a local Dutch boy than some Italian guy who looks like a mob lawyer.

Chuck didn't like it, but he had to agree.

On the other side, the DA himself, Robert Van Hoove, showed up to prosecute us. No assistants there. Van Hoove acted like he owned the magistrate's office, and the magistrate let him pretty well get away with it. The big Texan blustered and blubbered and slammed shit around on the table. Meanwhile, the tweedy little twerp just sat smoking his pipe and smirking at him.

When Van Hoove finished strutting his stuff, Bernhart began asking the magistrate all sorts of annoying technical questions. He demanded to see signed copies of the local ordinances we had supposedly violated. The magistrate said he didn't have any, and Van Hoove said he didn't need any. Bernhart said that it was illegal to proceed without them. This sent the magistrate to his filing cabinets, muttering and cursing Bernhart. Finally he came up with some papers and showed them to Bernhart, who flung them contemptuously back at the magistrate and said, "The law says signed copies, signed by the township supervisors. Since when do typewritten names constitute a signature?"

The magistrate said they were good enough. Then Bernhart began asking him more questions, and generally insinuating that the guy was running some kind of half-assed courtroom. Van Hoove was becoming visibly annoyed and started complaining.

Meanwhile, the magistrate was becoming visibly annoyed, too, but also confused and frustrated by Bernhart's demands that he proceed strictly according to the book. We later found out that Bernhart was fresh out of Yale Law School and Giorgi had sent him precisely because he knew his shit and could keep cool. In the end, the magistrate was forced to drop the "pointing and discharging a deadly weapon" charge because Bernhart pointed out that the DA had produced no evidence that any of us had even possessed a deadly weapon, much less pointed or discharged it.

Van Hoove hollered that the police had dug bullet slugs out of the wall, but Bernhart reminded him that given the age of the building they could have been there since the Civil War. Van Hoove left in a huff, while a grinning Bernhart shook our hands and told us that we at least got one charge dropped. He said that "out here they pretty much do as they damn well please and quite honestly, given the notoriety of you guys, I didn't even expect to do this well."

For the time being we were screwed, because Van Hoove still had two felony charges on each of us. Given the loose way they were worded, he could have convicted high school students on riot charges for having a cafeteria food fight as long as there were at least three people involved, or just in the room for that matter.

Giorgi and Bernhart told us that we were in for a fight. "We just have to stall," they said. Maybe, in time, they could convince the legal establishment that the charges were a farce and then embarrass the DA into a plea bargain that would land us in jail for a couple of months. In the meantime, they said we would have to make bail and stay out of the newspapers. "Every time you guys get your asses on the front page," they told us, "you give this guy another reason not to cut us a deal."

When I got back to jail, I wrote a letter and sent it home, explaining that we were in jail on felony charges for a barroom fight. My father didn't buy it for one minute. "I've been drinking in bars my whole life," he told my mother, "and I've seen plenty of fist fights, and no one goes to jail on felony charges for a barroom brawl." He was convinced that someone had been shot or stabbed. So he drove down to find out for himself.

First he talked to Chuck Ginder and Big Ski, both of whom had been released on bail. He was taken in by their down-home straightforward manner, as well as the fact that both of them had impressive military records. But he still had his doubts. Then he talked to Gibraltar Joe Biancone, a guy who wore regular street clothes and hadn't gone to college, but who knew how the courts worked and, what's more, could explain it without sounding like some pompous wiseass *scheisster*.

Between the three of them, they now had him convinced that it was all bullshit. So by the time he got to see me in the jail, he was more pissed at the cops and prosecutors than at me. A guard brought me into the visiting room and sat me in front of a large unbreakable glass window. In front of me was a shelf and a phone. On the other side, I could see two chairs and a phone. My parents were brought in by a guard and they sat down. We were all impressed; it was just like in the Jimmy Cagney movies.

While we were talking, Righteous Fuckin' Elroy was brought in by a guard and he sat down in a chair next to me. I introduced him to my parents, handed him the phone, and they said hello. Then a large Dutch farmer in a too-small homemade gray suit came into the visiting room. He was accompanied by a plump little woman in a long black skirt, black lace-up half high-heeled shoes and a black shawl and white bonnet. My mother was stunned. Being from New York, she had never seen anyone dressed like this except my great-grandmother from the Black Forest. And she had certainly never seen a woman her own age dressed this way, except maybe on postcards from Pennsylvania or the Black Forest. She was obviously impressed by the fact that such sectarian and deeply religious people could raise sons who joined motorcycle gangs, just like any other mothers' sons.

After the visiting session was over, Leroy's father spoke briefly with my parents about their common problems with raising kids. The little woman said nothing, but when she left she thrust a card in my mother's hand. It read: "Man is made in the image of God and it is his duty to serve

God; but woman is made in the image of man and it is her duty to serve man: Leola Mennonite Church."

Blackie and I were the last two to get bailed out and we got out the same day. While we sat in jail, Blackie had been talking to all the jailhouse wiseacres, looking, as usual, for some new angle on life. And sure enough, someone had told him that if you get out of jail and show up at the unemployment office, they have to either find you a job or you can go around the corner to the welfare office and get a $35 check.

"That's 70 bucks," Blackie said. "Ain't nobody gonna give us a job the way we look."

So the next morning we were down at the unemployment office, dressed to the nines, complete with black leather, chains, swastikas, earrings, and leather boots, expecting to get sent packing. But to our surprise the clerk merely handed us blue "report-to-work" cards.

"Fuck," Blackie said, flipping his on the floor in disgust.

But after I read mine, I yelled, "Hold it! Pick that back up and read it."

It said: "Clyde Beatty Cole Bros. Circus."

The next morning we were at the fairgrounds, by six o'clock. It was already hot and humid. We stashed our colors in Blackie's saddlebags and walked up to the site just wearing Levi's and t-shirts. They soon had us unloading poles and canvas from flatbed trailers. Then we had to unroll the canvas and stretch the canvas over the tent poles. As members of the Pagans Motorcycle Club, no matter what the situation, we had to be tougher than everyone else. This meant that while other people sweated and complained about the heat and humidity, we just spat and worked harder. The foreman picked up on this and kept telling us that he could find a spot in the truck and a spare bunk if we wanted to stay with the circus for a while. Blackie was game until I reminded him that we weren't supposed to leave the county yet.

Meanwhile, I wondered how we were going to get the tents up. But then after we had the poles out and stuck in the grommets, a guy came by with an elephant that had a chain around its hind leg. It wasn't a big African mastodon; it was just a little Indian elephant. The guy hooked the chain up to one of the poles.

"This ain't gonna do shit," I told Blackie.

"Just watch," he said. "I saw this in California once."

The elephant started walking, the slack came out of the chain, and without missing a step the elephant started pulling up the tent.

The elephant had the big top up in no time. Then they chained the elephant to a pole and gave it some hay and water. In the meantime we had to tie ropes and pound stakes into the ground. Here again, the guys with the Pagan tattoos had to look better than everyone else. So Blackie and I took turns pounding like hell with the sledgehammer. It was almost noon now, the sun was overhead and the sweat poured off us until our pants were soaked.

Finally we were done, and the foreman came up and handed us two tickets. He pointed to a window in a trailer where he said we would get paid. He told us that we had a breakfast coming, too, and that we could come back tonight and take down the tents. If we wanted, we could ride to Scranton with them after that.

The breakfast was typical institution food: coffee, powdered eggs, overcooked bacon, hash browns, and dry toast. Not as good as the Berks County Prison, but we could have all we wanted. While we were finishing up our last cup of coffee, I brought up the idea of coming back at night and making another 10 bucks.

Blackie was against it. He claimed that in the morning you got paid because they had no choice. But when you finished at night, you couldn't find the trailer to get paid because it was halfway to Scranton.

"So then we just beat the fuck out of the foreman and take it out of his wallet," I said.

"Now that's exactly what Bernhart and Giorgi said we're not supposed to do," Blackie reminded me.

We hit the first bar we found, right across from the fairgrounds, which several of the circus people had already found. Blackie ordered two bottles of Old Dutch. We had been working hard in the sun all morning, we were all dehydrated, and this was our first real drinking bout in a month. We were loaded in 15 minutes.

But we didn't stop. We kept on drinking, and Blackie used to get goofy ideas when he drank, which is why he had more tenure than the rest of us guys in the Berks County Prison. He had just been in jail for a month and now he had the wanderlust. So he started talking about going to Wilmington. He claimed that Dirty Louie had told him that there were union construction jobs available for the summer. We could earn money and stay out of trouble in Pennsylvania at the same time.

It was a crock. We weren't even supposed to leave Pennsylvania yet, but he just wanted to get on the road. So here we were on the hottest day of the year, riding through Chester County and into the most mosquito-infested state north of Florida. But I have to admit, it felt great to be on the road again.

Dirty Louie kept a farmhouse outside of Wilmington, where some of the guys lived. There were plenty of mosquitoes and no screens. There was also a large billy goat on a chain. One of the guys had a dog who kept sneaking up behind the goat and barking. At first the goat tried to ignore the dog, but the dog wouldn't quit. Finally, the goat spun around and put its head in the dog's face, its beard touching the ground and its horns thrust forward. The dog jumped back like it had been hit by a car and ran around the back of the house yelping. I could see that the dog had played this game before and lost.

Blackie and I had eaten enough that morning at the circus to keep us going for three days. Dirty Louie rode up with a keg of Budweiser on the back of a three-wheeler. We were set.

It turned out that John-John from the Mother Club was there. Later, when we were too drunk to notice, Big John from the Mother Club also showed up. There is something about the name John and outlaws. For one thing it is the most common American name, thanks in part to the Pennsylvania Dutch, who sometimes named all their sons John—John Peter, John Jacob, John Frederick—and then they just called each one by the middle name. But it also seems that there is something conducive to outlawry about the name: John Lafitte, John Wesley Hardin, John Brown, John Wilkes Booth, John Dillinger, John Vernon Marron. And for whatever reason, the Pagans seemed to be loaded with them.

I woke up the next morning on a mattress in a room on the second floor. Blackie was out cold on another mattress. The sun was streaming in, and I felt like shit. When I got downstairs, John-John was sleeping on the couch with a tweed cap pulled down over his eyes. He wore the same cap every day of the year, and he always slept all scrunched up like he was freezing, even on the hottest night of the year.

I walked outside. The sun was already high and it was hot. Big John was the only other person up, and in spite of the heat, he had started a fire. I walked over to him and asked him when he had arrived.

"Last night," he said. "Don't you remember talking to me?"

"No, I don't."

I noticed he was pulling slips of paper out of his wallet and throwing them into the flames. He let me watch for a while. He was obviously enjoying my interest.

Finally I asked, "What the hell are you doing?"

"Burning all my ID," he calmly replied.

And that was it. Like he was brushing his teeth or popping zits. The most self-explanatory answer in the world. He continued pulling out slips of paper and scrutinizing them in an exaggerated manner, almost defying me to ask the next question.

"Is this something you do whenever your wallet gets too heavy?"

"No."

"Okay, then why?"

"Because if I get picked up by the police, I'm better off with no ID than my own ID."

Then came the explanation, which he had been dying to give me, but he only wanted to build suspense for the proper dramatic setting. It promised to be whopper. You never knew what Big John was going to do next. In this case he had been going out with a girl in high school. The guy was going to be 30, and in 1968 the difference between high school and 30 was about two centuries.

In any event he went to get the girl after school, and he was wearing a three-piece gray pinstripe wool suit. That's right, a three-piece wool suit on an outlaw, in Washington, D.C., in June no less, like he's some kind of congressional aide. John-John used to tell us that it was called "schizophrenia," but in our world that was another word with as much meaning as "aneurysm."

So Big John came looking for this girl, and a couple of black kids noticed the crazy redheaded white mother in a suit in June. And in spite of the name Big John, he was only 140 pounds. So two big black kids decided to jerk him around. They walked up to him and said, "Hey, white boy."

And Big John stuck his right hand under his left armpit and said to me, "So I went like this. And one of the niggers says, 'Sheet, you got something under that coat, you better use it.' And I said, 'OK.'"

He pulled his hand out from under his armpit and held it up like a gun. "That was the last thing they ever heard," he said.

He shot them both through the head with a .357 Magnum. And now he was on the run. While we were talking, one of the guys from the Delco chapter pulled up on Beeser, and Big John said that he had to go. I wished him luck. He climbed on the back and I watched his red hair disappear down the highway. That was the last time I ever saw him.

When I got back in the house, John-John was still on the couch with the cap pulled over his face, but he was stretching and moaning like he was waking up. I asked him what he thought about Big John.

"The guy's a fuckin' idiot," he said without lifting the cap from his eyes.

I wasn't quite sure whether he meant for going out with a girl in high school, or shooting the kids, or dressing like a congressional aide for that matter. After all, in our world, when somebody steps on your toes, you take their head off. The shooting was more than justified. But John-John went on and elaborated: "Do you know how many times I've told him, you can't just leave bodies lying in the street like that. You gotta stuff them in the trunk and bury them. Without a *corpus delecti* they can't charge you with murder." Then after dispensing that little tidbit of wisdom, he rolled over on his side, pulled the cap down even further over his eyes, and went back to sleep.

Ten dollars went a lot further in those days than it does today. So when Blackie got up, we decided to ride to Baltimore. We headed straight for Dundalk, where we soon found Foggy, who pulled up his shirt and showed us the two holes in his stomach. Foggy was a union longshoreman, so he made good money and he was determined that his guests would not be allowed to spend any of their own. He took us to all the titty bars in Dundalk, which is the neighborhood around the marine terminal loaded with sailors, sluts, and stevedores. He broke out speed pills and acid, and God-only-knows what else, and offered them to everyone. Meanwhile he kept ordering bottles of National Bohemian, whether we needed them or not, and soon we had two or three of them in front of each of us.

Somewhere along the line I picked up a stripper, a tall, big-chested Valkyrie woman with long, dirty blonde hair. Then there was something about a fight in a parking lot with a bunch of sailors, and Foggy was screaming something at me. The next thing I remember, I woke up back in Mohnton, on the couch in Blackie's living room, flat on my back with the large stripper woman laying on top of me, her large bare boobs pressing down on my bare chest like two large, fleshy pillows.

Blackie staggered out of the bedroom wearing only a pair of Levi's with the zipper open and his hair all messed up.

"My old lady says that we gotta get rid of her," he said.

"How the hell did we get back here?"

"Fuck if I know," he said. "But the bikes are out front and we're not in jail, so it really doesn't matter. But we gotta do something about her before we have a war on our hands. Let me see her tits before she gets dressed."

I rolled the girl over and started waking her up.

Contrary to what Hollywood and Demi Moore like to think, the overwhelming majority of strippers are not single mothers who are working their way through medical school. Most of them, in those days, were pathetic burned-out nincompoops, and many of them had been so physically, psychologically, and sexually abused that they could never be made right.

And this one was no exception. She didn't have a brain in her head, and when she talked she made less sense than Skip and Oakie put together. Her clothes didn't even fit right and she only had one shoe. We had to use some of Baby's old clothes just to get her dressed right so that we could take her out on the street. We tried to figure out what to do with her, but after riding around in the Cadillac and listening to her for 15 minutes, I finally told Blackie to drive us to the bus terminal, where we bought a ticket with the last of our money and stuffed her on a bus for Baltimore.

Then we went back to Pennsylvania, and to the welfare office, where we again told them we had just got out of jail and needed money. This time the office gave me a blue card that said "Alstan's Scrap Yard."

Reading was becoming a rustbelt town fast, and nowhere was this more apparent than Alstan's sprawling scrap yard, where the main business was the demolition of the Reading Railroad. The anthracite coal industry had been dead for over a dozen years. You could probably count on one hand the people in Philly who heated with coal. Between that and the fact that the Susquehanna River had caved in and flooded most of the mines, the Reading Railroad yard was left with hundreds, perhaps thousands, of idle, rusting coal cars. Every day they brought them into the scrap yard, where a team of welders cut them into strips of steel about 10 feet long and 4 feet wide. A crane with an electromagnet then lifted them onto a steel roof on top of a shed. The roof had a slight pitch, and running down the center of it was a conveyer belt in a pit about 5 feet wide.

They gave me a pair of gloves and a steel hook, and told me to climb a ladder onto that roof. Up there, with the noonday sun radiating off the shiny steel, I pulled the steel slabs of railroad car into the pit, where they where carried by the conveyer belt to a hydraulic guillotine. There, an Old Dutchman in one of those black-and-white striped railroad hats cut them up into small pieces that fell into a railroad box car, which hauled them away to the blast furnaces.

With the sun reflecting off the steel roof, it was about 110 degrees by nine o' clock every morning. I pulled off my shirt, but my hair and pants were soon soaked. There was a water spigot in the room under the roof. Every half-hour, I ran down and gulped two half-quart soda bottles of cold water. The guy running the guillotine told me to hurry because the boss would get upset if he looked out and saw him doing nothing. At lunchtime I got a half-hour. The welders brown bagged their lunch and drank coffee out of a thermos. But I ran down the block to a bar, where I told the guy to stick a hamburger on the grill right away and make it rare because I only had a half-hour to eat. I then ordered two pitchers of beer. The first one I drank in about two minutes; the second one I nursed while I ate the hamburger. I made it back just as the old Dutchman in the railroad cap was climbing the ladder to the guillotine.

In those days, beer pitchers held about two quarts; every year since then, they seem to get smaller while the price goes up. With a gallon of beer in me, I felt great in spite of the heat, and I actually was working a lot faster. For about an hour or so, I couldn't feel anything, but then I began to sober up and feel like shit. After a couple of trips downstairs and a couple of gallons of water, things were all right again. All the while, I sweat so much that I didn't even have to piss, no matter how much beer or water I drank.

This went on for a couple of days. At first the Dutchmen with the cutting torches just looked at me kind of funny, because of my beard and all. But when they saw that I could keep up with the guillotine, they began talking to me and seemed to like the way I was working. In fact one of them later told me that before me they had three guys in two weeks up there, and "even the nigger quit."

I couldn't understand why they seemed to care so much that the guillotine kept moving. Then one of them explained the situation. The boss had told them that they were all a bunch of great workers, and he really felt terrible that he couldn't pay them what they were really worth. But since he didn't have any kids, he was going to make it all up to them by leaving them the company when he died.

"So vee don't make a whole lot of money now, but someday this whole place vill be ours."

"In the meantime, get yourself a union," I said. He looked at me as if I had just told him that I was a Communist.

I dragged around dismembered railroad cars for a week and a half. Then one day three open coal cars were pulled into the yard. They were loaded with shredded aluminum that gleamed in the sun.

"Fuckin' aluminum," I thought. "Great, that will be a break from steel."

The electromagnet could barely lift the aluminum out of the boxcar. It came out all tangled and stuck together like the rags at the Berks County Prison. When they finally got some of it on the roof, it was a tangled, shredded, shining mountain of aluminum.

What the fuck am I supposed to do with this, I thought.

The answer wasn't long in coming. One of the Dutch hicksters climbed up the roof. After me, he was the youngest and had the least seniority. He had two long-handled hooks in his hands and he didn't look too happy.

I soon found out why. He gave me one of the hooks. Then he showed me how to stick it into the mass of aluminum and pull like hell. We both did it. Nothing happened. We put the hooks in a different place and pulled like hell. Again, nothing. Finally, on about the sixth try, the aluminum moved a little. We continued doing this until we had the aluminum untangled enough that we could work it into the conveyor pit.

For the next three days I did steel in the morning and the hickster and I did aluminum in the afternoon. When Blackie picked me up at night he screamed, "Look at your the size of your fuckin' arms!" They were pumped up and huge. Meanwhile, I had lost 10 pounds. I had gone from the outlaw motorcyclists of America to the industrial workers of the world. It was different, but I was enjoying things. And I knew that I could stand it if I could someday come home to a row house in downtown Reading with Jane waiting for me.

Blackie had found a job as a maintenance man for a motel, and the two of us sat around drinking beer at night and tried to figure out how we were going to come up with Fred Giorgi's legal fees when we were only bringing home $51.52 a week.

People were also beginning to wonder what was going to happen with Jane and me. She was still under her mother's spell, but Rayels had been dead for almost two months. Although that may be no time at all in the citizen world, it was light years in our universe. It was obviously time for her to "shit or get off the pot," as the old Germans in Ridgewood used to say.

Then one night Blackie and I were sitting in the living room when I heard a knock on the door. Then I heard Baby open the door and say, "Jane's here." My stomach started to flip, and when I ran into the kitchen, there she was, standing by the door with her reddish brown hair and one kid by the hand and the other in a stroller.

We went for a walk. She told me that her mother was in the shower, so she grabbed the two kids and ran out. For some people this may not make much sense; after all she was 21 and had two kids. Unless you were brought up in a German household, though, you cannot understand the unquestioning *ordnung muss sein* institutionalized respect for authority. And she was also, after all, a widow with two kids and no means of independent support. Germans didn't go on welfare, and this was back before they had day care or job training programs for single mothers.

We walked down to a park, where we sat and talked for the first time since the day after Rayels died. She was better, but not much. She still wasn't herself. Today there are words like "depression" and "grieving," but back then they would have meant as much to us as words like aneurysm and schizophrenia. Neither was there such a thing as counseling yet, but even if there had been, outlaws and Dutchman wouldn't have believed in that either. We simply got up everyday and did what we had to. And if things weren't worse at night than they were in the morning, it was a good day. Jane got up every morning and washed and fed the kids. Then she played with them in the backyard. Meanwhile, I went to Alstan's, where I pulled steel and aluminum on a hot roof. Sometimes I almost wished I were back in the Berks County Prison pulling the crank on the wheel for free.

As we sat in the park, Jane explained her mother's plans. She had said that Jane should marry an older man, maybe even a widower with a home and kids of his own. That way Jane could take care of both their kids while he went to work. Very practical, very German, very medieval. Not that it really mattered, since with my track record and impending jail term I would not have made any parent's shortlist of potential husbands for a widow with kids.

As we talked, I suddenly felt a cold, icy presence descending on me. Jane must have felt it too, because she spun her head around. When I looked behind us, I saw the large, Wagnerian form of her mother standing in the road up on the hill behind us. Nothing was said. Jane just grabbed one of the kids and started pushing the stroller home. The mother said nothing, either. She just started walking slowly home behind her.

I realized that the breach in her mother's security would tighten things up even worse, and there was no telling when I would see her again. It was obvious that she wasn't going to openly rebel against the woman, and the mother wasn't about to warm up to me anytime soon.

But it didn't matter; the next day I received a phone call at Chuck Ginder's house. It was Flipout.

"Come home, come home," he said. "You've got to come home, Brother. Davy Kerwin and the Mortician are trying to take over the club."

Fifteen minutes later, Chuck and I were loading the Triumph in the trunk of the old '56 Pontiac. By suppertime I was back in Maspeth, where I parked the car in front of my grandmother's house.

That night I walked into a dirt-floor garage in Polack Alley. The Gypsy and Stevie Hippie were sitting on the greasy floor working on Gypsy's chopper. Sleepy was sitting on a milk crate watching them. After a bunch of enthusiastic "hellos," I sat down on a wooden milk crate next to Sleepy. He reached into a brown paper bag, pulled out a brown quart bottle of Rheingold beer, and handed it to me. As he was handing me a church key, I heard a shrieking falsetto voice come over the radio and start singing "Tiptoe Through the Tulips."

"What the fuck is that?" I shouted.

Sleepy slapped me on the arm with the back of his hand.

"That's my man, Tiny Tim," he said. "Ain't you even heard of him yet? You been away in the country too fuckin' long."

I popped the cap and took a long hard drink. It tasted great—my first Rheingold in four long months.

CHAPTER 18

In a land where justice is outlawed,
The just must become outlaws.

— Zorro

One of my first and more light-hearted adventures on arriving home occurred when someone told one of us that they had seen an FBI poster with a picture of one of our brethren hanging on the wall in the Ridgewood Post Office. It was Big John, and we were delighted. We felt that we had made it to the big leagues, in a manner of speaking; no longer were we merely harassing the Nassau County Police and intimidating the hinds out in suburbia. This was the FBI. We were now in the same class as John Dillinger, Pretty Boy Floyd, John Wesley Hardin, and Jesse James.

"We need one of them for our garage," Sleepy said.

"I'll go down and rip it off the wall in the post office tomorrow," I told him.

Then Stevie Hippie said, "Maybe you better not do that."

Sleepy thought a second and said, "He may be right. It's a post office and everything in there is technically federal property, and walking out of there with it might be a federal felony, And if they really wanted to be dicks, which they probably would when they found out who we were and why we wanted it. . . ."

"But why don't we just go in and ask for one?" Stevie Hippie suggested. "After all, they are trying to catch the guy and you would think they would want as many of them as possible out there in circulation. They might even give us a whole stack if we tell them we want to hang them up in the bars."

It sounded good. So the next day Sleepy and I rode down to the Ridge-wood Post Office where we admired the poster on the wall, and then we waited on line with the Ridgewood burghers. When we got up to the window, an old Dutchman said, "I can't give you boys any posters because I don't have any. The FBI comes by and puts them up, but I'm sure if you fellas go down to the FBI building in Brooklyn, they'll probably give you all you want. After all, they want as many people as possible to see it."

That made sense, but it was also out of the question. Normal people can simply walk into an FBI office building and ask for a wanted poster. They either get them or they don't. But outlaws can't walk into a police station, much less an FBI office. After all, what would people think if Big John were picked up the same evening after I walked into the FBI office? True, I didn't have a clue where he was. But as in the case of politicians, it's what the media refers to as the "mere appearance of impropriety."

However, the matter soon resolved itself. Pappy called from Jersey one night and said, "They got Big John. The FBI picked him up in Danbury, Connecticut."

"Danbury! Why the fuck would anyone want to go to Connecticut?" I said.

But then Sleepy said, "Why the fuck not? Isn't that the last place you would look for anybody?"

"Good point," I thought. I called Big Dutch for confirmation, and he told me that yes, they had picked him up in Connecticut.

The next day Sleepy showed up in the garage with a jug of chianti. As we sat drinking it, we got a bright idea. We rode to downtown Brooklyn, where we chained our bikes to parking meters and walked into the FBI office.

"I'm here for a wanted poster," I told the clerk.

"Just a second," she said.

Then she got on the phone and explained to someone that she had a person at the desk who was looking for a wanted poster. When she got off the phone she sent me to a room on the second floor. Sleepy waited downstairs.

When I walked in, there was a guy in a gray suit behind the desk, and I started to think that maybe this wasn't such a good idea. He asked me to sit down in a chair by the window. When I told him what I wanted, he got on the phone and told someone to bring down one of Big John's wanted posters. A couple of minutes later two more guys in gray suits came through the door behind him. One of them was holding Big John's wanted poster. The three of them started whispering and scrutinizing the poster, while periodically looking up at me. It was obvious what the three stooges were up to.

"Do you think that I'm him?" I asked.

"We have to check it out," one of them said.

I was almost 10 years younger, 3 inches taller, and 60 pounds heavier than Big John. I had straight blonde hair, not curly red hair. I looked like a Bavarian Nazi and nothing like the elfish Irish mug staring up at them from the poster. But all of this seemed to have eluded them.

Finally, I rolled up my sleeves and suggested that they compare my tattoos with those in the description, which they did. None of them matched. Big John had paratrooper wings where I had a swastika. Fortunately for me, between the three of them they were able to discern the difference.

"It's not him," one of them finally mumbled. The two others nodded their heads.

"Do you think I would be so stupid as to walk in here and ask for my own wanted poster?" I asked.

"It's been done before" one of then said solemnly.

By whom, I wondered, *Grover Cleveland Bergdoll?*

Then one of them popped the $64,000 question:

"Do you know this guy?" he asked.

"Yes, quite well."

That got their attention good, and they were all leaning forward now. "Do you know where we can find him?"

"Yes. I do"

"Where?"

"Call your office in Danbury," I said. "They picked him up last night."

They were on the phone to Connecticut in a heartbeat.

"Are you sure? Are you sure?" the guy kept asking. Then he put the phone down and said to me, "You can get the fuck out now."

"Do I get the poster?"

"No."

I left empty-handed, but on the way back we passed a Post Office. I walked in and ripped the poster off the wall while Sleepy watched for trouble. It had been fun, and actually it was the first time I had been in a police station with nothing to hide.

We had an easy, laidback summer, but then things began to deteriorate. I was on bail and I needed money. My club finally split into two separate chapters. It had been coming for some time. The Mortician and Davy Supermouth were getting fed up with the outlandish behavior of some of the brothers. Also, half the guys were now living in eastern Suffolk County, and the other half were living in western Queens and Brooklyn. Davy and the Mortician took Geoff, Stretch, and a couple of other guys and, along with the Mortician's brother, Paul "Ooch" Ferry, formed a new chapter in Suffolk County, which flew a Long Island patch.

We stayed in Maspeth, Ridgewood, and Greenpoint, and we reverted to the original New York patch. Things continued heading toward the shithouse. Flipout finally went to jail. Bobo got in a jam and split for Florida, but not before apologizing for not being able to pay me for a motorcycle I sold him and handing me 1911 Colt as compensation.

Then Stevie Hippie came up to me one afternoon with his club patches in one hand and a white envelope in the other. He handed me his patches.

"What's this?" I asked.

He handed me the envelope. I opened it. It was his draft notice.

"You might be able to get out of this," I said.

"Nope," he said. "I'm going." And he did, which is more than can be said for at least two recent presidents of the United States.

At the time, the Pennsylvania Court of Common Pleas was structured so that they held trial four times a year: March, June, September, and December. Your case was always scheduled for the next session, so every four months you had to quit work and go sit in court for two weeks. But more often than not, your case ended up getting postponed until the next session.

So every four months, I lost my seniority down at the 816 Teamster shape hall and took off for Reading, wondering if I was going to come back or not. The first three times our case was continued. Each time I stayed with Chuck, who was having the same problems that I was. For starters, the police had undertaken a harassment campaign of the landlord, until he kicked Chuck and the club off Mount Penn. Chuck was now living in a small row house in town. They no longer had a clubhouse, and half the time he didn't even know where his people were. He was busting his hump to come up with legal fees and at the same time support his family, while trying to keep his people's noses out of shit until the current mess was cleaned up.

But when the bull moose is wounded, that's when the wolves close in for the kill. And while we were hurting, another club was flourishing.

The Breed first appeared on Long Island in the summer of '67. A lot of them were older guys, many Vietnam veterans who had seen all the fighting they needed for a lifetime and now just wanted to ride in peace. They took a big red-white-and-blue, 13-star colonial American flag and sewed it on the back of cut-off denim vests. They forbade their members from wearing swastikas or any other "un-American" emblems. They also forbade their members from wearing one-percenter patches.

They soon had the best of all possible worlds. With their Revolutionary War flags, army patches, and buttons that said things like "Bomb Hanoi Now" and "Kill Jane Fonda," the cops left them alone and the rednecks loved them to death. By wearing denim vests and sporting long hair, they disassociated themselves from the old '50s Marlon Brando and AMA images. They looked like outlaws and the girls loved them. After all, as Chuck Ginder so eloquently put it, "what did some leaky 20-year-old cunt who's looking for a ride on the back of a motorcycle know, or even care, about the significance of a one-percenter patch and outlaw brotherhood."

On the other hand, by not trying to fly one-percenter patches and insisting that they were not outlaws, but just good old boys who started a club and wanted to be left alone to ride in peace, they avoided heat from the outlaw clubs. Besides, most of the outlaws knew and got along with many of the guys who were joining the Breed. We knew that they were nice guys who didn't want trouble, and they were certainly not about to go to jail for a club. The guys were simply not outlaw material. We knew it and we left them alone. And they were damn sure to leave us alone—at first.

But with their all-American—if not exactly clean-cut—image and hassle-free lifestyle, their membership exploded and they were soon starting chapters all over New York, Jersey, and Pennsylvania. Soon there seemed to be more Breed members on the road than Honda jockeys. You would go to a bike show and there would be a half-dozen outlaws and a hundred sets of Breed colors. At times, you would even see Aliens and Pagans hanging together, joined in common cause for the first time ever. Many of the older Breed members dropped out, and eventually the club made the transition over to outlaw. This caused some turf problems with outlaw clubs that had coexisted with the Breed. And soon it was obvious that a reckenin' was coming down the road.

For years Chuck had made sure that the Heathens and Pagans were the only club in Reading. Citizen bikers were cautious about riding in large packs, and they didn't dare wear cut-off denim jackets with any sort of patches. But then in May of 1969, some Breed members and their women rode into town and settled into a rundown second-floor apartment on Laurel Street in South Reading. One of them was 22-year-old Robert Makowski, a Breed member from New Jersey. One Sunday morning he got up and decided to take his girlfriend for a ride in the country. He was also flying Breed colors.

Late that afternoon, as he was riding across the Schuylkill River on his way back into Reading, he noticed a small pack of bikers approaching him. He thought that they were Breed so he pulled his bike over and waved to them. The first two blew right past him, but the third one stopped. He was big and had a beard and greasy hair. He glared at Makowski. Then he tried to look behind him and read the patch on his back, but the girl was in the way.

"You Breed?" he demanded.

"Yeah, I am," Makowski shot back.

The other guy reached for his waist with a big hairy paw. He came up with a steel chain with a lock on the end of it and began flailing it around his head King Arthur style. "There ain't enough room in Reading for the Breed and the Pagans," he snarled, as he brought the chain down on Makowski's skull with such force that it split open the fiberglass helmet he was wearing. The girl jumped off the bike and ran screaming like hell for the Laurel Street apartment, while the unidentified biker administered a chain whipping to Makowski as the horrified burghers of South Reading watched from their porches.

That night, the Breed members sat in their apartment behind a locked door, making plans to return to Jersey. But it was too late. A sledgehammer shattered the door and took it right off the hinges. In a berserker rage, Chuck Ginder burst into the room at the head of a band of Pagans. They began ransacking the apartment and pulling the Breed colors off people's backs. The donnybrook spilled out into the hall, where they were putting people's heads through walls and throwing them down the stairs. At this point it was a simply a rumble between two biker clubs, but all that changed dramatically when a 60-year-old Dutchman who lived down the hall popped his head out to see what the ruckus was all about.

Any other place in the world, a 60-year-old man would be scared shitless and stay locked safely in his apartment while the hallway was being ransacked by two biker clubs. But there is a reason why the Irish, Italians, and Hunkies refer to them as "dumb Dutchmen."

Instead of closing the door and calling the cops, the old man stepped out in the hallway and began reading the riot act and ordering the warring bikers out of the house. Finally, someone took notice and punched him in the mouth to shut him up. But this only brought the Dutchman's son out the door and into the hall. He was carrying a loaded shotgun, which he was holding at his waist like a carbine, and he began pumping off shots indiscriminately into the crowd. He caught Skip with a load of buckshot right in the gut, between his pubes and his navel. Then he leaned over the landing and shot Righteous Fuckin' Elroy in the ass as he was running out the door.

Skip was obviously dying. They tossed him in a car and raced him to the hospital. It was only after they got Skip to the hospital that someone noticed Elroy was missing. The cops found him later that night in West Reading near an abandoned mineshaft where he had been living. He was passed out in a pool of blood with a load of buckshot in his ass.

Skip lived, and so did Elroy, and the next morning they were both in the prison ward at Community General Hospital, in critical and guarded conditions, respectively. Chuck and Blackie were in the Berks County Prison, but at least the Breed was out of Reading.

A year earlier, they all would have been charged with disorderly conduct. But the police were getting wise. They realized that the difference between a fraternity prank and a felony is often a mere technicality. They charged them with burglary (breaking into the apartment) and larceny, theft, and receiving stolen goods (the Breed colors). This not only increased the seriousness of the charges, but also enabled the magistrates to jack the bail up through the roof. So things were not looking good, in New York or Pennsylvania. Exactly one month later, all of us went on trial in the Berks County Court of Common Pleas on felony riot charges stemming from the brawl at the Pleasantville Hotel a year earlier.

At a time when many outlaws were learning the importance of playing by the rules—which is to say cleaning up, washing your hair, and leaving the leather and chains at home when they went to court—and at least one big outlaw club was forbidding its members from wearing swastikas in an effort to clean up its public image—Chuck Ginder refused to be intimidated by any of this and decided to take his club out as the last true outlaws.

He told us that putting on citizen clothes and playing by their rules was a sign of submission, and that was not what outlaws were all about. When the trial opened, he marched his club into the courtroom, decked out in chrome chains, black leather jackets, beards, earrings, long hair, and swastikas. And there he stood glaring at the judge and jury, defying them to convict him.

Right beside him was Skip, at 20, not even old enough to drink legally in Pennsylvania, but with a 17-year-old wife and a screaming baby at home, a month-old shotgun wound healing up in his belly, and 10 years of state time staring him in the face. And none of it had ever put so much as a gallon of gas in his car or a Philly cheesesteak on his table. Nevertheless, there he stood, decked out in black leather, denim and swastikas, sneering at the judge and letting him know that he could take his whole act and shove it up his ass if he didn't like it.

Again, this is what the old outlaws meant by "true class." As I pointed out earlier, the Mennonite martyr Simon de Kramer was executed in the Netherlands when he refused to bend his knee and genuflect before a Spanish bishop who, in a lavish display of piety, was carrying a consecrated host through the marketplace in Bergen op Zoom. Whether we look at Simon swinging on the gallows for refusing to genuflect in the Netherlands, Lucifer getting cast into Hell for refusing to kneel before the throne of God in Heaven, or Skip, Chuck, and the whole crew getting carted off to jail for refusing to kowtow before judge and jury in Berks County, Pennsylvania, it is all the same colossal *chutzpah* that makes real outlaws what they are. And this is exactly what I meant when I said that the original outlaw bikers in Pennsylvania were imbued with the same spirit of religious fanaticism that their ancestors imported from the Rhine River valley.

So there I now stood, next to Chuck Ginder and the Reading Pagans, sneering at judge and jury. And we made our point. We scared the shit out of the entire courtroom, including the jury. And they responded by convicting us on all charges, including the felonies.

The Heathens and the Pagans of Reading may not have been the most flamboyant, the most colorful, or the best party people among outlaw clubs. How could they be? They were Pennsylvania Dutchmen. But they were the most righteous. When the end came, they had lived as outlaws and they went down like outlaws. All of them sat next to Chuck ready to give up home, jobs and family, rather than compromise with the society they had rejected. None of them became informers, none of them offered to join the army and go to Vietnam if the charges were dropped. None of them even sought a plea bargain.

Four years later, I watched the U.S. government self-destruct over the Watergate scandal. I was shocked. I had expected the leaders of our country to be as tough as George Patton, or General Custer, or Davy Crockett, but instead they turned out to be a bunch of whining, sniveling, pleacopping, born-again weenies. Only one of them seemed to have as much class, character, and intestinal fortitude as Chuck Ginder and the Reading Pagans, and that man was G. Gordon Liddy.

After we were convicted, our bail was revoked and a new bail was set pending our sentencing, which could take up to a year. The judge could have simply continued the old bail and let us go home, but by setting a new bail we had to come up with the bail bondsman's fees all over again. This was about $500 at the time, which meant that we were on our way back to the Berks County Prison.

Blackie and I were again handcuffed together. It seemed to be our fate that we were bonded with steel bracelets, and we ended up handcuffed together every time we were transferred from one prison to another, right up until we were released in the Berks County Courthouse a year and a half later.

On the way to the prison, one of the sheriff's deputies, a gray-haired old man who spoke with a heavy Dutch accent, warned us to watch ourselves. As it turned out, there was a new warden. Conditions were deteriorating—particularly the quality of the food—and it was not the Dutch country club that it had been. What's more, the black population had more than doubled in the past year, many of whom were Muslims and black militants. Furthermore, there was a local character named Ray Krackhauser, who claimed to be the head of the Ku Klux Klan, the American Nazi Party, and various other organizations of the same political leaning. It seems that he got a bunch of young white kids all psyched up, and they drove through the black section of Reading shooting people in the ass with BB guns. Now they too were in the Berks County Prison, and the warden was braced for the arrival of about a dozen members of the Pagans MC.

"You boys watch yourself," the old Dutchman said. "The new warden's expecting big trouble from you guys." Blackie and I assured him that we had enough problems and weren't looking for any more.

When I got to the prison, one of my first stops was the prison library. I had become a voracious reader over the past year. It all started shortly after I got out of jail the previous summer. One day out of boredom I got on my bike and took a ride over the Williamsburg Bridge into Manhattan. I parked the bike and while I was walking around Greenwich Village, I passed a small book store, where the window was filled with about a hundred copies of the same small black paperback book: *The Diary of Che Guevara.*

At first I did a double-take and looked a little closer. *The authorized text with an introduction by Fidel "fucken" Castro,* I thought, *they're both Communists. What is this country coming to?* But then I thought about it and realized that's what a free country is all about. We're free to read their shit, but they're not free to read ours. *Maybe,* I thought, *I should take advantage of it and see what the guy actually has to say for himself. After all it's only $1.25.*

I went in and bought the book. I read it in about two days, and the day after that, I was back at the book shop, where I bought a copy of Guevara's *Reminiscences of the Cuban Revolutionary War.* I decided that a lot could be learned from books. I was shaping up at a local 816 Teamster job, delivering liquor. I earned more in two days than I did in a week at Alstan's scrap yard. But there were times when we were slow, and I didn't work for two or three days in a row. Then I spent all day reading. I read *The Communist Manifesto, The Federalist Papers,* the works of Thomas Jefferson, the plays of Sean O'Casey, and Brendan Behan's *Confessions of an Irish Rebel.* Then I looked for German-American writers and discovered H.L. Mencken and a guy my grandfather's age who grew up only a couple of blocks away from me in Brooklyn. His name was Henry Miller, and he had a typical New York German cynical *klugscheisser* attitude about everything. Because I was reading this stuff untutored and from the perspective of an outlaw biker, the above list of authors tended to confirm my beliefs that society was all fucked up and the people running it were either crooks or outright scumbags. In any event, I returned to jail a lot better educated, and probably a lot more dangerous than I had been a year earlier.

At the prison library, I picked up a copy of *Moby Dick* and *The Count of Monte Cristo.* One of our lawyers, Bill Bernhart, was highly amused that they would allow people in jail to read *The Count of Monte Cristo,* which tells the story of a wrongfully imprisoned man who takes a horrible revenge on the authorities who sent him to jail.

When I got back to my cellblock, Chuck Ginder was talking to a young black man about my age, who showed a great deal of interest in the books under my arm. His name was Ed Butler, and he was a black militant who believed that black Americans could start solving most of their problems if they simply made sure that they read more books than white people did. Butler and I became good friends. Blackie had gone to Reading High School with a lot of the black guys, gotten in trouble with a lot of them, and gotten kicked out of school with them. And as I already said, most of the black guys in Reading might as well have been Dutch. They did not swagger like Philadelphia jitterbugs, and they had a Dutch, "I respect you, you respect me, and we'll get along fine," attitude. As long as different people show respect and courtesy, the Dutch are probably the most tolerant of all rednecks in America. So the whole prison got along fine, except for Krackhauser's boys, who felt that the Pagans should have formed an Aryan alliance with them.

One day, someone came up to me and said that one of Krackhauser's boys had said that the Pagans ain't nothing but a bunch of nigger lovers. I headed straight for the cellblock, but when I got there, two black guys blocked my way.

"Please," one of them said, "Let us handle this. We deal with this all the time. Every time a white person treats us decent, they start getting shit from their own people."

"I take care of my own problems," I said, as I pushed them out of the way.

But it was too late. When I got to the kid's cell, there was a big black guy there with a broken arm, using his cast as a club to beat the kid unconscious. So I just returned to the main block thinking what a funny place this world is.

There continued to be a lot of discontent. The old Dutch sheriff's deputy had been right. It wasn't the club it had been. Eventually, some of the black militants got together with the Dutch Mafia that ran the jail. They decided to go on strike and refuse to lock up. I was honored when they asked me and Ed Butler to write up the list of grievances. But Big Ski said that "you're just gonna get yourself fucked. Stay out of it."

I didn't. Ed and I drew up the list with a lot of pomp and heavy Latinate diction that self-educated convicts tend to be so proud of. The leaders of the strike decided to wait until the day when the warden went on vacation to Atlantic City to pull it off. Chuck said, "That's dumb. He ain't gonna come back to talk to us. He's just gonna send in the state police to beat the shit out of us with clubs."

So there we were at nine o'clock on the night of the strike, all the Pagans huddled together in the main block. A guard announced, "Lock up time." And we all walked over to the wall and sat down.

"Vot's dis?" one of the guards demanded. Then Duke Mason and one of the black guys stood up and explained that we were on strike.

They called the warden in Atlantic City. For two hours, we sat on the floor arguing over who was more likely to come through the gates: the warden or the state police with clubs. To his credit the warden came alone, and he was cool. He said he would discuss the matter tomorrow. In the meantime, he asked us to return to our cells. And he promised that the ringleaders would not be dragged off to the state pen in the middle of the night.

He was a Dutchman; he kept his word. There was some discussion, but little happened. Before the matter was resolved, we were again out on bail and scrambling for money to pay for an appeal.

CHAPTER 19

The stars move still, time runs, the clock will strike,
The Devil will come, and Faustus must be damned.
— Christopher Marlowe, *Doctor Faustus*

I was back in New York scrambling for money to pay for an appeal and trying to stay out of trouble. My club disintegrated into nothing. Sleepy ran off with Tony the Gypsy's wife, but Gypsy wouldn't let her take the kid, so she came back a week later. I had to pull Sleepy's colors. Did that ever hurt. Then Gypsy moved to Florida, where his wife's people were from, in order to try to patch up his marriage. Bobby Flipout was still in jail, Bobo was still on the run someplace in Florida, and Stevie Hippie was in the army. I was alone, and I spent most of my evenings sitting in Wally's Bar and Grill, a place down Polack Alley so ethnic that they had a version of Harry Belafonte's "Banana Boat Song" in Polish.

There was still some hope that Fred Giorgi and Bill Bernhart might convince the judge that it really was just a barroom fight and that he might let us off with three to six months in the county jail. But that seemed ridiculous. Van Hoove and the judge had the Pagans by the balls on two state felony charges, and neither of them was not about to let go. So we lived with the reality that any day, we might get a phone call from our lawyers saying that we were due in court for sentencing.

Finally, Chuck called the week before Thanksgiving and told me that we were going to be sentenced on Tuesday. Then he added that we were really fucked now because they moved our sentencing date up on account of "Dreamland Park."

"What the fuck is Dreamland Park?" I asked.

"Dreamland Park. Haven't you heard about the Dreamland Park murders? It's been on national TV all week."

"I don't watch much TV," I told him. They didn't have a TV in Wally's.

He then relayed the bare outline of an eerie tale, which I later found out went like this:

A biker they called the Arab showed up and began hanging around. He wasn't really an Arab; his mother was Dutch, but his old man was some sort of foreigner from the Middle East. Not a real Arab or even a towelhead, but some sort of Armenian, Turk, or Lebanese. Not that any of the guys gave a shit, they were all foreigners, camel jockeys and towelheads to them, so they just called him the Arab and pronounced it A-rab.

The Arab's old man was quite a wealthy and successful businessman. Rumor had it that he owned the water company, the electric company, and bunch of other prime real estate around town. One of his holdings was a defunct amusement park out on the Pricetown Road called Dreamland Park. Back in the 1940s and 1950s, it was the hot spot to take a date, but it was a boarded-up white elephant with weeds growing around the wooden roller coaster.

In the middle of the park was an old casino with a roller-skating rink. The Arab was using the place as a hangout for bikers, hippies, degenerate drug users, and runaway girls. Eventually Righteous Fuckin' Elroy found the place and was using it for a crash pad, since it sure beat the abandoned mineshaft in West Reading where he had been living. Chuck didn't like the idea. He could see nothing but trouble coming down the road from a mile away. But with his clubhouse gone, there was little he could do.

Then at the beginning of August, a pack of bikers blew into town from Florida. They called themselves the Thunderbolts, and their leader was Bobby "the Juice" Martinolich, the guy who pistol-whipped the suspected narc when he found out the gun wasn't loaded. He used our name and our connection to ingratiate himself with Chuck. Then he settled in with his club at the amusement park on Pricetown Road, where everyone seemed to exist on a diet of speed, booze, pot, and acid.

Ten miles out of town, in a heavily wooded rural area, it would seem that they couldn't get in much trouble or hurt anyone other than themselves. But then a series of bizarre events began shortly after dark on the night of August 12, 1969. Just before midnight, 20-year-old James Buchter and two companions arrived with multiple injuries in the emergency room at Saint Joseph's Hospital in Reading. Buchter had a large, gaping hole in his shoulder and claimed that he had "fallen on same glass." But the ER doctor took one look at the X-ray and called the state police. When they arrived, the doctor told them that there is no way that a wound that deep was caused by "falling on some glass." After some prodding by the cops, Buchter and his companions related the following tale:

They had gone to visit a friend out on the Pricetown Road, but they got lost. Shortly after dark, they turned on to a macadam road which led them to a locked gate at Dreamland Park. Realizing their mistake, they turned around, only to find the road blocked by a van. Several men, who they described as "bikers," jumped out of the van, pulled them from the car, and began beating them with chains and clubs. One of the bikers stabbed Buchter in the shoulder with an "elaborately decorated knife." Then the bikers warned them not to say a word about the incident to anyone or they would kill their families. Shortly afterwards, Buchter arrived at the home of his brother-in-law with his two companions and a badly bleeding shoulder. The brother-in-law then sent him to the hospital with a concocted story about falling on glass.

The police were confused. They were beginning to learn more and more about bikers and their lifestyle, and this story just didn't sound right. Bikers could be violent when provoked, but they managed to get into enough trouble as it was without arbitrarily running people off the road and stabbing them for no reason.

Nevertheless Lieutenant Robert Schuck obtained search warrants, and at about 3:30 a.m. he and a dozen state troopers raided the compound at Dreamland Park, where they found six people huddled in sleeping bags around the embers of a dying fire. When asked what they were doing at the park compound, they explained that they had rented it from the Arab's old man for 50 bucks a month. The police then arrested four men, all members of the Thunderbolts, and two 18-year-old girls, and charged them with about a dozen crimes, ranging from assault and attempted murder to conspiracy and narcotics possession.

The following day they placed the area under helicopter surveillance and that evening the police picked up Bobby the Juice Martinolich and Righteous Fuckin' Elroy as they were walking along the road. The next morning, Bobby the Juice was recovering in the prison ward at Reading Hospital after emergency surgery for mysterious internal injuries. Commander Philip Chulick of the local state police explained that while Martinolich was being questioned at the police barracks he began "to show signs of drug withdrawal and went berserk. He then had to be restrained, and in this condition," Chulick added, "any number of things could have happened to cause his injuries."

The following afternoon, a cop saw another Thunderbolt, Harlan "the Wolfman" Bailey, along with the Arab buying gas in Muhlenberg Township. They too were arrested, handcuffed, and shipped off to join the others at the Berks County Prison. The bail bondsman wouldn't even touch the Thunderbolts from Florida. Elroy was in so much trouble by now that the bail bondsman figured he might as well just stay and start serving one of his sentences for which he was about to get time anyhow. But the Arab was bailed out by his old man and promptly split for Texas.

And there things sat for the next two months. Preliminary hearings were postponed because prosecutors were having trouble with witnesses who could say little more than that they were attacked by "bikers." Two of the alleged attackers were actually little girls, and four of them had not even been present when police raided the compound the night of the assault. Defense attorneys were whining about probable cause and lack of positive identification. The whole thing did not look good for District Attorney Robert Van Hoove or the Pennsylvania State Police.

At this point, it did appear that they had just gone out and arrested longhairs on motorcycles just because the victims said their assailants looked like bikers. Now if the victims had said "hippies" or "niggers" did it, the cops would not have gone out and randomly busted longhair students at Albright College or Sunday worshipers at the local African Methodist Episcopal Church. Something clearly had to be done to save face and strengthen this case.

So on a bright October morning, when nothing much was going on at the local police barracks, State Police Commander Chulick told Trooper Robert Kaunert to take a ride out the Pricetown Road and have a look around the park grounds for some as-yet undiscovered evidence.

Trooper Kaunert obliged and drove out the Pricetown Road expecting a pleasant, peaceful, and uneventful afternoon. For a while he was walking around the woods, kicking the brightly colored dead leaves without much luck, but then he noticed the sun glistening off some bright object a short distance away from him. He walked over to investigate, and there, sitting on what looked like a pile of dead leaves, he found a pair of eyeglasses. As he reached down to pick them up, Kaunert discovered that the eyeglasses were sitting on a skull. And when he moved some of the leaves, he found the skull attached to a badly decomposed body. Then, under closer inspection, Kaunert discovered that the skull contained two small holes, which he thought looked suspiciously like bullet holes. Kaunert was on his car radio in a heartbeat, and within minutes the place was swarming with state and local police. The skeleton was taken to Saint Joseph's Hospital, and that evening the Berks County Coroner's Office identified it as the remains of Glenn W. Eckert. This kicked everything up a notch and soon put the investigation into high gear.

It seems that two months earlier, Glenn Eckert himself had been the subject of a newspaper article. The night of August 12, the same night that Ronald Buchter showed up at the ER with a hole in his shoulder claiming that he been attacked by "bikers," was the last time anyone saw Glen. Eckert's father operated Boscov's Country Kitchen, a restaurant in Robesonia, a small town clear on the western side of the county, where Eckert arrived at closing time, as was his custom, and picked up the receipts. Employees claimed that he left with the cashier, 18-year-old Marilyn Sheckler. They said that the two of them "had a date."

The following morning, when Glenn was not in his bed, Charles Eckert reported his son missing. That afternoon Marilyn's brother, Grant Sheckler, told police that the couple had stopped at his trailer, where Marilyn lived, and told him that they were going out for a while, but he had not seen his sister since. The car that Eckert had been driving was later discovered by the railroad station in Leesport, a small rural town on the Schuylkill River about five miles north of Reading. Two pairs of loafers had been found in the car, along with some of Eckert's clothing and a bag containing $489.23.

Leesport Police Chief David Kintzer claimed that there was no evidence of foul play, for residents had seen the two walking barefoot down Railroad Avenue on Thursday or Friday night. He had also checked with New York State Police to see if the two had been seen at a large rock concert in Woodstock that weekend, but the New York State Police simply told him, "You've got to be kidding." Now, two months later, Pennsylvania State Police were staring at the badly decomposed body of Glenn Eckert with what appeared to be two bullet holes in his skull.

The following morning Trooper Kaunert returned to the woods around Dreamland Park with three mine detectors and an army of state troopers from three separate barracks. After about an hour of searching, Kaunert again hit pay dirt when he moved some rocks and discovered a skeleton with what appeared to be a crushed skull. That afternoon the county coroner identified the skeleton as the remains of Marilyn Sheckler.

The autopsies determined that Eckert had been shot and beaten, and that Sheckler's skull had been crushed by a rock. The case was soon plastered on the covers of supermarket tabloids. The entire county was outraged and the newspapers immediately connected the bodies and the bikers. Howls went up demanding justice. And Robert Van Hoove had yet another corncob to work out his ass. To him, like most other people, "the bikers" seemed to be the obvious answer.

But the police were not so sure. In fact they were puzzled. They were bothered by the fact that Eckert's car had been discovered 10 miles away and that no money was taken. Also, they doubted seriously that six bikers would have crawled into sleeping bags after such a crime and just waited for the police to show up. And why would Harlan the Wolfman Bailey be standing around a gas station a few hours later flying colors, or why would Rightous Fuckin' Elroy and Bobby the Juice be casually strolling around the site of a double murder the next day, just waiting for the police to drop by and pick them up? If police had learned anything about bikers, it was that they had the survival instincts of coyotes. They were paranoid, they were highly mobile, and if they had anything to do with the murders, they would be gone. Quite frankly, the cops really were puzzled, and they concluded that the two incidents were just coincidental.

But if the police were puzzled, at least one person was not. And that was the Arab's old man. He was a foreigner and a shrewd businessman who was familiar with the American system, but he harbored no altruistic delusions about freedom, equal opportunity, or justice for all. He was also intimately familiar with the Berks County political machine, and he harbored no delusions whatsoever about that either. He knew that politics in Berks County were every bit as corrupt as the bodies of Glenn Eckert and Marilyn Sheckler. The machine was under intense criticism for corruption, and like all the politicians, the district attorney was under pressure to do something, and do it fast.

As the Arab's old man sat reading the papers, a gruesome picture began to emerge in his mind. The corpses of two young people, who were obviously the victims of some horrible crime, had been discovered on *his* property. Nine people, who were allegedly *his* tenants, were in jail. And *his* own son was out on bail, but had split for Texas. The police may have been baffled by it all, but the old man was certain of one thing: someone was going down for this. Baffled or not, the cops and the courts would eventually have to blame someone, anyone, and guilty or not, that someone would have to pay. He was determined to make sure that all of this shit would not eventually come down on *his*, or *his* son's head.

While police and reporters continued to ask questions, the old man got busy. First, he picked up the phone and began calling in favors. Within hours he was on a plane for Texas, accompanied by a uniformed

Pennsylvania state trooper. When they got to Texas, they rented a car and drove to the motel where the Arab was holed up. The cop sat in the car while the old man went inside to talk to his son. An hour later, the two emerged and the son surrendered to the cop, who brought him back to Pennsylvania in handcuffs.

The Arab claimed that he had no part in the murders and that he had not witnessed them, thus in no way implicating himself. But he claimed that while he was sitting around a campfire, Bobby the Juice casually mentioned to him that he had just shot Glenn Eckert, who, according to the Arab, had been kidnapped along with his girlfriend and brought to Dreamland Park. In return for this testimony, the Arab never went to prison.

This was enough to charge Martinolich. And police then planted the word in Berks County Prison that they had a snitch. The Arab was back from Texas and had flipped. They wanted more witnesses, and they were willing to deal.

Harlan the Wolfman Bailey, the Thunderbolt who had been arrested with the Arab at the gas station, took the bait and swallowed it hook, line, and sinker. In return for his freedom, he offered up the following tidbit of information. Leroy Stoltzfus had murdered Marilyn Sheckler. Now he too had not been there to witness it. But after the corpses were discovered he claimed that he had heard Elroy walking around the jail saying, "It was me. It was me. I did it. I crushed the girl's head with a rock and it felt soooooo goooood."

Wolfman then spun out a tale for the DA that would have been worthy of Baron von Munchhausen, the greatest liar in history. He claimed that the couple had been abducted, or escorted, to the Thunderbolt campsite at Dreamland Park. The girl then had sex with several of the guys. When she finished, she joined Wolfman, who was sitting by the campfire. She then told him that she had enjoyed him the best, and the two supposedly made a date for the following Thursday. Somehow things got out of hand, according to the Wolfman, and Eckert was shot, then Elroy crushed the girl's head with a rock. Of course, Wolfman was out in the woods taking a wizz, or something like that, while all of this happened. So he didn't actually see any of this happen and, most importantly, was not there when it happened. In fact, the way he told it, he had wandered off for a while and a double murder had taken place, yet he knew nothing about it until he read about it while he was sitting in jail two months later.

Jurors are told that they may believe all or part of any witness's testimony. In this case, they chose to believe the Wolfman when he said he heard Elroy in jail say that he did it. In the end, the only two people who admitted to having any knowledge of the murders, Wolfman and the Arab, went free. And the only two convicted were Stoltzfus and Martinolich, who supposedly had the stupidity to return the day after the murders to the very site of a double homicide where everyone else had been arrested the night before.

After we went to jail, we spent many a lonely night speculating on what actually happened. Leroy said that he didn't do it, and that was good enough for us, so we didn't push him. Some guys said that given the wicked combination of street drugs they were doing out there at the camp, anything was possible. Other guys insisted that it was out of character for Elroy, but not for the Juice. Finally, Chuck blurted out one night, "I don't care what anyone says, that guy used to babysit my two little girls while I took my wife to a movie. In fact," he emphasized, "I would still let him babysit my daughters."

But none of that mattered. For years Chuck Ginder and the Heathens and Reading Pagans operated with class and dignity, even if it was in an outlaw manner of speaking. As noted before, the *Reading Eagle* investigated reports that three police officers bolted out the back door in terror when we burst into the Pleasantville Hotel the previous spring. This type of awe-inspiring reputation, however brutal, was built by ass-kicking, shit-stomping Dutch rednecks, not by people who shoot helpless men and bludgeon little girls to death. Then suddenly another club blows into town, and they are involved in a murder. A Pagan goes to jail on the word of a Thunderbolt who bought his freedom by fingering somebody else.

To this day the Thunderbolts are forgotten and people still think only of the Pagans every time they hear the word Dreamland Park. This goes a long way in explaining why you don't allow other clubs in your town, why you bust them in the head with chains for flying their colors, why you burst into their apartment, pull their patches, and end up taking a gut shot like Skip did. Because you learn from experience that no town is big enough for two outlaw clubs.

I once told the story about Skip getting shot over the hassle with the Breed to a member of the Vietnam Vets Motorcycle Club. He shook his head and said, "And what for? Over a stupid jacket."

"No," I said "Think about it a minute, and you tell me what makes more sense. Getting shot defending *your* reputation, in *your* hometown, where *you* were born, and where people respect *you*? Or going halfway around the world and shooting some poor gook in the ass while he's just trying to take a shit in his own backyard? And what for, because the Archbishop of Boston told JFK that it might be a good idea to prop up a corrupt government because it was, nevertheless, being run by devout Catholics?"

A week after Elroy was arrested, the rest of us were all in court standing before the judge. We weren't supposed to be sentenced for a couple of months—something about completing a "pre-sentencing investigation." But such things didn't matter now. They yanked our case, yanked our bail, and yanked us into court immediately. When they had us lined up, a door opened behind the judge, and two uniformed state troopers brought Elroy into the courtroom in handcuffs. Then they took the handcuffs off him so as not to prejudice the judge, and they stood him between me and Eggy. He gave me a big "hello" and a hug. Bill Bernhart reminded the judge that we should all be sentenced as individuals. The judge agreed, and then he went down the line and sentenced each and every one of us to "one-and-one-half to five years" in a state penitentiary. Bernhardt asked that we be released on bail since he had filed a direct appeal to superior court. The judge shrugged his shoulders and said that it was the superior court's problem.

With our options exhausted, we were led out of the court in handcuffs and driven to the Berks County Prison, Blackie and I again make the trip sharing the same set of bracelets. It was the Tuesday before Thanksgiving, and they had a new policy. They kept you locked down in your cell for the first three days that you were there, figuring that if you were going to wig, you would do it by then. They stuck us all in C-Block in a row, except for Elroy. He was in the hole.

The hole wasn't very sophisticated; in fact, it was right out of the Middle Ages. The last three cells on both sides of C-Block were separated from the rest of the block by a screen wall. The door was secured by a simple Yale lock. I used to stick a match in it every chance I got and then watched the guards have to cut it off with a hacksaw. You couldn't get near the people in the hole, but you could scream back and forth.

The reason Elroy was in the hole was because they thought he had wigged. And I guess he had. It had become a nightly ritual, and the black guys in particular loved it. Shortly after lock-up Elroy would begin screaming down the cellblock and taunting the guards.

Every night it was: "You motherfuckers! Hey assholes, I'm talking to you!"

And every night, the Dutch hicksters responded the same way, with the same surprise and confusion as if it was the first time. First they ignored him, but this didn't work. And Elroy kept it up: "Fuckin' motherfuckers, you hear me assholes!"

Elroy kept it up until finally a guard shouted down the block, "Hey Leroy, shut up!"

Now he knew he had their chain and he knew he had it good. "Shut up and go fuck your mother asshole!"

"Hey Leroy, I'm not kidding this time, shut up."

"I'm not kidding either this time. I thought I told you to go fuck your mother. What in hell are you still doin' standin' there, runnin' your mouth!"

Finally, they would get a bunch of guards to shout down the cellblock, but that didn't work either. Then they would take the guy with the least seniority and make him walk down the end of the cellblock to the wire mesh wall and yell at him to shut up. They hated this. The fat little guard had to walk all the way down the cellblock, past all the cells with every-one of us grinning through the bars. He stared straight ahead, his face turning red. Dutchmen can't hide embarrassment.

At first he tried to talk. "Hey Leroy, a choke is a choke, but that's enough now, you hear me."

"I hear you motherfucker, and if you don't shut up I'm gonna come out and cornhole you right up your fat ass."

The guard would then have to walk all the way back down the cell block, with all of us grinning through the bars and with Leroy shouting at him that if he didn't get out of the cellblock, he was gonna ram a bat up his ass, or something to that effect.

The guards would then get in a huddle at the end of the cellblock, with Leroy taunting them the whole time. Finally, the delegation would come down the cellblock, about five of them with stern faces and wooden clubs.

They opened the door and went back in the hole, where they stood by the door of his cell and asked him if he was going to shut up.

"Fuck you."

They opened the door to his cell and gave him one last warning, to which he responded, "Let's get it on, motherfuckers."

Then they rushed into the cell and laid into him with boots and clubs. We could hear the blows and the screams and the kicks and the moans. Finally, the guards came out and walked down the cellblock with sweat pouring down their red faces.

Leroy just laid there and moaned. After a few minutes he began singing "We Shall Overcome," his voice laced with agony and pain. The black guys loved it, and you could hear them singing along with him all over the jail. Chuck and I just stared at each other through the bars from opposite sides of the cellblock, wondering what had happened to him.

The next morning Elroy just slept; by the afternoon we could hear him moaning in pain. By dinnertime, he could actually hold a short conversation. And by bedtime, he could actually scream. So the whole thing started all over again and the guards had to kick the shit out of him all over again. Some people said that Leroy had gone crazy, but I like to think of it as the spirit of Simon de Kramer, just another example of the pure fucking defiance and fanaticism of a Mennonite martyr.

The next day was Thanksgiving. We were still locked in our cells. At noon they brought us dinner on a steel tray. Corn (what else?), a baked potato, and a half a baked chicken. The chickens were from the prison farm. Every year, the week before Thanksgiving, they slaughtered the post-menopausal egg-layers that were so tough we had trouble ripping them apart with our hands. We couldn't eat them; they tasted like rubber. Finally, we gave up and threw them through the bars on the doors and onto the floor of the cellblock and told the guards to shove them up their asses.

So there we were: Thanksgiving Day in the Berks County Prison, locked down in our cell, each of us with a porcelain toilet with no seat, a mattress as thin as a doormat, and one skinny wool blanket so rough it would have scratched a horse; rolling our own cigarettes, with our Thanksgiving chickens lying on the stone floor of the cellblock; Leroy moaning in pain from down in the hole, and the rest of us laughing our asses off at our predicament. Two and a half years earlier, I didn't even know these people, but here we were, all together again in the Berks County Prison for the third time. The following Tuesday they would again shackle me and Blackie together, put us in a sheriff's car and drive us to the Diagnostic and Classification Center at the Pennsylvania State Correctional Institution at Dallas, high up in the old anthracite coal region. And not one of us had ever made a dime out of the whole thing. But then again, we were not your ordinary criminals. We were the last of the all-American outlaws.

AFTERTHOUGHTS

Forty years have now passed since the events described in this book, and many of the people are long dead: Sweet William Parker, Richie Gavin, Bob Rayels. In June 1980, police found Blackie dead on the floor of a Fern Street apartment in Reading with a .45 caliber bullet hole in his head. Bob "Bobo" Dillingham rose to national sergeant-at-arms before he was shotgunned to death in Seldon, Long Island, by two scumbag junkies who tried to rob him in April 1980. Fred "Dutch" Burhans was shot to death while trying to defuse someone else's domestic dispute. The list goes on: Pappy, the Galloping Guinea, Dirty Hombre, all shot. Renegade was killed in a motorcycle wreck. And these are only the ones I know about. The question is, did they need to be dragged from their graves and brought back to life on the pages of this book? I say the answer is a resounding yes. And I address these words primarily to anyone who ever wore or will wear a Pagan patch.

Consider the following two incidents:

In January 2002, a large group of Pagans entered a catering hall on Long Island, where a motorcycle event was taking place. A disturbance broke out and one Pagan was shot and killed. Within seconds, an army of state police officers, Nassau County police officers, Suffolk County police officers, FBI and BATF agents, and God only knows who else descended on the place and the Pagans were carted off to jail. It was the Newark hotel donnybrook all over again. The following week 73 Pagans were charged with felonies under the federal RICO laws, and newspaper reporters went on a feeding frenzy.

Their stories mostly followed the same pattern. Long Island had been a Pagan fiefdom until 1998 when federal agents arrested the entire member-ships of five Pagan chapters on Long Island, this time for allegedly scaring a titty-bar owner. But one article stood out from the rest. It described a bunch of cars with out-of-state plates waiting in parking lots along Wellwood Ave. in Lindenhurst. It seems that the Pagans had stopped here on Sunday morning, drank beer, ate hamburgers, shot pool, and in general left a bunch of happy bar owners counting an unexpectedly large amount of cash, before they moved on to the motorcycle event.

As I read these articles, I wondered how many of those jailed Pagans who were drinking beer that morning on Wellwood Avenue even knew who Sweet William Parker was, much less how he stood up to the Aliens that hot summer night in 1967, or the fact that he was buried only five miles away right up Wellwood. All the newspaper articles mentioned was that Long Island was Pagan country, but none of them explained why. The answer was buried in a grave in Pinelawn National Cemetery with Sweet William Parker, who, along with other now-dead brothers, created an American folk legend that will endure forever. Although the legend endures, these brothers are now forgotten. Many of them left kids who never got to know their fathers. It is now time to bring these guys back and let the whole world know who they were. I have tried not to sensationalize or sentimentalize them. Nor did I spew bullshit about them; I simply tried to bring them back and put them out there as I remember them so that the world will remember them.

That is one incident that inspired me. Another one that kept me going when I thought that no one really gave a shit about the Legend was the story of the Amish drug ring.

Back in June 1998, every newspaper in Pennsylvania ran a front-page story claiming that the Pagans Motorcycle Club was behind a drug ring that was selling drugs to Amish kids. The gist of the story was that the Pagans were big-time drug lords who recruited two Amish boys to sell drugs for them. That was the story on page one. But if you followed it as it drifted from page one to page eight over the next several weeks, a different picture emerged. First, the two Amish "boys" turn out to be "twenty-something-year-old" Amish businessmen who were selling drugs in the Amish community. One of them owned a roofing company. When they were arrested, the two drug-dealing businessmen agreed to make a deal.

They fingered two roofers on one of their construction crews and claimed that they were behind the whole thing. In return for this tidbit, the two Amish men were allowed to go free after they stood up in court and apologized to the members of their community, who had packed the courtroom in support of their drug-dealing brethren.

Three things stand out here. One, after scrutinizing dozens of articles, there is no substantial evidence that the two roofers were members of the Pagans. Number two, even if they were, we must remember that drug kingpins are capable of devising many elaborate and amazing schemes to launder money and conceal the true nature of their business, but schlepping shingles up on rooftops in August for Amish construction companies is not one of them. And finally, when all is said and done, there was no evidence that any Pagan ever sold any drugs to any Amish kid. Now reporters get paid to amuse readers with sensational stories, and these readers are not really interested if the story later falls apart like a house of cards, so why should reporters be?

Then you have the problem of the self-anointed experts: writers like Yves Lavigne, snitches like Anthony Tait, along with college professors, retired cops, and federal agents who write articles and collect fat consulting fees for lecturing people on the menace of outlaw motorcycle clubs. It is time that someone talked back to them. I'm not saying that all one-percenters are saints. But neither are all cops, priests, or politicians. Someone had to do what I did in this book. Many of the guys I rode with are dead. Others are in jail. By a twist of fate, I got to learn how to write, I got to be the college professor, and I got to be a journalist. Like Ishmael in Moby Dick, I alone am left to tell their story. For better or for worse, I did it as best I could. Take it as a whole, brothers, and don't pick it apart one sentence at a time. If you can do a better job of telling the story, do it. If not, enjoy reading, and keep the faith.

John Hall
Sieg oder Untergang
"Victory or Annihilation"
Allegheny Mountains, Pennsylvania, 2008